KT-578-883

A JOURNAL OF CONTEMPORARY WRITING

IRISH PAGES

DUILLÍ ÉIREANN

IRISH PAGES is a biannual journal (Spring-Summer, Autumn-Winter), edited in Belfast and publishing, in equal measure, writing from Ireland and overseas. It appears at the end of each sixmonth period.

Its policy is to publish poetry, short fiction, essays, creative non-fiction, memoir, essay reviews, nature-writing, translated work, literary journalism, and other autobiographical, historical, religious and scientific writing of literary distinction. There are no standard reviews or narrowly academic articles. Irish-language and Scots writing are published in the original, with English translations or glosses. IRISH PAGES is a non-partisan, non-sectarian, culturally ecumenical, and wholly independent journal. It endorses no political outlook or cultural tradition, and has no editorial position on the constitutional question. Its title refers to the island of Ireland in a purely apolitical and geographic sense, in the same manner of The Church of Ireland or the Irish Sea.

The sole criteria for inclusion in the journal are the distinction of the writing and the integrity of the individual voice. Equal editorial attention will be given to established, emergent and new writers.

The views expressed in IRISH PAGES are not necessarily those of the Editors. The journal is published by Irish Pages Ltd, a non-profit organization.

Submissions, by post only, are welcome but must be accompanied by return postage or an international reply coupon. No self-addressed envelope is required. Reporting time is nine months. If work is accepted, an electronic copy on disk may be requested.

Your subscription is essential to the independence and survival of the journal. Subscription rates are £20stg/€30/$60 for one year. Visit our website at www.irishpages.org for a subscription form or to order online. Credit cards are welcome.

IRISH PAGES
129 Ormeau Road
Belfast BT7 1SH

Advisory Board
William Crawley
John Gray
Darragh Mac Intyre
Manfred McDowell
Ruth Carr
Bernard O'Donoghue
Noel Russell
Daniel Tobin

Legal Advice: Elliott Duffy Garrett, Belfast

IRISH PAGES is set in 12/14.5 Monotype Perpetua and printed in Glasgow by Bell & Bain.

This issue has been generously asssisted by the Arts Councils of Northern and Southern Ireland.

Copyright remains with IRISH PAGES and the authors. All rights reserved. No reproduction, copy of transmission, in whole or part, may be made without written permission.

ISBN 978-1-8382018-3-8

Supported by
The National Lottery®
through the Arts Council of Northern Ireland

IRISH PAGES

CHRIS AGEE, *Editor*

CATHAL Ó SEARCAIGH, *Irish Language Editor*

KATHLEEN JAMIE, *Scottish Editor*

MEG BATEMAN, *Scottish Gaelic Editor*

JACOB AGEE, RUTH CARR, STEPHEN DORNAN & RUTH PADEL
Contributing Editors

EDITED IN BELFAST
VOLUME 11, NUMBER 1

IRISH PAGES
DUILLÍ ÉIREANN

VOLUME 11, NUMBER 1

CONTENTS

The Anthropocene

"At any given moment there is an orthodoxy, a body of ideas which it is assumed that all right-thinking people will accept without question. It is not exactly forbidden to say this, that or the other, but it is 'not done' to say it, just as in mid-Victorian times it was 'not done' to mention trousers in the presence of a lady. Anyone who challenges the prevailing orthodoxy finds himself silenced with surprising effectiveness. A genuinely unfashionable opinion is almost never given a fair hearing, either in the popular press or in the highbrow periodicals."

George Orwell

PORTFOLIO

PANDEMIC

The Patron of This Issue

ANDRÉ GUMUCHDJIAN

FRIENDS AND SUPPORTERS OF *IRISH PAGES*

Anonymous (Glasgow)
Gerry Bell
Lucy Brennan
Vincent Browne
Paddy Bushe
John Cassidy
Manus Charleton
Charles Coventry
Joan Dargan
Donnell and Alison Deeny
Joe and Geraldine Duffy
Gandolfi Fish (Glasgow)
Elliot Duffy Garrett
Jack Gillespie
Philip Haughey
Marie Heaney
Celeste King
Brian Mac Call
Tom Mac Intyre
Enda McDonough
Robert McDowell
John McGinley
John McMahon
Colette Ní Ghallchóir
Joe Prendergast
Gillian Reynolds
William Reynolds
Carolyn Richardson
Tony Skelton
Anne Smith
Alex Stafford
Timothy Vignoles
Bret Walker
David Woods

Subscribe / donate online at www.irishpages.org

A Singular Perspective on Dalmatian Marriage
By Tisja Kljaković Braić

(See "Portfolio")

A PATCH OF MOONLIGHT

Ruth Padel

Darwin's warning.

Rustles of the night in the Nilgiri Hills. I sit behind the low wall of a veranda beside Priya who invited me here, her husband Jean Philippe and her brother Peter. They are scientists and naturalists. This is what they do every night. I am very lucky to be their guest and doing it with them.

It is February 2020. The first Covid case has just been detected in India, a pandemic is ambushing the world but we don't know, we are intent on what is near us in the dark.

In daylight, this stony soil is the colour of milky tea overlain by dry grass. The horizontal rays of early morning will turn all this to honey gold, but under a night sky and a full moon everything is a lacework of silver and black.

Dense forest starts a few hundred yards away but the clear ground round the house, dotted with trees and bushes, is pale and lit. I stare at the outline of a chin-high square of cement, the water tank behind a fat tree, where the ground slopes towards the river.

Behind that tree, half in shadow, are the tusks, trunk and double-domed forehead of a wild Asian elephant. He has come to drink, silk-silent. We never heard a sound. The Nilgiri biosphere has the largest population of Asian elephants in the world.

His trunk dips into the water, curves up, pours water down his throat in the moonlight. The night rustles, he drinks, we watch.

Behind this veranda is the kitchen. Last night, Jean Philippe showed me the spot in it where he once stood underneath the thrusting tusks of a wild bull elephant, mad for fruit, doing his best to rip off the roof. Jean Philippe lit flares to scare him away. Afterwards, they reinforced the roof with steel girders and bought zinc-lined containers which even the longest, most sense-receptor rich noses cannot smell through, to store fruit.

He knows we are here. Any noise or sudden movement and he'd be off. His fragile trust in this place is the result of 50 years' work protecting this 30-acre patch of forest between two villages.

Priya's father bought the land in 1964 and built this bungalow. (I cherish his books about this forest, especially *Whispers from the Wild*.) If he hadn't, the villages would have merged and wild animals would lost access to the river. Priya, Jean Philippe and Peter protect the forest from anyone who tries to harm it. By grazing cattle in it for instance, or taking timber, or building illegally at its edge. They keep their impact on it as light as possible, don't try to make friends with animals or feed them, simply protect access to the river and fill the water tank.

My first afternoon, we watched from this veranda a family of dhole, India's wild red dog, trotting along the river bank. Last night, a bear and her cubs walked across in front of us, snuffling the ground. I often see drifts of chital, the spotted deer, and sometimes sambhur, grazing, browsing, drinking at the river. Sometimes a tiger calls at night.

15 years ago, I wrote a book about wild tigers and their conservation. Starting at the millennium, I explored tiger forests on foot, in jeeps and on trained elephants, in India, Bangladesh, Nepal, Bhutan, South East Asia, Indonesia, Russia and China. I dreamed tigers. I thought I could never feel so connected to any other wild animal.

Given the degradation and shrinking of forests, the loss of wild habitat everywhere on the planet, I wondered if that was the last time anyone could go into all those forests and see signs of tiger. Growth in human populations, expansion of agriculture and livestock farming, means more tigers are coming into conflict with humans all the time. They eat goats and cows, sometimes kill people too, and get poisoned in revenge.

But in India, there seem now to be more tigers than there were then, because those years coincided with a big surge in tiger poaching which in some places has been beaten back. The media hail optimistic tiger surveys which say tigers are on the up.

However, counting animals that don't want to be seen is a tricky business, and scientists say the surveys are flawed. Also more trees are being cut, more roads are being built, more people are driving, and so more and more wild animals, including tigers, are getting killed on India's roads. The tigers are still here though, and meanwhile I am starting to write about elephants.

I never expected to. In Indian forest, elephants were the ones I was most afraid of. They kill so easily, are so quick and so emotional, and hate being disturbed. Other animals try to get away from human beings. But elephants evolved to think everyone should get out of their way. Today, with so many more people, elephants are under pressure as never before. Maybe that is how mammoths felt before they died out.

Africa's elephants are not worked. Fascinating and complex as they are, they are purely wild animals. The ones Hannibal took over the Alps were probably a smaller North African species which has since gone extinct. Africa also has a smaller forest elephant, genetically different from the best-known elephants, the giants of the savanna who have genetic and biological differences from Asian elephants. They are larger, with larger ears. Both sexes have tusks. And they have never been tamed and worked.

Asian elephants are very different. Down the millennia, the relationship human beings have created with them, on the subcontinent, in Sri Lanka and South East Asia, and more far-reachingly the imaginative relationship all of us have with them in our heads, is far more complex than with a cat that keeps to itself.

We have hunted tigers, displayed them in zoos, made them do circus acts. Selling their skin and bones illegally makes some people a lot of money. But we can't make tigers do anything actually useful to us, whereas Asian elephants have been caught in the wild and kept captive, have been trained, and worked in transport and logging industries, also in hunting and in mass ceremonies demonstrating kingly power and religious worship. Also used, until very recently, in war. There is a procession of horses, dogs, mules and pigeons carved on a Hyde Park war monument, in London, to animals killed on active service. It is led by an Asian elephant.

———

An elephant is the most ancient image in the world for the different ways different people try to make sense of how they perceive the world. Six blind men encounter an elephant. They feel it, and then theorise about what they perceive. The story probably began here, in India, in the first millennium BC. Relativism was cool in the first millennium: somewhere between 1500 and 1200 BC, the *Rig Veda* said, "Reality is one, though wise men speak of it variously", and the men in this story do what humans do, variously: try to explain what an elephant is. Or rather, since we invoke metaphor to explain the unknown and don't always realise that what we are using is metaphor, they explain what it is like. One feels the trunk and says the elephant is a snake. One fingers an ear and calls it a fan. One feels the round of its leg and thinks it is a tree, one runs his hand along its flank and calls it a wall. One grabs the tail and calls it a rope, the last discovers a tusk and calls it a spear. In some versions, they come to blows over their competing interpretations.

About 500 BC, a Buddhist version of the story spread to China, then to the Arab world and Sufism. Philosophers have used it to argue for the intangibility of truth, and respect for different perspectives; they have drawn more morals from it than there are blind men in it. The elephant is reality. Or God, or truth. We use our limited subjective experience to decide what is true and brush aside other people's ideas. Sometimes, to defend our own opinion, we go to war.

The story has not done much to resolve human conflict but does illustrate the many contradictory aspects of our relationship with elephants themselves.

———

Writing about an animal is also writing about yourself. Even if you have never seen one in real life or in the wild, or if you blank out that dimension of your writing, you are still working out of your own imaginative relation with it. Thinking about elephants, and our relations with elephants, means examining how human beings treat captive and working animals, as well as wild ones. Despite their extraordinarily different bodies, elephants seem to share with us a lot of emotions and social behaviour. Strong family bonds, for instance. They recognise themselves in a mirror. They mourn their dead. They seem to feel and express gratitude, even to us.

I have watched over and over again a YouTube video, made very near here on an I-phone, in which a wild elephant thanks workmen for rescuing a baby elephant.

The baby has fallen in a very deep muddy ditch. The adults squeal and trumpet and worry, mill around, reach down but cannot help. Their weight makes things worse, the ditch walls fall in more. Then the labourers who made the ditch bring up a bulldozer. The wild elephants, very upset, retreat and watch while the men use the bulldozer to pile up mud at the bottom of the ditch and the baby manages to scramble out.

It wobbles off to re-join the herd in nearby jungle. There is a lot of joyful trumpeting. Then one adult elephant rushes out from the trees, stops and stares at the men from a distance. Finally she raises her trunk at them and disappears.

No one can really say for sure what most animal behaviour means. She could be saying, with good reason, *If you didn't mess with our landscape this would never have happened.* But what it looks like is a wild salute, a *Thank you.*

Above all, there is empathy. Elephants care how others feel.

I once had a bareback elephant riding-lesson in Nepal. I was there for tigers, but I hung out with the elephants trained to carry tourists into the grasslands to look for tigers, and the people who looked after them. Who, after my lesson, told me about the birth of their one tusker, many years before.

They had not realised the mother was pregnant. She was ridden that afternoon but at night there was a wild noise in the elephant lines, trumpeting and squealing. The mahouts dashed over and found the other elephants had broken their picket chains and were standing either side of her, holding her up while she gave birth. Then they all clustered protectively round mother and child.

Elephants respond immediately to another elephant calling for help. Just as we put an arm round someone in tears, they reach out their trunk to embrace them and calm them, they even put their trunk in the other's mouth, which seems to be a way of saying, "I'm here to help you".

The only other animals who identify another's distress, and try to comfort and console them physically are the great apes, some members of the crow family, and some dogs. And some humans. In this year of 2020 it would be nice but maybe over-optimistic to think most.

—

In 2001 when I started researching tigers, I soon learned that there was everywhere, as the field zoologist George Schaller put it, a great dying. Field zoologists knew then, better than anyone, that we were staring into an abyss. Kayaking down a side-river in Laos, lurching nervously towards the mighty Mekong River, I came to a stark realisation. Darwin reached his insights into how species evolved by sailing round South America. 150 years later, I understood that my small journeys through South Asia, in search of tigers, were going to end in the opposite understanding: how species go extinct.

I asked experts in the field how they dealt with despair.

"We do what we can, those of us who love the wild", said a conservationist in a mangrove forest in Bangladesh.

"You have to switch off on Friday nights or you'd go mad", said an ex-commando who taught forest guards in Cambodia and Vietnam how to deal, physically and legally, with armed gangs of illegal loggers.

"You have a choice, do something or do nothing", said a wildlife vet, the first person to radio-collar a wild tiger in Sumatra. "And I know what I decided."

20 years on, forests everywhere are in crisis. Human population growth and pollution, the plunder of timber, animals and forest land, are all made a million times worse by galloping climate change. This past decade has been the hottest in Earth's history. Rivers are drying, even the wonderful Mekong, now threatened by Chinese dams. Flooding, fires, hurricanes and heatwaves. Storms, droughts, melting permafrost. Fires in the Amazon, glaciers collapsing in front of our eyes.

Already in February 2020 feels like a year of reckoning in the ledgers of the earth. Last year, over four environmental activists *every week* around the world were killed by companies destroying nature through mining, agribusiness and logging.

In this last month of innocence before the world wakes up, to a virus we brought upon ourselves by our intrusions into the wild, we are reeling from what has been happening in Australia, where scientists have been warning for years that clearing land for agriculture, mining and development was making the bushfires worse. At this very minute, 33,000 square miles of forest are burning, along with nearly three billion wild animals.

In the developed world, environmentalists are not usually murdered in the interest of making money, just side-lined, and portrayed as marginal by media on the side of the vested interests, while wild habitat is lost and wildlife extinctions increase.

How does all this affect elephants in the Nilgiri Hills?

This island of forest lies on one of the ancestral elephant migration routes that vein the sub-continent. Jean Philippe has been mapping these routes. They are the ancient connectivity, the blood flow of the land. Tigers are solitary and territorial. Once they have won a territory, they stay in it. Elephants are social nomads. They evolved to move on and then return when plants they fed from, and fertilised, have grown back. To eat the enormous amount they need each day, they have to migrate over long distances.

Human barriers now block these routes. Cities, factories, farmland. Busy railways, ditches, highways, vast dams. Elephants are electrocuted by electric fencing and sagging high voltage power lines, try to cross fences of wood and metal, get hung up on them and die halfway over. The photos are terrible. Huge animals, folded in half, dying on a railing like grey deflating laundry.

There are also miles and miles of mines, for gold, diamonds, bauxite, manganese, iron, you name it. Asia is too rich, in what we call resources, for the elephants' good.

So are the elephants themselves. In the last four decades, seventy per cent of elephants worldwide have disappeared. International trade in ivory is at last illegal but each country makes its own laws about domestic sales, of ivory from elephants killed before it was made illegal. The cut-off year was 1990. Today, nearly all countries have banned domestic trade entirely. Even China, the largest consumer of ivory in the world. But a few countries still allow it. Ivory is very difficult to date, so it is easy for ivory from elephants killed illegally, since 1990, to enter the domestic market in, for example, Canada, where selling pre-1990 ivory is still legal. And the black market worldwide is huge. A pound of ivory sells for 1,500 US dollars.

Every year, around 20,000 elephants are killed for their tusks. Among Asian elephants, it is only the males that have tusks, so they are the ones that get poached.

All this tumbles through my head as we watch our visitor tip his head to pour water down his throat. His tusks glint in the moonlight.

Long tusks can weigh 250 pounds. The ivory he is carrying, through a countryside where the average family has less than 20 dollars surplus income a month, may be worth 350,000 dollars.

In the early days here, the sixties and seventies, Priya's family saw elephants with huge tusks, and quite calm. Poaching was low, no one was harassing them. But we have been such bad predators to them and one by one those males were poached. No more enormous tusks.

Today, there is so much poaching, and so much of the land where the elephants' natural food grows has disappeared, that conflict has increased between hungry elephants and poor people protecting their crops. Poisoned, shot at, electrocuted, elephants are becoming more and more – well, to themselves, anxious, angry, suspicious, embittered, het up. And to human beings, dangerous.

In the last five years, 2,036 humans and over 500 elephants have been killed in human elephant-conflict. (Conflict with tigers killed 275 people in the same years.) Last year, nearly 500 people died. North-east of here, in Orissa where my brother has spent most of his life, 115 people were killed, and 132 injured, in human-elephant encounters. Orissa's Keonjhar district, torn by large-scale iron and manganese mines, reported 112 elephants in the 2002 elephant census. In 2017 it reported only 40. The destruction of elephant habitat there, and elephants, had made human-elephant conflict worse. Just last month there, in January, in Hariharpur village, a tusker trampled to death a ten-year-old girl playing outside her home.

———

The tusker in the moonlight finishes drinking and stands very still beside the tank.

Adult male elephants generally live and travel alone. The small herds are made up of closely related females, babies, and half-grown children, led by a matriarch. This quiet lone standing is classic male. They do it for hours, like meditation.

What is going on in his enormous head? Their brains are four times bigger than ours. What is he thinking about, what is he feeling?

We do have a lot in common, emotionally and socially, with elephants. But suppose they have more emotions than we do? Deeper, subtler, more sensitive?

We know there are worlds beyond our limited senses, that animals know things in ways we can't. Other animals see different wavelengths and colours than us. Bumblebees sense the electrical field of flowers ripe for pollination. Birds live in a richer-coloured world than us, full of signs and messages we'll never see. Hummingbirds distinguish sources of the nectar they feed on because they can see colours outside the spectrum of the rainbow.

Elephants call to each other in bass rumbles too deep for human hearing, and feel vibrations through the soles of their feet and hairs on their trunk from miles away. Maybe they have emotions, too, which we cannot imagine, or social and even moral feelings, beyond the rainbow of our own.

This is his forest. We don't go in. Even in daylight, I have been warned to look round very carefully, walking the few yards to my own one-room bungalow. Elephants might be anywhere. They are surprisingly silent and are the colour of dust, of shadow. You don't see them till you are on them, and they can move amazingly fast.

The only thing a bull elephant has evolved to be afraid of is another like himself, but he won't want any other animals in his space. I've seen an elephant chase away a pack of dhole, furiously, squealing, ears flapping.

In a mock charge, designed to frighten off enemies, that is what they do — make a loud noise and flap their ears. That is how they chase off a mongoose or a harmless spotted deer. But when they mean business, when they want to eliminate an intruder, a danger, they attack in silence. And they are suspicious, with very good reason, of human beings.

Last year, Priya and Jean Philippe heard goons throwing firecrackers into the forest just beyond this slice of river.

"Goon" is a technical term for hired thugs. These ones work for a neighbour who keeps trying to encroach on the land. The goons, afraid of the elephants, were throwing firecrackers into the forest to scare them away.

Jean Philippe said he would go in and tell them to stop.

"Be careful", Priya said. "I saw an elephant there this morning."

But the elephant seemed to have gone. Jean Philippe, furious about the firecrackers, walked down to give the goons a serious piece of his mind. Everything was dead quiet in the forest. But then a twig snapped at the edge. He stopped. He was just turning back when a tusker charged him out of the trees. He raced back towards the house but the elephant, also furious, very upset by the firecrackers, was much faster.

He looked behind and saw the trunk lifting up almost above him. Priya saw him sprinting desperately towards her, jumped up on this veranda wall, shouted, then leaped down and ran towards them both to deflect the elephant.

It swerved a little, which just gave Jean Philippe time to get into the house. It stopped, then careened off into the trees.

"He meant to kill", Jean Philippe told me. "Running at me, utterly silent."

Last year's dry season was one of the worst. The drought went on and on. Terrible heat and the river ran dry. One afternoon, they saw 13 elephants standing there by the water tank. The babies were on the point of collapse.

The tank was empty.

"I'm going out to turn on the tap", said Jean Philippe.

Priya couldn't stop him. He walked out. He didn't look at the elephants in front of him, just as I don't look at the blackbird who waits on the fence for me to put crumbs on our kitchen windowsill. If I look at it, the bird flies away, it is used to me doing something purposeful for myself, weeding, digging, putting out crumbs, the natural things for me to do, but relating to it scares it off. I walk to the sill, not looking at it, put down the crumbs, and leave. As soon as I am back in the kitchen doorway, the blackbird flies to the sill. But a blackbird can't kill me.

Elephants are far more dangerous than tigers. Tigers kill for food, or in defence. Elephants, wild or captive, kill because of how they feel. They kill with their head, feet, trunk or tusks. They trample, swipe, gore, crush; they can pick you up with their trunk and dash you on the ground. In zoos, the keepers killed most often are those who look after elephants. In forest, elephants will go for you just because you are there.

In front of 13 pairs of wild eyes, Jean Philippe walked to the tap and turned it on. It began to fill. But it's a big tank. It took time.

There's a subtle undertow of movement in elephant stillness. The tip of the trunk keeps delicately moving, testing smells in the air. And in great heat, the ears keep fanning out and back like gills of a fish because the veins of the ear help cool the blood.

As the tank slowly filled, the sun blazed on the parched soil and the parching elephants. Priya watched, terrified, from the house, Jean Philippe looked at the tap, not glancing up or facing them, and the elephants loomed. 13 gently pulsing enormous bulks, 13 trunks each packed with 150,000 muscle fascicles. The tip is like the tissue of our lips, packed with nerve endings, but one blow from a trunk can kill.

When the tank was full, he turned it off and walked slowly back to the house.

They came forward and dipped their trunks in the water.

The one who speaks for the wild, speaks for the world.

Ruth Padel (born 1946) has published twelve poetry collections, most recently Emerald *(Chatto, 2018). She has also published a novel acclaimed for its nature writing,* Where the Serpent Lives *(Abacus, 2010), and a memoir of tiger conservation,* Tigers in Red Weather *(Little Brown, 2005). The great-great grandchild of Charles Darwin, she is Professor of Poetry at King's College London, Fellow of the Royal Society of Literature, and Council Member for the Zoological Society of London.*

From A FIELD GUIDE TO PEOPLE

Greg Delanty

An hourglass running down.

BOS TAURUS

The raising of cattle in different ways is significantly adding to climate change and one of those ways is due to bacteria in the stomachs of cows producing methane.

So much to say about the herds of Bos Taurus.
They supply the silk of milk for the tea or coffee,
bullions of butter, a panoply of cheese, plus:

haul heavy loads, pull ploughs, act as money,
a dowry, are a daily staple, and so much more.
You browse the meat aisle: filet mignon, sirloin, kidney?

Something tender? There's a deal on veal? Forget the poor
trapped calf. Scruples flit like flies around the tail of a cow.
Quell your qualms, man. You're a natural carnivore.

Whatever you do, don't look down at your hooves now.
You're standing in their skins. Such a bleeding heart.
Your default: headless hen, bleat-less lamb, ass of sow.

And gas, you ruefully laugh, as you load milk in the cart,
thinking of what the billions of cattle burp and fart.

CHIMPANZEE

As a chimp, usually the adult male,
approaches and the roar of the water
booms louder, you see him, without fail,

speed up. His demeanor starts to alter,
hair bristling. Arriving at the fall,
he stands, sways from one foot to the other,

bows, genuflects. Answering some call,
he dips his hand as if in holy water, splashes
himself along the tassel border of the silk wall,

climbs the bell ropes of draping vines, lashes
his body to several, takes flight
over the deafening water as it crashes.

He swings like a thurible above that veil of white;
the spray is the incense of the monkey's rite.

ELEPHANT

Sometimes you see something so
dreadful that the mind's camera snaps a shot,
shoots a video of the scenario,

lasers it into your retina's screen on the spot,
impaled in you for as long as you live:
the memory of an adult thrashing a tot,

or the elephant Dan and I saw given a sedative
so she could rest, sleep, that time in Dublin Zoo.
The aged female was trapped in a repetitive

back and forth on her haunches, unable to
stop herself, a tormented beast of Orcus.
Her attendant explained, feeding her bamboo,

"It was her one way to move, trapped in the van of a circus
so long. We adopted her, our unforgettable bonus."

IBEX

*In January 2000, the Pyrenean ibex (Spanish common name "bucardo")
became extinct. Scientists cloned DNA from a last female.*

In the end, no cliff or impossible crag
could save them from plantation or gun.
Their heads hang on walls. Hunters brag.

Many were taken down for sheer fun.
The king pucks – their antler plumes
rising magisterially – plugged one by none.

Gone the clash of horn scimitars, grooms
battling to mate, the *bucardo* of lore.
White-coated gods in lab rooms

summoned one back from the dark shore
of the underworld. They should have known
from the ancient myths what was in store.

She returned after seven minutes, lone clone,
relieved to be back among the herds of her own.

THE LION

has the humorless, bearded face of an Amish elder
as he patrols the edge of his pride. The females
nurse the cubs with a strictness that's tender.

The young gambol, snap at each other's tails,
prelapsarian, oblivious of threats,
typical of youngsters. He catalogues details,

sniffs the humid atmosphere, frets.
Something alerts him — a hunger or rogue lion
in the tall savanna grass? Whatever upsets

the pride is unknown, but, like a wagon train,
they form a circle, as if with the one will,
the same that earlier brought down, *coupe de main*,

an elephant with the natural savagery of the kill.
The savannah draws taut, finger-on-the-trigger still.

ORYZA SATIVA

Something to behold, how this crop succeeds
in such diverse moraine. Best of all, see row
after row descend gradually from the gods

down mountainsides to the valleys below,
tiers of a great amphitheatre,
their heads craning to watch the show:

the traffic, rickshaws, the general theater
of our priceless world. On the slow train
to Kandy I was a passing spectator,

watched locals kneeling to the god of rain,
lay offerings to the assisting oxen and ant,
petition the god of rice for healthy grain.

I wanted to join them, genuflect, pray, chant
praise to the plant that's half the world's constant.

QUIZ TIME

Surely, you will get, know, guess, who
this one is? They go with the current,
never against, in contrast to

the nektons. As varied and different
as an ox from a bee, lizard from kangaroo.
To say they are diverse is understatement.

We know them not so much by who
they are but by where they float and sway.
Perhaps one stung you out of the blue

while you were in for a swim. What an array.
We can't manage without them. They detox
the air. If only we learned to live the same way,

flout extinction's law, all live together in flux:
google "Gauze's Law" and "the Plankton Paradox".

WHEAT

The old gods are defunct, but not the old necessity
to give thanks. This god spread from the Levant
forgotten religions ago, bestowing prosperity.

He is goodness incarnate, the Midas plant
without the Midas curse, turning a field
into plains of swaying gold. He is our constant

from dawn to dawn, strength concealed
within burnished stalks of energy,
grounded goodness variously revealed.

This great shape-changer: the deity
of porridge, pasta, bread, the English taco
has more lives than Buddha. We

become him, where he grows we grow,
rising each morning, leavened dough.

A poet, translator and anthologist, Greg Delanty was born in Cork in 1958 and studied at University College Cork, where he was taught by the poets Sean Lucy and John Montague. He is the author of seven collections of poems, most recently Aceldama *(Carcanet, 2006), and one of the foremost translators of the Irish poetry of Seán Ó Ríordáin. For past 30 years he has lived in the United States, where he is currently Professor of English at Saint Michael's College in Colchester, Vermont.*

GANGA

—

Malachi O'Doherty

After forty years.

It was Christmas Day and I almost didn't notice. I had been settling into my new home by the river Ganges at Brijghat, where the main road and railway line due east from Delhi cross the river.

I had a room in the corner of the courtyard of a pilgrim hostel called *Teen Bandar ki Dharmashala – The Three Monkeys Hostel*.

Pilgrims came here from all over the state and Delhi on four holy days of the month: the full moon, the no moon and the eleventh phases of the waxing and waning moons called Ekadashi, a fast day for the devout.

But I had little idea yet of the scale of the invasion Brijghat experienced in warm weather. December on the north Indian plain was like a half-decent summer for me. To the people who lived there, it was winter. I walked out in a short-sleeved shirt past people who huddled by the tea shops wrapped in heavy woollen shawls.

I had come to India in response to an ad in the personal column of *The Guardian* to help a Hindu swami to write a commentary on the *Bhagavad Gita*, one of the holy scriptures.

I was there for my own benefit as someone who wanted to travel and, eventually, to write. I didn't have a lot of faith in the project I was contributing to yet. Swamiji was an imposing and needy man. He strode rather than walked, stroking his wispy black beard, his stomach several inches ahead of the rest of him.

People around us assumed that I would take an increasing interest in Hinduism and meditation and indeed I would.

For now I was tentative but I would mark the day a little ceremoniously in my own way. I was going to take a dip in the Ganges.

"Raj Pal", I said, "today I will take bath in Ganga."

Raj Pal was my closest companion. He ran the hostel. He was a few years younger than me, busy but playful, fascinated by me and determined to be helpful.

"Yes, Mr Malky. Yes."

I walked along the river every day. It was about half a mile wide there. The sand of the banks was dark grey. Pilgrims set up camp there and lit their little fires on the night before holy days and spent the dark hours chanting under the moon.

There is no official religion of moon worship that anyone will own up to, but both the Muslim and the Hindu prostrate themselves before her. I have seen a Muslim tie his camel to a palm tree in North Africa and bow to the east, to Mecca, the full moon low in the sky, right in front of him. Further east, when they bow towards Mecca once a month, they face the new moon setting.

The river is the Goddess Ganga. Applying a Latinised masculine name to her is an impertinence that Indians are content to overlook but no one ever talked of having a dip or going for a swim. They suggested I take a bath.

By the river I had to steer past the over-curious, the wandering bull and the little family huddle that was right in my path.

People waded out in their sarees or loose wraps and plunged three times, holding their noses, and said some prayers and came out, the cloth clinging to them, marbling the surface of rippled flesh. I stripped down to my bathing trunks. The water wasn't too cold. It was murky but Swamiji assured me that it was clean. The holy river is self-purifying.

I was self-conscious standing in the water, realising that Raj Pal expected to see me do something, bow to my god, something.

I joined my palms as in prayer and said *namaste* to the river, then plunged forward, swam for about half a minute and waded out again to dry myself, shivering now.

Up on the bridge cars, buses and tongas waited to take pilgrims home. The *tonga* was what we used to call a jaunting car in Ireland, a horse and carriage where the fulcrum of the axle makes all the difference to how you position yourself when you climb on. Sometimes there are so many people with baggage at the back that the horse is almost levered off the ground.

The driver flicks a cord whip at his ear to start him off.

There is no joy in being a horse in India.

Instead of going straight back to the hostel, I took a walk and stopped to have chai at a little tea shop where the tea was boiled in an old and blackened metal pot, over a fire in a range fashioned out of dried mud. The ingredients were sprinkled in, the milk added. Then the man squatting on a table by the range in his tartan wrap and woolly hat would pour it into a little earthenware cup like a misshapen flowerpot. It had taken me a while to accept that the occasion's end was for me to signal by throwing the cup into the gutter for someone else to sweep up later.

The worst pollution in India back then was shit and woodsmoke. When tens of thousands of people flowed into the town on holy days they bathed, drank tea at the little stalls and defecated in the drains or on open ground.

The first sight of this is appalling but defecating was a social occasion for some.

On my evening walk out past the cane fields I often saw a group of men squatting together, smoking, their little *lothas*, or water pots at hand, their bottoms bare.

The custom was not to look, or at least not to stare.

At Three Monkeys we had two toilets but Vajpayee the cook preferred not to use them and often in the morning he would rattle the gate, summoning Raj Pal to let him out so that he could go and shit by the river.

I liked the smell of woodsmoke. In those days the sky was clear. There was a powerful whiff of coal smoke that hit me as soon as I stepped off the plane in Delhi. I was immediately enchanted by it. That was the smell of my childhood.

I stayed four years in India, and I have many stories to tell, of how I became a disciple of Swamiji, practised meditation and *hatha* yoga, debated with myself the difference between psychological and spiritual explanations for my experiences, then asserted my independence again and came home.

For years I had dreams that I was walking back to the Ganges, past bullock cart and cane fields and I always woke up before I reached the water's edge.

In one dream I did arrive at the river and there was a carnival going on, wild animals sporting in the water. I took it to mean that I had lost my yearning and my fascination with the river and that seemed confirmed by the dream never coming back after that.

But last year I got a Major Artist Award from the Arts Council of Northern Ireland to fund a return.

The population had more than doubled since I had left, forty years before. India had changed in many ways and I realised that I knew an India that people under fifty, which was most Indian people, had not known.

I recognised it as a country I could almost feel at home in. I knew what kind of curiosity to expect. The taxi driver from the airport asking me how many children I had, how many cars I had, was just doing what so many others had done before him, placing me inside a hierarchy in his head. He made no effort to conceal his disappointment with my answers.

But before the rush of impressions about the new metro system, the lavish hotel, the migrant workers camped under flyovers, there was the filthy air.

The glory of India that struck me on my first day with a shock in 1975 was the crystalline sharpness of the light. The sun was brighter than I had ever known it at home.

I read a comment from a writer I would attribute if I could remember: that the boys in India wore bright coloured trousers and shirts to compete with that light.

It was gone. Instead a pallid smog dimmed the sky. On my first morning back, I wondered if it might just be a seasonal mist that dissolved the view in the distance.

Imagine letting something like that happen to a beautiful country.

I took a taxi to the Ganga. This was a bit difficult because the receptionist at the hotel in Delhi could not comprehend that I wanted to go to a place that no tourist went to. "You mean Agra?" A man behind me interjected, "No, he wants to go to Hardwar."

This is an Indian thing I know, people stepping forward to speak for you.

I showed them the map on my phone and they shook their heads.

I said, "I have been there before. I know what I am doing."

Tourism in India is not about acquainting people with the country but shielding them from it.

I had not understood the privileged access I had had to religious Hindu society in the 1970s. Before I left Belfast I contacted a charity which ran pilgrim hostels and was told there was no possibility of me getting a room in one.

The taxi to Brijghat took me over the Jumna River which was now almost inaccessible though there had been a promenade along a riverside park there and I had watched the *dhobis* washing clothes in the water and slapping them to dry on a flat rock. I had sat there and gazed out across farm land between there and Ghaziabad.

The river was now a disgrace to the city and we were sheltered from it.

There was no way to shelter us from the sight of the city rubbish dump which rises as high as Cave Hill does over Belfast. Eagles hover in their hundreds, having evolved into scavengers now, the way seagulls have in British and Irish cities.

When I lived there before I was in open countryside as soon as the river was behind me. Now the city and the towns that have grown round it extend almost all the way to Brijghat. The traffic was as chaotic as I had known it;

there was just an awful lot more of it, dense over a vaster area. Family groups on motorbikes wove through the trucks and taxi scooters. Where the road was diverted onto broken concrete under the unfinished metro flyover, the shambles of mixed vehicles nudged and beeped their ways through.

In the city the *tuk-tuks* didn't tuk-tuk, their engines having been converted to take organic fuel to reduce the pollution. The problem is acknowledged in different degrees in different states.

The tea shops along the way served drinks in plastic cups. Each shop front was garlanded in crisp packets. India has discovered cheap snacks.

The road into Brijghat has been widened. There is now an interstate checkpoint that taxi scooters have a feeder lane through. Market stalls selling cane furniture line the roads on the edge of the town as before.

I walked around expecting some kind of curiosity about me and there was none. There were new cafes and shops. I had developed a cough and went into the pharmacy to ask if I could buy an inhaler. The man offered me a choice of two. No prescription needed. It cost about £1.50.

Was I putting people off in some way by my own manner? Perhaps my disappointment was obvious. Forty years ago I had been a familiar face in Brijghat and the shop keepers waved to me and smiled.

The old style of tea shop was gone. There were little sit-in cafes with red plastic seating. Along the river, stalls sold white plastic canisters for pilgrims to gather the sacred water in. The cremation business was big now.

On my walk there in the following days I would sometimes see a dozen fires burning at the same time. And litter everywhere. I walked up to one of the pyres and watched the incense being spread on the body of a woman wrapped in a yellow saree. Her face was covered but her hands and bangles were exposed. Her family set logs about her. One took a light from the brahmin and circumambulated before touching it to the kindle. The brahmin, like the others, was dressed in casual clothes. No dressing up for this funeral.

The next fire along had died down and a dog was settling to enjoy the heat. All along the edge of the water was litter, scraps of cloth, plastic, indeterminate filth.

The Gita says, *The ladle is Brahman, the oblation is Brahman, it is offered by Brahman in the fire that is Brahman; who in all things sees Brahman to Brahman attains.* It is a poetic description of the divinity of everything, inside the ritual and outside.

Today the *rishi* would have to write that *the litter is Brahman, the dog is Brahman, the plastic is Brahmin, the dead sky is Brahman.*

There are now public toilets, so less of the shit; but shit at least decomposes or gets washed away. All that plastic that starts out nice and shiny just lies on the ground forever.

Even the traditional earthenware urn for water from the well is now replaced everywhere with a plastic imitation in a wide range of colours.

Raj Pal has not changed. We fell into each other's arms without reservation at first sight.

I sat with him in the courtyard as he stripped the stalks from dried chillies and he laughed when I offered to help with such a dangerous job. *You will wipe your eye and blind yourself.*

In the forty years since I had seen him, he had had three children and his wife had died. I remember her well. They spent their early marriage in the room next to mine and laughed constantly like children at a new game.

I realised that I had never had such love for a man as I had for Raj Pal and yet I hardly know him. I know nothing of his politics.

He took me up onto the roof where I had slept in hot weather or lain awake among other sleeping pilgrims and watched the moon. Now another building blocked the view. Raj Pal took me to a corner, from which we could see past that building, and gestured to Ganga – his face full of pride – joined his palms and bowed to the river. For him this is still one of the holiest places on Earth, where the Goddess washes the land and all the sins of all the humble sinners bathing in Her waters.

Malachi O'Doherty was born in 1951 and raised in West Belfast. He is the author of nine books, most recently Gerry Adams: An Unauthorized Life *(Faber, 2017) and a novel,* Terry Rankin Has a Gun *(Merrion Press, 2020). He continues to live in Belfast.*

A COMPLETE TOURIST'S GUIDE TO NORWAY

Morten Strøksnes

Running amok — like the rest of the West.

1

Norway used to be a poor and scarcely populated country on the fringes of Europe. Visitors from the continent were few, but some wrote books about the very exotic experience. In the nineteenth century, many travelers commented on the backwardness of the Norwegian people, especially if they were intrepid enough to travel through the mountains and valleys inland. For instance, the British officer William Henry Breton painted a rather bleak picture in his *Scandinavian Sketches, or A Tour in Norway* (1835). Norway was poverty-ridden, and the people were often plagued by vermin, disease, drunkenness and inbreeding. People and their animals slept together in small, smoky cottages. Villagers were dormant and rarely travelled anywhere, not even to the next valley. News from Europe took years to arrive, and there weren't many modern inventions around. Breton got the feeling he was travelling back in time, towards some stagnant primordial past.

Photos of people living in these regions, even if they were taken fifty years later, are striking for their aboriginal appearance, staring into the lens with ferocious eyes, like people who only follow their own ancient laws. You would be forgiven for thinking they were taken in some remote valley of Albania.

Norway may have been poor, but the locals were also described as proud, helpful and generous to strangers. Many of these visitors were deliberately going to remote and exotic places to explore something genuinely different. They often did not report much from the coast, because it was much the same as other places in coastal Europe: highly connected and surprisingly integrated into European civilization. A thousand years ago, the people along these coasts went deep into Russia, to the Middle East and to North America. A city like Bergen had grown in considerable size and affluence already in the early medieval period, due to the export of fish. The abundance of the sea, and our ability to master it, has always been our blessing.

Let's admit as much: most people visiting Norway come for nature, not culture. Our first tourists were often upper-class Englishmen. They used to be called *salmon-lords* because they came for the abundant wild salmon in our rivers. Kaiser Wilhelm II of Germany was another pioneer, who loved the Norwegian fjords more than anything. Almost every year he took his warships along the Norwegian coast, just to relax in a wild landscape that he found totally irresistible.

He set the tone. Most modern tourist guides to Norway will start something like this: you should go to Norway to admire the "overwhelmingly beautiful landscapes" at the "fresh fringe of Europe" or "the land of the mid-night sun". Mass-tourism was invented only a few decades ago (by General Franco of Spain). In 1905, when Norway became independent, about 25,000 tourists visited Norway. Today, millions of tourists travel around the country every year. They do not come for the food, the value for money or the quality of the service. They come for the landscapes, like they always have.

The *Lonely Planet* guide to Norway starts like this: "The essence of Norway's appeal is remarkably simple: this is one of the most beautiful countries on earth. Stirring Landscapes. Impossibly steep-sided Norwegian fjords of extraordinary beauty cut gashes from a jagged coastline deep into the interior. Glaciers, grand and glorious, snake down from ice fields that rank among Europe's largest. Elsewhere, the mountainous terrain of Norway's interior resembles the ramparts of so many natural fortresses and yields to rocky coastal islands that rise improbably from the waters like apparitions. Then, of course, there's the primeval appeal, the spare and staggering beauty of the Arctic. And wherever you find yourself in this most extraordinary country, these landscapes serve as a backdrop for some of Europe's prettiest villages."

The Norwegian tourist authorities are trying to sell the country in exactly the same way: as a pure wonder of nature with sparkling glaciers dropping into pristine fjords bursting with marine life. Visit Norway, the state agency for the promotion of tourism, has found their slogan in "Norway: Powered by Nature". The drone-prone videos they produce are almost always of the fjords. They are the pride of Norway and are therefore used to promote the country all over the world. It's an easy job since the fjords are already on the cover of every travel guide available, and the travel magazines are equally enthralled.

2

It is easy to pinpoint exactly when-and-what changed Norway more than any-thing else (with a possible exception of the bubonic plague): on 23 December 1969 commercially exploitable oil was discovered in the Norwegian sector of the North Sea. To make a long story short: over the next few decades, oil and gas worth thousands of billions of dollars was exploited, making Nor-way into one of the richest countries on Earth. As we speak, the oil-fund, formally called the Government Pension Fund, is the largest fund in the world. Most of the revenue from oil and gas is invested in stock exchanges or property in places like Tokyo, London, Paris and New York – or else is used to buy government bonds. Billions find their way into coal, nuclear subma-rines, weapons and companies with quite deplorable environmental records. There's hardly any end to the ironies. The Norwegian state is giving billions of kroners (NOK) to poorer countries to make them drop coal and replace it with renewable energy. At the same time, the Government Pension Fund is investing even more in companies building 39 new coal power plants in the very same countries.

Like other investors and companies, the Norwegian oil fund puts profit first. Its purpose is not to benefit mankind, except the Norwegian part of it. A website, which tracks the fund's exact market value in Norwegian kroners, updates from millisecond to millisecond. Like a cash register running amok, hundreds of millions are added or lost in a couple of seconds. Today, as I write this, it has reached 9,000 billion kroners (around 1,000 billion euros). That is about 200,000 euros for every Norwegian.

There are only a few things the oil fund will not invest in. One of them is, believe it or not, oil. Or at least that is the plan from 2019 onwards. Divestment in oil is done explicitly to make the Norwegian economy less exposed to oil and gas, and thus less vulnerable. That said, Norway is on a global spending spree. We have more money than we could possibly spend at home, without causing massive inflation. At the same time, we are selling Norway by the pound. Public institutions, infrastructure and natural resources are being sold or privatized as if they were approaching their expiry date. Dr. Jekyll sells. Mr. Hyde buys. Schizophrenia is a long-term mental disorder of a type involving a breakdown in the relation between thought, emotion and behavior, leading to faulty perception, inappropriate actions and feelings, withdrawal from reality and into fantasy and delusion.

Surprisingly, many Norwegians still think Norway is on higher moral ground than most other countries. They see themselves as more democratic, more just, more environmentally aware, and … just better in almost every respect. On the New Year's Eve of 1992, our former Prime Minister Gro Harlem Bruntland even tried to rally the nation around the slogan "it is typically Norwegian to be good". A few years later, she coined the expression "sustainable development" as the leader of a key UN report on global environment and development (*Our Common Future*, Oxford University Press, 1987).

Even our bombs seem to have magical qualities. We dropped 588 over Libya in 2011, more than any other country. But our bombs never killed any civilians, according to our Minister of Defense. The NATO war destroyed Libya, rendering it into a criminal fiefdom with gangs, clans and sects controlling different parts of the country. The lackadaisical Norwegian politicians responsible for our involvement seem to think our bombs are, by definition, humanitarian, simply by virtue of being Norwegian. If any mistakes were made, it must be down to the responsibility of the international community (the UN), or the Libyans themselves.

There was something in it for Norway. Jens Stoltenberg, our Prime Minister at the time, remarked that the war gave Norwegian fighter pilots excellent training. This attitude made the Americans fall in love with him, and he is now the head of NATO. His main job is to make threatening remarks towards Russia and bend the arm of every NATO member-country, including Norway, to get them to buy more American weaponry. Stoltenberg's relationship with Donald Trump is not only cordial, it's downright affectionate. Norwegian media is very proud of the fact that Trump is so chummy with Stoltenberg. Apart from this, the American President is being described, by the same media, as a deranged and very dangerous person.

3

It's easy to spot a Norwegian abroad. Especially the older generation, who never got used to the idea of belonging to a global one percent. They often stay at luxury resorts, but that is not really what they feel they're cut out for. So they embarrass themselves by being over-friendly with the cleaners and waiters, people who are often working much harder, but only earning a fraction of an average Norwegian's salary. By pretending to be their peers, Norwegians often make it difficult for workers to get their job done. The decent thing would be to tip them generously at the end of the stay. But Norwegians don't believe in that. We think people should earn decent hourly wages, like we do. If the world turns out to be unlike Norway, and of course most places are, they've only got themselves to blame. We wouldn't want to dirty our hands and corrupt it further by giving them a solid tip.

We honestly want to be humble, hard-working people devoted to fairness, equality and solidarity. We wish we deserved all the good things we have. But it is getting harder and harder to justify, especially when talking about sustainable development, which we constantly do. Our national oil company used to be called Statoil, not an unreasonable name for a state-owned oil company. But last year, the board of the company (now partly privatized) decided that the old name had to go. The new name is Equinor, which means precisely nothing, but that seems to be the whole point. Nothing plays better than any association with oil, gas – or the state. The old name has been slightly tarnished by corruption, in Norway, Iran and Angola. Also environmentally-speaking, by producing oil from tar sand in Canada. The change of name, however, doesn't change much. Equinor now plans to drill for oil in the middle of the unique Great Australian Bight, much to intense protests from Aussie surfers, fishermen and environmentalists.

Speaking of new names, something is definitely going on. In March 2019, the old state railroad company NSB – Norwegian State Railroads since 1883 – also changed its name. The new name is Vy. Like Equinor, Vy doesn't really mean anything, and that appears to be very important. The new name severs the link to history, tradition and the state, even if the enterprise is still one hundred per cent owned by the Norwegian state. According to the wishful thinking of the consultants, the public would associate Vy with Vision, and Equinor with Equilibrium and the North. But for Norwegians and English-speakers alike, Vy sounds like "Why?" and few seem to know the answer to that question, though it is quite obvious. Vy will be dismantled, split up and sold. Then the private companies will create more expensive monopolies; but when the scandals hit the headlines, it will be too late. The fruits of the hard labor of previous generations are being sold like we were broke and in need of a quick buck to fill our empty stomachs. Norway seems to be the place where neo-liberal ideas go to die. We don't need to control that kind of infrastructure anymore. You see, we've got money now.

They are even in the process of selling Oslo Børs, the Norwegian stock exchange, to either Nasdaq or Euronext. I care less about that than the selling of our waterfalls to foreign companies.

Yes, we are Western Europe's main producer of oil and gas. But look at us. We are also the world's leader in electrical cars. They are heavily subsidized in Norway, and fossil fuel cars will soon be obsolete. "We are about to succeed in making the green shift, by using the market for the sake of the climate" our Prime Minister Erna Solberg stated last year. To justify this claim, she pointed to Norway's unparalleled share of electrical cars.

The import of biodiesel is also rising sharply. Most of this fuel derives from palm oil, produced in what used to be rainforests in Brazil and Indonesia. The CO_2-footprint of biodiesel is often many times higher than our own gas and diesel from the North Sea. But we only want to sell it, not use it ourselves. We have, in this sense, become like the worst kind of dope dealers: the ones not using themselves, only selling to make money. Life can be hard when you want to be seen as a green nation and are, at the same time, a petromonarchy, the Kuwait of Europe. The rhetorical efforts to conceal or camouflage this simple fact are often quite impressive, but even an idiot will see through the self-delusion in no time.

But we really yearn to be a progressive force for good in the world. We do pay a lot in remission and indulgence, through foreign aid, by helping international peace processes and by cashing out to save tropical rainforest. Our left hand is often not aware of what the right hand is up to.

The Prime Minister has also redefined the ice-border in the North. Global warming is moving the ice-cap northwards, but the Prime Minister's intent was not to sound the alarm. By redefining Norway's Northern border, vast new areas were opened to exploration for oil and gas. When she was criticized, she replied that the ice-cap had moved itself. She was not the one to blame.

What is more, ice from retracting glaciers on the Norwegian mainland is going to be exported as exclusive ice cubes, branded "svice", to be put in drinks. You see, through eons of time, the ice-molecules have been compressed under the glacier's massive weight. For this reason, "svice" is guaranteed to keep your drink cold a bit longer.

No. I am not making this up.

It would be unfair not to admit that some action is indeed being taken against climate change, but only if there's money in it. Specifically for what our former Prime Minister Stoltenberg dubbed "the environmental industrial complex", as a warning to his successors. For instance, more than three thousand wind turbines are currently being built. All of them in untouched nature, turning these wild places into grand industrial construction zones with roads, cable gates and other installations. We don't actually need this energy and, typically, German investors own the sites. The logic seems to be that the destruction of some of the last areas of wild nature is welcome as long as the word "green" can be tossed in there somewhere.

Wind turbines are being built all over the world, for very good reasons. But only Norway, which is already self-sufficient with green hydroelectricity, let the construction companies blast their way through pristine wilderness – to produce very limited quantities of electricity for export. How green was my valley.

4

What *is* typically Norwegian? Being a lightly populated country with a sound distance between cities, villages and people in general, some characteristics have developed through time. A rugged individualism and stubborn self-reliance are on the positive side while the attitude of the old Norwegians is often presented as negative. They are seen as small-minded, envious, rigid and suspicious of change and otherness.

The essence of this attitude was famously expressed by the Dano-Norwegian writer Aksel Sandemose (1889-1965) in the ironical "Law of Jante". The rules of this imagined law-state are as follows. *You're not to think you are anything special. Don't think you are as good as we are. Don't think you are smarter than we are. Don't imagine yourself better than we are. Don't think you know more than we do. Don't think you are more important than we are. Don't think you are good at anything. Don't laugh at us. Don't think anyone cares about you. You're not to think you can teach us anything.*

Nowadays, people trying to get away with nasty stuff appeal to the Law of Jante. It is very convenient. Nobody wants to be seen as upholding the Law of Jante. So the person claiming to be a victim of this law will always have the moral high ground. Even when they have been malicious, greedy, selfish, stupid or tried to get away with exploitation or nepotism (or what is called corruption in other places), then they can make one last appeal. Namely, that they are being judged by of the Law of Jante.

We've always overlooked the possibilities of any good sides of the Law of Jante. It describes the mental mechanisms of a collective trying to safeguard its own survival, promoting a degree of humbleness, caution and respect amongst its members. What would the opposite of the Law of Jante look like? You're to think you are better and more than we are, more special, knowledgeable, important and smarter than us, etc.? This is perhaps more the credo of the neo-liberal sociopath, thinking only of himself and his own gain.

And today, that is more typically Norwegian than I like to consider. Where is the Law of Jante when we really need it?

Often, the universally known fairy-tale figure of Askeladden is used in combination with the Law of Jante, to much the same effect. Askeladden (literally "lad in the ash") came from a Norwegian folk tale, where he was bullied by his two older brothers. Nothing was expected of Askeladden, but he was good-natured, selfless and always keen to help others. Long story short: Askeladden ends up winning the hand of the princess and half of the kingdom. Today, Norwegian billionaires and oligarchs are being compared to Askeladden. But our billionaires did not succeed by being kind-hearted and unselfish. They succeeded by bending and breaking the law.

Unfortunately, the old puritanical Norwegian is a dying breed. "Framsnakking" (literally: *to talk something forward*) is a catchphrase of our times. It means that you will be branded as a grumpy, negative person if you criticize anyone or anything, no matter how much they deserve it. You are even supposed to cheer for something as fundamentally destructive as salmon farming. If not, you are a proponent of the Law of Jante.

Being proud, principled and a bit morose, like the Norwegians were often said to be, is not necessarily the solution to all problems. But has the pendulum swung too far in the other direction? And is the result dignified? The Norwegian language is under constant attack and often tears itself away from what used to be considered reality. The shackles have been broken, and truth is trouble, like a fugitive on the run. Traditionally, we are not smooth talkers, or even much for talking. But these days it sometimes feels like a self-help guru has hijacked the collective mind through spin, branding and a positive rhetoric, made by an armada of consultants and PR-people, experts in blurring the distinction between truth and lies. The parliamentarian Torgeir Knag Fylkesnes recently pointed this out in an interview: "Spin used to be added on top of something real. Something built on facts was spun, some version of the truth was at the starting point. But now it starts and ends with spin."

Norwegians used to be called *citizens*, which implicates a collective in a sense of togetherness. This collective of Norwegians constituted the nation. Nowadays the word citizen is very rarely heard or seen. In our dealings with the state, we are now "customers", "clients" or "users". It may seem trivial, but these words describe very different types of relations and are not about society, cooperation or anything like that. A customer or a client is an individual operating in a market and under market law. This is the identity the Norwegian state wants us to adopt. People behave like the system encourages them to. So it shouldn't be surprising that Norwegians started to behave like disgruntled customers in their dealings with the Norwegian state.

The language of New Public Management has spread to all corners of the land and it is constantly mutating, taking over new areas, often to a maddening effect. The public sector has been sent to school, and it has learned, through this process of re-education, to speak as if the free market was its native country. Democratic control of these new "public enterprises" is now lost.

5

For thousands of years, we've been a nation of seafarers and fishermen. But with oil, our connection to the sea went through a sea-change. The new harvest of the sea was drilled up from the seabed way out in the North Sea, from platforms beyond the horizon. We never see them and few of us have any contact with the oil and gas when it reaches the mainland into secluded industrial zones. In some areas (Stavanger, on the southwest coast, is the oil-capital), many people work in oil. But for most Norwegians this source of wealth is totally abstract. It's only been going on for 50 years whereas the old way of living from the sea goes back to time immemorial. In a short time span, oil has been immensely profitable for Norway. But in the long run, it is actually of little value compared to fish. Fish have been our main article of export and trade since the age of the Vikings. As a renewable resource, it has rarely let us down.

This part of our history, which could be said to be *the* history of Norway, seems largely to have been forgotten in a very short time. *The fish* is still common property, but only formally, as make-believe. These immense resources are supposed to be of use to the coastal communities, creating work and income where there's not much else to live by. But the ideas and ideals concerning access to the fish have been eroded, often against the letter of Norwegian laws.

Much control of fish has been taken from coastal communities to end up with investors in a liberalized market favoring people with capital. A substantial lot of the fish caught today is frozen at sea and sent directly by cooler-ships to the Baltic, China or Thailand for processing – and infusions of water and chemicals. Not at any point is it getting even close to Norwegian shores. No value is added by landing, processing, transporting or selling. Fish have become almost on par with oil as an abstract source of income. But at least the profit from oil ends up in the state coffers. The profit from the fish ends up in the hands of the few, leaving many communities along the coast depressed and stagnant. Coastal fisheries involving smaller vessels could create a lot more jobs and spread the value more evenly. The smaller vessels often deliver higher quality than trawlers and factory-ships, and the way they catch fish is much more sustainable (trawlers are very destructive of the seabed, and there's a lot of bye-catch thrown away). Their small boats are flexible and cost-efficient, compared to a trawler with a price tag of around a hundred million euros. Not to mention the fact that the coastal communities represent an old and unique culture worthy of survival. For generations they've been adapting to the seasons, local environments and natural fluctuations in the availability of different species of fish.

Now this culture is dying. The old fishing communities have lost their old right to harvest from the sea. The fish they depend on have in large part been given away to venture capitalists, who do not think about fishing as a form of harvesting, but more as industrial production. The bigger and more expensive boats you build, the more fish you will "produce", according to the prevailing logic. And when one of these companies has invested in a new trawler, you couldn't take any fish away from them. They've got huge bank loans and would go bankrupt in a short time. No one will allow that to happen. Being irresponsible will make you the guaranteed owner of millions of fish.

The quest for "the new oil" has already been going on for quite some time, and the Norwegian authorities have found some brave new candidates. Salmon farming is now at the top of the list. Tourism is a given because of the beautiful fjords, enclosed in many places by jagged, almost perpendicular mountains with snow on top. The tourists are encouraged to see pure, virginal beauty. But the salmon farming companies are, on the other hand, into a grand-scale pollution.

6

Most fjords end in a river, or if you prefer, begin there. These rivers have traditionally been the birthplace of one of the most spectacular fish: the wild salmon (*Salmo salar*). This super-fit, muscular torpedo of the open ocean and rivers is anadromous. It is born in rivers and then, small and vulnerable, it is released by the streams into the fjords. If it survives, it will swim thousands of kilometers in the Barents and Atlantic Ocean, feeding on fish, shellfish and prawns coloring its meat so deliciously pink. When the time has come, it will return to the river in which it was born, using some evolutionary GPS-technology that still makes scientists scratch their heads. In the home-river it will spawn and die and the cycle will start again.

This ultra-mobile top predator, one of those wonders of evolution, is the fish they decided to genetically modify and transform into a stagnant farm animal. Hundreds of thousands of farmed salmon are trying to coexist in relatively small open-net pens. They are fed soya from Brazil and given chemicals to color their flesh red to fool consumers all over the world into thinking that they are eating salmon. In commercials, they use wild salmon swimming up roaring rivers with ecstatic energy as stand-ins for the lice-bitten creatures they sell.

The salmon-lobbyists claim, in spite of all available evidence to the contrary, that there is room for five times more farmed salmon than our fjords contain today. Many of our ministers and politicians, getting all their information from the same lobby, regularly repeat this claim. And they in turn are quoted by the salmon-lobbyists to reinforce the validity of this insane goal.

In Norway, there are now more than 1,300 locations for open-net-pen salmon farms. Each location holds several open-net pens, and each pen contain around 200,000 salmon. Do the math. The waste, that is faeces and spill fodder, from each of these open pens is comparable to that of a small town. But a small town would never get permission to let untreated sewage flow into the ocean. We are talking hundreds of millions of tons of waste. Under the pens, the seabed is often anaerobic, smelly and devoid of life. The seabed is also heavily contaminated by poisonous and nondegradable copper used in the thousands of tons to clean the net-pens of algae, effectively making the surrounding environment unfit for any living creature. Every year, more than 50 million salmon die in the pens. That's the official number at least, but some well-reputed sources claim the number in reality is at least twice that. Millions are getting eaten alive by sea lice, their red flesh totally exposed, which might compel some soft soul to ask whether this level of animal suffering is even legal. On an animal farm, something like this would obviously be considered criminal and be on the 9 o'clock news. The salmon is made to suffer by a long list of parasites, viruses and bacterial diseases; pathogens are spread freely into the environment. Desperate measures are taken in an attempt to keep the salmon alive. Millions of tons of chemicals are used against the sea lice alone. These parasites spread to wild salmon and kill them. The fish are washed in chemical baths (the idea here is to kill the sea lice by dissolving its shell), then the chemicals are dumped straight into the ocean even though they have been proven to kill crustaceans, small and large, from zooplankton to crabs. This is going on also in spawning grounds for fish.

Farming salmon has got more to do with the intense industrial farming of pigs or chickens and less to do with healthy marine life. Some people sarcastically call the salmon farm "sea-barns". The intention is good, but the comparison is misleading. Pig and chicken factories, hellish as they might be, are after all controlled environments. If there's an outbreak of disease, the whole unit is isolated and closed down. Salmon farms, however, are placed in the midst of a living ecosystem with no barrier between the farmed fish and the surrounding water.

Alarming phenomena occur as a result. People out fishing have been catching creepy, disfigured cod in the areas with salmon farming. These grotesque fish are called "monster cod" and nothing like them has ever been seen before. But like most problems that could diminish the profit of salmon farming, it is not being investigated or researched. So the salmon farmers can deny any connection to their activity and to all problems for lack of hard evidence.

Fun facts: sick salmon suffering from deadly diseases, like pancreas disease, are often slaughtered and sold on the market. But there's not much fun being a salmon under these conditions. Farmed salmon are given massive quantities of tranquilizers or antidepressants. Millions of salmon stop eating because of the dismal conditions they live in. They stop growing and eventually die – due to salmon depression. Yes, I know. Even I needed to check if it was an April Fool's joke the first time I read the headline, "Farmed Salmon Plagued by Depression". But it is unfortunately true. Antidepressants are not only administered in the fodder, but also injected into the suicidal fish. In Norway we used to call exuberant and life-affirming people "a happy salmon" ("en glad laks"). That expression will need to go.

7

On behalf of the industry, ministers and departments lobby the EU for permission to increase the levels of toxins in both salmon-fodder and the resulting food (like endosulphan and ethoxyquin). Maybe the presence of such harmful chemicals can explain why researchers working in the industry have tailor-made the salmon to do research on. These "Potemkin-salmon" are given another, healthier diet than the salmon for sale in the shop in order to reduce the level of toxins and increase the Omega-3.

It is not an exaggeration to claim that the salmon business and the state have quietly merged. The Norwegian salmon-lobby is even present in almost all Norwegian embassies through The Norwegian Seafood Council. In fact, they hold diplomatic passports, as though Norway had become some sort of weird sect intent on spreading farmed salmon to every corner of the globe, no matter the consequences.

Undoubtedly, they've been very successful, and the industry has built a global marked of innocent, often environmentally conscious sushi-lovers. Marketed access for farmed salmon has become a national priority, and billions are used on commercials and marketing. Chefs, and associations of chefs, all over the world are sponsored by the industry. When a Norwegian salmon company offered a deal to an association of Icelandic chefs, they rioted. We all need money – but chefs with integrity can't be on the take.

The Norwegian authorities have tried to exclude salmon farming from environmental obligations like the EU's water directive, though Norway's decision to unilaterally exclude salmon farming is legally contested. Even the largest and supposedly most responsible companies have been shown to take part in criminal activity. Like when Salmar was exposed for using formalin – a carcinogenic chemical that is normally used to preserve already dead animals – on salmon in a desperate attempt to clean it of sea lice.

Lerøy, another giant of the industry, was caught burning their documentation on the parasites in their open pens with no other plausible motive than to hide their criminal activity. But the fines they receive are normally less than what they have gained by breaking the law. Isn't this highly unusual? Bank robbers, for instance, are rarely sentenced to return half of the exploits from the robbery. When it was exposed that the industry had for decades been dumping these chemicals in the fjords, without a license to do so, the authorities' reaction was to dismiss the problem and change the law because "everybody was doing it".

To shape the minds and habits of our youngest, the salmon industry has even invaded kindergartens by orchestrating campaigns to get children under the age of six to consume more of their product. Kindergartens are neutral in regard to religious confession, but not when it comes to the religion of farmed salmon. These are just a few facts about the industry. Critical information has up until recently been hard to come by. One obvious reason is the campaigns the PR people of the industry would mount against scientists and journalists they found unhelpful. To be accurate and honest (i.e., to adhere to basic journalistic principles), when writing about this business, can be risky in Norway. Lobbyists from the industry will be in touch with your editors and try to get you suspended or moved to the sports section. They regard unfavorable information, however true it might be, as "biased".

The bullying tactics extend into the realm of "independent" science. Like when one of the industry's lobby organizations (NSL) harassed the State Institute of Marine Research, the oldest, largest and most prestigious of its kind in Norway. The lobbyists hired lawyers to demand tens of thousands of scientific documents, with the intention of taking scientists to court, for scientific findings that could put some limitations on salmon farming. If they discovered something wrong, or something that could be disputed by *their scientists*, the plan was to demand economic compensation. This in a situation where most problematic topics are not being investigated, obviously because the findings would make people demand action from the authorities. However, the plan finally disintegrated when it was revealed that the "brain" behind it all had tried to establish a secret channel to the Ministry of Fisheries, in order to evade the Norwegian laws of public transparency. It was a Keystone Cops' sort of mistake. The emails were supposed to go to the private inbox of the Minister of Fisheries, but they were misaddressed and ended up with a private Swedish individual. The content ("how can we get someone on the inside of the Office of the Auditor General of Norway?") shook the Swede enough to go to the media, and the scandal broke.

Still, many raised their eyebrows when the previous Minister of Fisheries, Per Sandberg, in a 2016 interview with Norway's largest newspaper

Aftenposten, called for a showdown with the "dark, negative forces" unhelpful to the salmon farming industry. When asked to specify, he did. The dark forces are professors and academics at universities and within academia in general. In other words: scientific results that could diminish the profits of the industry, or the people "talking the industry down" were branded as forces of evil. It's the bloody Law of Jante again.

Is Norway becoming some sort of banana republic? What's important for such republics is not what is being produced, but how it is done. Sandberg later stated that he could see himself working for the salmon industry. Like he wasn't already doing so. Many of the politicians and administrators whose job it is to regulate the business have invested in salmon.

Salmon farming is putting a huge burden on the ecosystems of our fjords. But it could have been worse. Someone must have made this observation and decided to do something about it. Let's use some of the fjords as deposits for mines! Only Turkey, Papua New Guinea and Indonesia allow marine deposits for mines, but even these countries are revising the policy. Norway now wants to be on that list as the government has decided to allow mine deposits in Repparfjorden and Førdefjorden. At the same time, while Norwegians are constantly targeted in aggressive government campaigns about the importance of recycling garbage, and new environmental regulations of practical or symbolic value are being implemented all over, the government has allowed tens of millions of tons of waste from copper and rutile mines to be dumped in our fjords. Every environmental organization in Norway, but also the State Institute of Marine Research, has protested at these decisions, to no avail. The "miners" are just a few well-connected investors backed by American banks. Having no capacity for mining themselves, they will sell this license to pollute to a foreign company, which will pay a tax rate of 0.5 per cent. Why do we do it? For environmental reasons, the minister Torbjørn Røe Isaksen claimed. He claims the minerals are necessary for "the green shift". To save the environment, we will first have to destroy it, unfortunately.

Norway is quite vast and the birth rate is low. Most people live in the south, around a few big cities. This gives us a lot of magnificent wilderness, more than most other nations. Do we have a special responsibility to take good care of it? Like most people, I think so. So does the UN. In May 2019 the IPBES Global Assessment Report on Biodiversity was finally published, following many years of hard work by 550 top scientists from all over the world. The headlines from the report surprised many: destruction of habitat is just as much of a threat to biodiversity as global warming. The warnings were unusually stark, due to the seriousness of the data. 82 percent decline in global biomass of wild mammals. 47% decline in natural ecosystems. 25% of plant and animal species threatened with extinction.

Last year, on 25 February 2018, at the World Economic Forum in Davos, Norway launched an initiative for a "global ocean panel" led by the Norwegian Prime Minister Erna Solberg. The aim is to put the health of the oceans and marine economic sustainability on the global agenda. The Prime Minister thinks Norway is a shining example for the world. Look to Norway, they say. It's beyond chutzpah. The equivalent of Saudi Arabia appointing itself as leader in teaching the world about women's rights. The salmon industry breeds a lot of salmon, but also piranhas and red herrings.

8

Fish rot from the head down according to an old Russian proverb. Norway has become a petromonarchy with a global farmed salmon empire on the side. The industry is not only creating damage at home, but also in places like Scotland, Canada and — everywhere it is profitable to farm salmon the way they do. As I write this, I hear on the news that the Norwegian king, queen, foreign minister, minister of fisheries and an entourage of more than fifty business people, almost exclusively from the salmon industry, have arrived in Chile. In Santiago, the Norwegians were met by angry protesters. They hoped King Harald would protect them against the Norwegian salmon-farming companies devastating the coasts of Chile — now expanding all the way into the pristine waters of Patagonia.

The protesters were indigenous people, fishermen or environmentalists, and they have learned their lesson the hard way. In Chile, where Norwegian salmon companies are the main operators, disease, pollution and intense over-exploitation has led to a veritable eco-collapse already in 2007. The deadly ILA virus was accidently imported from Norway, via infected roe. Media exposed the dismal treatment of employees working for Norwegian companies as well as the criminal neglect of safety routines. Between 2005 and 2009, 63 people working for Norwegian companies were killed. What's more, enormous quantities of antibiotics where used, causing resistance. The salmon hit the fan and the industry was devastated.

Now the Norwegian Salmon Empire is back, fronted by the king. The production levels are almost back to what they were before the collapse. So is the pollution. Toxic red waves of algae of "biblical proportions" have arisen over the two last years along the southern coast of Chile, destroying the livelihood of poor, often indigenous people. Most problems are linked to farmed salmon, particularly the dumping of enormous quantities of dead salmon. And now, as I am about to end this essay in late May 2019, the top news story is millions of salmon are dying in the pens in the North of Norway, due to toxic algae. Most commentators just think it's a "tragedy". By pure luck, that could be a more accurate description than the commentators know. In the old Greek tragedy, the protagonist is often the last one to see the truth about his or her destiny. One commentator points out that the industry has itself to blame. Fiords with hardy any flow of water through them have been filled with millions of farmed salmon. The mess from fish-shit and spilt fodder could, artificially, have created ideal conditions for massive rises in toxic algae.

The king and queen of Norway are being used to promote farmed salmon at the expense of Norway's reputation abroad. I don't know if the royals are being duped, but their role is symbolic and they tend to do as asked, in this case by the Department of Trade and Department of Foreign Affairs. The king made a comment to the media after their encounter with the angry protesters: "I take it for granted that Norwegian companies follow all rules and regulations. If something is wrong, it must be that the regulations are not strict enough." Saying so was a gaffe, considering the situation at home. In Norway, we have plenty of laws and regulations, like the law of biological diversity or §112 of the Constitution (about responsible management of the environment and natural resources). International conventions too, like OSPAR. None of these protect us much. So what to expect in Chile?

Already in 2012, the Office of the Auditor General of Norway, the central and independent state-agency for auditing the activities and practices of the state, published a crushing report on the environmental record of the industry, and the slack attitude of the Norwegian authorities. Normally, a report like that would have serious consequences. Not this time.

"The new oil" is in many ways worse than the old oil. The oil industry never polluted our fjords, at least not on such a massive scale. They are offshore. And the profit from the oil industry benefits all Norwegians. Incredibly, the salmon-farming corporations do not pay any tax or environmental fees for polluting, on such a massive scale, the common property that are our fjords. Even if they often are owned by tax refugees (the main shareholder in Marine Harvest used to be the super-rich John Fredriksen, who has since moved to the tax haven of Cyprus), gigantic multinational corporations (Cermaq is fully owned by the Mitsubishi Corporation of Japan), or a long list of international investment funds. All along the Norwegian coast, there are salmon millionaires and billionaires. Many of them live in small places, and there's a social dimension to the presence of a new class of the "salmon-flush". They are often the only people with real money to invest, allowing them to buy anything worth buying, be it property or other businesses, which not only gives them huge political and social leverage, but ultimately allows them to decide the fate of individuals and communities. It can be compared to a re-feudalization in a country that never had nobility.

In downtown Oslo, by the shore of the Oslo-fjord, a brand-new part of the city is being built. It is a gigantic monument to the oil-era, with thousands of apartments, public institutions, museums and office blocks. The new Munch museum and the Oslo public library are both opening in 2020, right next door to the beautiful Opera House of Oslo. It's said to be this decade's largest urban building project in Europe.

Looming over it all is a row of high-rise office buildings called "the Barcode". On the front of these high-rises, occupying the most expensive part of real estate in the land, are the names of companies. All 180,000 square meters are, almost without exception, occupied by companies doing "consultancy", PR, lobbyism, tax evasion – and salmon farming. One of the high-rises is called the PWC-building (PricewaterhouseCoopers), another the Deloitte building.

These are the new rulers of Norway.

The richest person in Norway, and the richest person in the world under 30, is Gustav Magnar Witzøe. He got his 20 billion kroners by inheriting the salmon-farming company called Salmar from his father (the kid is pursuing a career in modeling). Every krone is made by exploiting what used to be considered a national, communally-owned treasure. And that very exploitation is the industry's main competitive advantage. That's why they are so resistant to available technology, i.e., closed pens that would eliminate all the sinister spillage.

Black Metal, music inspired by dark forces, is also a huge Norwegian export industry. As a witty person pointed out, the Black Metal bands might be worshipping Satan, but they are definitely more environmental-friendly than the oil and salmon industries.

Against the advice of scientists, the grand-scale harvesting of kelp (where most of the fish live), and zooplankton (what fish eat), is allowed. The zooplankton is being made into fodder for salmon, as "lesser" species of fish (like sand lance, blue whiting, Norway pout) are already decimated. As resources have been depleted at one of the upper levels of the food chain, the industry has just moved one step down. Now, with zooplankton, they are approaching rock bottom. The next level is phytoplankton. They get their energy directly from the sun. Fortunately, the sun is probably too hot and far away to be useful as fodder. But if the industry finds a method to feed it piece by piece to farmed salmon, it would soon be getting darker in this neck of the universe.

Also, Norwegian "supertrawlers", owned by a Norwegian oligarch, are catching vast amounts of krill along the South Pole ice-cap. The consequences are as of yet unknown, but ignorance is no longer seen as a reason for caution, rather as an opportunity, before someone comes along and points their finger at the environmental vandalism. If you go to Norway, every other person you encounter will ask: "What do you think about Norway?" They will have a special, delightful glow on their face. It comes from the anticipation of praise. Will you give them what they ask for?

All our new banknotes are embellished with maritime or marine engravings: the 200 kroner note has a cod; the 1000 kroner note has an oceanic wave. It is hard to miss the irony. Our maritime resources used to belong to the nation, as a group, or even a community, future generations included. Now, everything depicted on the banknotes can be bought with those same banknotes. If you want to pollute, exploit or use them as dumping grounds for mining deposits, you are welcome to do so. Norway is in the middle of an era of extreme financial opulence. But what will be remembered about this period? Probably not all the things we bought, but all the things we sold, when Norway turned into Moneyland.

The play *Peer Gynt* (1867) by our famous Henrik Ibsen has, more than any other work of literature, become a part of the Norwegian psyche. An abundance of quotes and figures from this epic play, built on an old fairytale, is incorporated into the Norwegian language. One of the most known quotes is from the hall of the Mountain King. The Mountain King teaches Peer the difference between being a troll and being human. Humans say, "be yourself", whereas trolls say, "be yourself enough". In Norwegian "enough" is the word "nok". Coincidentally NOK is also the acronym for our currency Norwegian Kroner. As the poet Torgeir Rebelledo Pedersen once remarked, the real message from the Mountain King concerning trolls must be reinterpreted:

the King has abdicated for the crown, or more specifically Norwegian crowns. So: "Be yourself, Norwegian Kroner"!

9

The Vosso River, in the mountainous wild western part of the country, used to be one of the most famous salmon rivers in Norway. The local "salmon-stem" in the Vosso was known to be larger than most other places, and most likely the largest anywhere on the planet. Salmon of more than 30 kilos were quite regular, and the Vosso became a magnet for "salmon-heads" from all over. From the mid-nineteenth century, British "salmon-lords" paid substantial sums every summer to secure the best positions along this river.

But this champion of the sea, and the fast-flowing river of Vosso, fell into sharp decline. God only knows how many million years nature needed to make this creature. The time it took to destroy it is on the other hand well known. It is infinitesimally much shorter. In just a few decades, the Vosso salmon became endangered. Already in 1992, the situation was critical, and all fishing has been banned since then.

The collapse of the Vosso salmon coincides *exactly* with the rise of farmed salmon. Smolt needs to pass narrow fjords on their way to the ocean, and open pens containing millions of farmed salmon occupy these fjords. The surrounding waters are packed with sea-lice, killing the small and vulnerable salmon on their way to the open ocean. It's not only a question of numbers. Farmed salmon on the run pollute genetically wild salmon. The Norwegian authorities have, together with local experts and enthusiasts, tried to restore the species, by directly releasing smolt into the river system. They have spent something like 20 million pounds on this effort. In May 2019 they gave up. The legendary Vosso salmon is not coming back. The Vosso is not an exception. As the farmed salmon empire has colonized the Norwegian coast, all the way up to the Arctic North, no river in Norway is unharmed. Leading scientists, like professor Are Nylund, also warn that there is "no doubt" deadly viruses are being spread from farmed salmon to wild salmon.

2019 is the international year of the wild salmon. Most Norwegians don't know about that. If it was made better known, it would draw attention to the plight of the wild salmon, and many people don't want that. They know Norwegians are not supposed to accept environmental crimes like this for money. Most people are embarrassed by it, except those who have no shame to speak of.

10

In Norway, there's been continuous media coverage of the movement of a mountain called "the Man" (Mannen). It's been on and off for the last decade. The Man looms over the village of Horgheim, an old Norse name, signifying a place where cultic sacrifices were made. The needle-shaped top of the mountain has been closely monitored since 2009. It is highly unstable and can fall at any moment. When this happens, up to one hundred million cubic meters of stone will roll down the mountain. The village will be crushed. The river Rauma will probably be blocked. Catastrophic floods will likely ensue. It's like something from Henrik Ibsen. Every time movement is detected, all 11 inhabitants of Horgheim are evacuated. In between the hasted evacuations, they are waiting for the Man.

Nobody knows when exactly: it could be sooner, or later. That's the way it is with disasters waiting to happen. They wait. And then they happen. But a hard mountain is gonna fall.

This essay was written in English.

Editor's Note: 26 hyperlink footnotes were provided along with the above text, providing the necessary factual substantiation at a precise variety of points. These can be provided to readers upon request, by post or email. It is our general policy not to include such footnotes or hyperlinks, so as not to interfere with reading fluency.

Morten Andreas Strøksnes (born 1965 in Kirkenes) is a Norwegian journalist and non-fiction writer. His books include Hellig grunn *(2001),* Snøen som falt i fjor *(2004),* Automobil – Gjennom Europas Bakgård *(2005),* Et mord i Kongo *(2010), and* Tequiladagbøkene – Gjennom Sierra Madre *(2012). For his 2015 non-fiction book* Havboka *he was awarded both the Barge Prize and the Norwegian Critics Prize for Literature. As of 2018 the translation rights of this book have been sold in 24 countries, and the English translation (titled* Shark Drunk, *Penguin Random House) was awarded the British Wanderlust Travel Book of the Year in 2018.*

TWO ESSAYS

—

Seán Lysaght

SPATE RIVER
Call of the wild.

The summer had been fairly dry, with only an occasional shower of rain. The spate river had not been properly in flood since May, when rain fell in a brief, violent burst and flushed muddy water through the system for a day. Then the levels fell back and gave little hope for weeks. There had been reports of sea trout taken in some bigger pools, but these fish had been caught by salmon anglers who stalked the stale waters even in heat; they were a small, grudging reward for long days spent in unfavourable conditions.

My spate river is a favourite place, a rocky avenue of shallows twisting across a lonely bog with occasionally a bigger pool where fish might be harboured in the months prior to spawning. I have fished it for about fifteen years, and have walked its banks during high floods and stale droughts. Its catchment is defined by a few shallow valleys of blanket bog contained within the boulder-littered slopes of a mountain massif rising to over 500m.

There are no lakes draining into its course, only a motley scatter of bog pools slowly leaking water into the peat; rain brings sudden flushes of water into the river, and once it stops the levels fall away just as rapidly.

Over the years, the most violent spates have knocked big chunks of peat out of the riverbank and have washed rubble, gravel, and clay out of the lower strata where they had settled after the action of glaciers. These deposits have been sifted by water and brought to quieter currents, where the sediments form gravel banks and sandy pastures all along the stream. Plants such as gorse, which hate the soggy conditions of the open bog, can grow here; so can grass, and where grass grows, people were tempted into the valleys in search of grazing for their livestock.

Looking after cattle along these bog streams is seen as hard work nowadays; only a few men bother with it any more, and they have quad bikes to take them across the bog. Sheep is the usual business now, supported by European Union subsidies. The history of booleying, of summer bothies, of milk and butter from the mountain, of potato ridges bearing the precious tubers like a lifeline, is over now; its visible remains are as obsolete, yet as intimate in shared memory, as the abandoned defences and hardware of an early twentieth-century war.

My interest in this place is focussed on the river at certain times during summer and autumn, when sea trout come up from the sea and can be hunted with a fly. At other times, during low water for instance, the frustrated angler can walk up to the top of a ridge to see if any grouse or merlin might be disturbed from the open bog, or he or she may be drawn there, distracted by the lonely call of a golden plover. Then there are long winter months when the river finds its way to the sea without any human presence. Salmon spawn in remote, unfrequented streams, an event rarely sought out and rarely witnessed. The bog is cold, days are short, and conditions on the high ridges overlooking the meandering river are monstrous.

I knew that July was the best time when there is water; rain had come as forecast, starting in the evening and continuing overnight. Just as crucially, the rain was due to stop in the morning, so that the flood would peak and then run off during the day. A big, falling flood is the optimal time for sea trout: in my river this allows a window of a few hours, when fish are agitated, eager to snatch at novelties swimming through the water. If you miss that window, as I have many times, there's a melancholy feeling that the few fish you stir are stragglers from a glamorous party now ending to which you were not invited.

On my way north through clearing showers I had an eye on the streams running under the road: quiet, modest little rivers usually veiled by alders and hazels were now a big agitation of brown water and froth. The powerful mass of seawater would swallow these freshwater streams presently; grey-brown distances of gently-profiled ridges had absorbed the night's rain into anonymity; there were just one or two known, crucial places where a cataract formed a white line of fresh floodwater plunging down a steep slope several kilometres away. My need was acute, to be assured by such signs that water is still running high, that the spate will not have drained away before I get there. The sight of the main river dispelled all doubt: it was a heaving monster struggling to get under the bridge before it surrendered to an indifferent sea.

All the topography of streams, pools and emergent rocks, which linked the river to its context of banks and adjoining fields, was annihilated in that process: a great excess of water heaped up into a raging stranger had obliterated those habitual forms and relationships, and the place wanted it to leave. I comforted myself with a much smaller thought: there would be more than enough water, I was not going to miss the flood; there might even be a crushing surfeit of brown water, making angling impossible for a while.

When the two biggest rivers in this region are in spate, there is no chance of fishing, and the anglers put away all thoughts of sport until the following day. But on my river there is a narrow window after the flood has peaked, which I had rarely managed to get to: I thought, the time is now, and I must keep going.

Timing the flood was one thing; the other was a decision to make once I had parked the car: should I go upstream or down? Downstream, the river runs past a conifer plantation into a relatively narrow cutting; there are two large pools, with a long history of poaching, and several broad streams where I have often encountered sea trout, but this lower section of the river lacks the elemental loneliness of the upper stretches. Downstream means approaching a bigger fishery beat, with the risk of meeting other people; on the other hand, once you set out upstream you are away from all human traffic into a pure encounter with mountain, bog and water. And this was the option I took.

A low bluff three hundred metres away from the parking place gave me the first proper view of the river as it ran in a relatively shallow stream between a high peat bank on one side, and a level green space the size of a football pitch. There was a soundscape here too, a streaming, chuckling, growling noise, the running total of a night's rain off the deserted mountain spurs and ridges. The noise of the stream became the noise of an entire stretch of upland: every leaking peat bank, every gargling fiddaun, every stony drain, every gravelled stream, pouring, trickling, dribbling, dripping, seeping, surging, cascading, drifting, becoming this restive, unfamiliar creature of the wilderness.

In such conditions the river is alive in a special sense: you know that summer salmon (also known as grilse) and sea trout are running. Not that there is much to eat in these barren waters – salmon don't feed here at all; it's the breeding instinct that brings these fish into the narrow, hazardous channel of the river, where grilse will risk their fortunes for a few months until the breeding time of short winter days. Somewhere in this noise of cold water there are streamlined, cold-blooded muscles of protein making their way against the flow; their backs are perfectly camouflaged from predators such as cormorants, black-backed gulls, poachers, and anglers. Occasionally, you hear a splash as a salmon crosses a shallow place, but by the time you turn to look, it has vanished into the turbulence.

I walked down the stony track and continued on smartly towards a ruined, roofless cottage half a mile away. A small tributary stream was so full that I had to make a wide detour in order to cross it. At the cottage itself I sat within the walls and set up my three-piece rod and flies, even though I had not yet come to the best pool where I hoped to start. The river was still virtually unfishable: water was toiling and twisting through the big holding pools, preventing the fish from holding their positions; they would be lodged at the bottom somewhere, in the shelter of a rock, until falling levels gave them back their world. Sea trout like areas of smooth current: they avoid the churning effect of high floods.

Close to the cottage, where the stream ran through old pasture, the flood had brimmed out over submerged silvery grass-blades: here I marked the level with a stick as a reference for later.

Then I took up my rod and kept going, crossing wet, peaty trenches, stepping on heathery tufts in the softer, sphagnum-filled sections. The river was the only mark in a vast, wide bowl of blanket bog rising to a smooth horizon of mountain ridges several kilometres away. The slow drift of cloud shadow on these slopes knew nothing of my agitation; and it also seemed to have forgotten the rain that had fallen, a story that was now gathered in the stream. Fatigue from the effort to get here was the only fact linking me to the scale of the place.

In its upper reaches the river meanders in wide, varicose loops, textbook style, across the valley floor. There are other memorials here, cabins and enclosures from booleying days, but I am a poor guide to them because the angler is fixated on the river and has little curiosity for other things. The stony flanks of the mountain loom high above these deserted expanses as you approach; this is as far as the catchment goes. Water drains rapidly from these slopes, meaning that the floodwaters do not stay high for long once the rain stops. I look at these upper reaches and wonder how far do sea trout go? They are famous for running high into catchments; I have dreamt of sea trout trying to get up mountainsides on the shooting spurt of a cascade – but even these great migrants have their limits, and once the pools have lost their floodwater, they will also lose their sea trout to the deeper stretches farther down.

Eventually, I came to the biggest pool in this upper stretch of river and studied the prospects. A broken stream runs into it at a shallow angle and turns sharply at the foot of a crag forming its western side. There is deep water here holding salmon and sea trout, a fabled spot for poaching and angling where I have taken sea trout and grilse. Most of the pool was a boiling mass of slightly coloured water, all topsy turvy from the volume of the flow, but at the end, just before it fell away into another fast run, there was a glassy stretch of several metres where the water flowed evenly. I cast the flies across the pool and let them swing into the smooth glaze of the pool tail. A fish rose at the fly but did not take. I tried again, and again a sea trout boiled at the fly without making contact. A few casts later, as I worked the same spot, a bigger fish locked on the fly and held it down in the depths. It must have been a grilse or a very big sea trout, because it did not show, but moved upstream into the churning commotion. A fine "v" spread out from the taut fly line where it entered the water. Then the line locked on the bottom and would not budge. I suppose that the second fly, which hangs on a dropper off the main line, had snagged on a tuft of vegetation. There was nothing doing when I tried to coax it off again. I had to pull with my hands until the line gave way and I pulled in the remains of the leader, minus fish and flies. I would have to tie on another set of lures and start again.

As I did, I saw signs that the water was dropping: fragments of moss and rushes washed up by the flood had got caught on the growth and were already a few inches proud of the river. Falling water levels, fish in the river, a respite from midges, and total solitude: the day was shaping up as one of those rare occasions, which happen just a few times a year, when all the variables are favourable to a drama of silver fish in dark water.

When it flows out of the big pool, the river enters a short series of fast streams and then follows a straight, narrow channel for a few hundred metres, with a high peat bank on the right, and a low stretch of pasture on the left. Here the channel deepens and the river slows for the last hundred metres before it enters another deep pool and turns left. This straight stretch should be a sea trout angler's dream, and I have fished it many times with great hopes and little reward. These dark waters tantalise and challenge; just as you decide that the prospects are hopeless, a vigorous "schtock" exploding near your fly, but not taking, reminds you that there is life in the cold, peaty element, and the moment evades you even as it is offered.

I hooked and lost a grilse here in high water on my first day on this river. The fish ran strongly downstream and went into the lower pool, where it tore the leader apart. My inexperience told against me: I should have been able to hold the fish in the stream and prevent it from running away beyond my control. The friend I was with had two grilse and five sea trout that day; I managed three sea trout. There had been heavy, thundery rain that morning, and more showers during the day, so that we were wet, tired, and hungry after our excursion. It was my first experience of the river in its living manifestation as a salmonid stream, and I have measured all my later visits by its standard.

On another occasion a few years ago, I fished here with a second companion in a torment of midges. He hooked and lost a grilse on the same stretch before more rain brought the river into a raging muddy flood within twenty minutes and ended our sport for the day.

Today I had to approach this stretch from the top of the peat bank, forcing me to clamber over peat hags and down onto a few grassy ledges where you can fish the water from a low position. (If you stand high on the bank, your figure looms on the horizon and you easily spook these shy fish.) The stream was a bucking bronco of water hurtling through its course, the swing of the line was too brief, and the current too rapid; I had to move farther down, to the final fifty metres where the current slackens in a deeper, slightly wider stretch. A deep drain cuts through the peat bank at this point and joins the river: this confluence of streams is a special, favoured place for sea trout; the black darkness of this water makes the sudden appearance of flashing sea trout a miraculous revelation.

My flies had a little more time here to take their course across the current, for their sooty black fluff with glints of silver to tempt the hungry creatures. After a couple of casts, two sea trout exploded at the leader, diving into the air as their mouths discovered the hooks. The flies had been hit simultaneously. Both fish went down, the reaction was sluggish at first, but then the movement became fluid, a single gesture, and it was clear that one of the fish had come off. The remaining one, weighing about a pound, came to my hand easily a couple of minutes later.

Most of the sea trout in this river, like the one I had in my hand, were hen fish; they run on floods from June onwards, are set to spawn in November, but can be curiously shy or absent in between times; perhaps the lack of feeding makes them return to their homes in the estuaries and bays for a while. Unlike brown trout, they are not active surface feeders in fresh water; there is little to keep them nourished in these bog streams; the appearance of an angler's fly must be as sudden and mysterious to them as a mirage to a delerious desert traveller. When a fly swims into a pool, or lands on the surface, taking trout are quick to respond: a quick detonation, and you are likely to have one. (Whether or not you get it onto land is another matter, ruled by mysteries of your skill and their mood.) You can cast many times with tact and delicacy at the same place and nothing will happen; these fish do not loiter, or sulk, or hesitate. There is no point in "flogging" the water, as some salmon anglers do, in the hope of coaxing a reluctant fish to take.

I now had a fish in my bag, and trout slime on my hands; that, along with the anecdote of a lost grilse, was enough to ensure that the day was "on", but the angler, rarely content, always hurries to get to the next pool after he has pocketed his first fish. The long straight stretch drains into a deep, stomach-shaped pool which curves to the left, and narrows; the main current runs close to a high bank on the right, but at the centre the pool is calmer, and this is the best place to present the fly. I did so, and another trout came instantly; it joined the other in my bag.

The river's course changes after this section, no longer shadowed by a high peat bank on one side; instead, it has flat pasture on both sides; the rim of the riverbank is no more than a foot or two above the water surface. While this makes this section easy to access, it also means that the angler looms as a monster of the moor without the cover of a high bank, so the approach to the water must be cautious. There's one beautiful stretch here, a long, broad pool that settles quickly after the agitation of its opening stream; even in poor conditions, there's usually a sea trout established here to challenge the angler.

I felt compelled to look up and around, and take in the day. The mountain top was draped with a steam-train puff of cloud; lower cloud formed a grey distance, but the sun was now dominating blue sky, and there were few clouds left to challenge it. Brightness is another factor for the trout angler. If water conditions are not optimal – as they were now – bright sunlight is a curse and puts off all but a fraction of the fish. You can toil all day in a well populated river with hardly a stir and, as your frustrations increase, you come to hate the river and everything associated with the hunt. One bright day I dragged my line for hours through tea-coloured water in the shadow of the wind farm at Bellacorick and despaired of the naivety that had brought me there, and of the tenacity of my companion, which kept me there. But there are sunny days when the river is alive with taking fish, when every pool and run has a grilse, sea trout or even a brownie knocking at the fly, when the sun loses its power and all the angler has to do is present the fly discreetly.

I stood back from this favourite pool and took a few photographs of the landscape as I waited for some cloud cover. Then a threadbare screen of cloud veiled the sun for an interval, giving me a chance to cast. One fish took, and came away from the hook after a few lurches; then another took the fly, and was hooked securely. When I got this one in my hand, a certain scruple took over and I threw it back to the water as an offering, to the planet, to the river, to some hastily concocted household god.

Something in me relaxed at this point; I was no longer anxious about catches and tallies as I followed the river down for another kilometre, crunching across gravelly levels, or thudding softly on the grassy margins of the stream. The water was clear, the day brighter than I would have liked, but sea trout continued to take in all the usual runs, including one big trout that steered my line around the depth of a pool for a couple of minutes before the hook flew up and he was gone.

Several more trout came to the fly, and made brief contact before I lost them; there was a margin of hesitation in their behaviour that day that I could not explain. On other days I have had fish taking the fly with more savage urgency – and these were more likely to hook themselves securely.

I made my last careful stop at the last big pool in this upstream section where a friend has had great tussles with salmon. The heavy flank of a salmon turned strongly close to the fly without making contact. I could have changed my lure, put on one of the bigger, proven salmon patterns in my box, but I chose not to, and fished on, still in pursuit of sea trout; here I caught my fourth fish of the day, another pounder which rattled onto the stony margin of the river.

The earlier mark I had made with a stick was just below this pool; it was now a foot and a half above the water level; the flood was running down rapidly, but there were still a couple of hours' fishing until dusk for someone with the energy to continue.

And there was also the option of night fishing for sea trout.

Some anglers such as Hugh Falkus, and a few in my locality, prefer to fish for sea trout at night, when their behaviour changes, and they move more freely about the pools under cover of darkness. In his book, *Sea Trout Fishing* (1962), Falkus describes setting out in pursuit of these fish only when the sun is declining, with no thought of casting a line before the sun is off the water. This noctural sport amounts to total acquiescence to the sun curse, and involves many hours alone, indifferent to family ties. I know of one group whose annual fishing holiday to north Mayo is completely focussed on night fishing.

On sea trout rivers in Wales, where night fishing is not unusual, anglers on busy beats will pass each other silently at night as blurry shadows with muted voices, taking care not to spook the fish with the glare of a careless head torch. In north Mayo, the night angler has to confront the demon of utter solitude in some of the wildest locations in the country. And unlike well-managed fisheries in Britain, the going underfoot along Mayo spate streams is a challenge by day, let alone at night, an hour away from the car, out of mobile phone coverage.

Night fishing for sea trout on Mayo's spate streams is a story that has not been told, although it happens. If we had a narrative of what it was like to go out across the bog in the small hours after sea trout we might be inspired to follow, with that story echoing in our memory as a drama of hope, frustration and fulfilment. The Welsh anglers have their lore of stories to take with them into the night, although their solitude is qualified by those others who go after the same sport in the dense mothy night. And their tenacity is sometimes rewarded with much bigger fish than any Irish fishery can boast of, with the exception of Lough Currane in south Kerry.

Language might be the best security we have against the anxieties of nocturnal solitude in a remote location. Language – that is the stories people tell about their experiences in such conditions – creates a network of under-standing, a memory-store of incidents connected with places that keep the shapeless darkness at bay. There is nothing like this on my spate river, which is why I think that going there alone at night would have more of madness than sport about it. There is no nocturnal songline along the river, no fence of language to keep you safe. Anyone setting out to build that story now would be like the first climber on a rock face, putting in the pegs for others, who climbs the rock unaided.

This part of Erris is for me at the very limit of our range. It may not be the most remote geographically, nor is the terrain the most dangerous, but the wide bog at night is a space our culture scarcely knows, not in the natural history sense, but as a place for our meanings. This is why I have never gone upstream there at night, even though I have hurried across its darkening margins many times on my way back to the car.

That feeling of wildness, of primal chaos (which is not the same as pic-turesque wilderness viewed from the terrace of a safari lodge) is compounded when rain sets in, especially the slow, drenching rain that is accompanied by fog over the mountains. One night, at the end of a day's fishing, as I was driving home on one of the small roads leading away from the bog, my eyes were straining to follow the road; the headlights probed a wet formlessness of weeds, tarmac, rain and conifer forest. If I had a couple of sea trout in my bag on that occasion, it seemed like a puny, irrelevant reason to be confronting such desolation many miles from the comfort of my house. As I leaned forward towards the windscreen glass, another shape appeared on the road ahead – less a shape than a glowing, unresolved agitation moving thirty metres ahead of me. The weedy strip of road and roadside vegetation were all streaming past me and under me, but this agitation in the headlights did not get any nearer; it was suspended at a constant distance, too far away to be seen clearly. I kept driving, and still this unknown wraith performed its giddy dance in air. The performance continued for a minute until the shape finally crystallised as a stray horse running ahead of the car, a dazzled, confused creature which found the sanctuary of a lay-by as we reached the main road. This banished any thoughts of supernatural revelations on a wretched night. Still, there was a lingering feeling of disorientation, of perceptions unharnessed with the animal, and space there as well for fanciful work of new associations.

———

I had fished down as far as the ruined cottage and didn't continue after that, although there was another mile of fishable water between me and the car. That lower section has never held much appeal for me; I have fished it with little success on many occasions; the real drama of the river belongs to the upper stretches, beyond the ruined cottage, as far as the big pool with its rocky flank where I lost the big fish.

This is what I have heard referred to as an outback of the mind, a place we inhabit only temporarily, given that our lives belong to civilised, domestic spaces. While there can be no enduring temptation to linger here, some of my strongest memories belong to that broad, shallow valley with its paucity of features. On that recent visit, clouds were performing impressive shapes in a clearing sky, draping mountainsides with sharply-defined shadow. There have been darker days, more congenial to sea trout and sea trout anglers, when louring cloud, and peaty darkness combined as a tone of bleakness, underscored by the memorials of rural subsistence and toil. Then, out of the grey cover of floodwater, a silver fish exploded off the surface. My friend was into a sea trout. The first that day. Like an essence of light from the sea in a wilderness designed to offset its purity.

AN EARLY START
The bonniest company.

I had set out early, the car headlights swept the hedges as I drove helter skelter along the curving boreens towards Newport; just a single moth was suspended ahead of me like a star.

I was heading to a rendezvous at seven, at the Letterkeen bothy in the Wild Nephin Wilderness area. Sheep had just begun to stir from their overnight sleeping positions on the road, and some looked towards the approaching car with eerie yellow eyes. A few cars were already in the car park, their red lights still smouldering, and a woman in a high-viz jacket was bent over a pannier on her bicycle. It turned out that she had cycled from Westport that morning.

By the time I got on my boots and jacket, the darkness had thinned somewhat; one of the leaders was checking a list of participants in the beam of a head torch; there were greetings and introductions: I recognised a silver hairstyle, a voice. Then the ranger's big vehicle arrived; our party of six was complete, and we were ready to set out.

The morning was cold in the plantation; as our track followed the main river upstream, there was high water noise everywhere, from the cascading river and lots of smaller streams running into culverts under the road, there had been so much recent rain. A mixed coniferous woodland was starting to materialise over the track, the oldest Monterey pines like huge cathedral pillars, with deep, dark fissures scored into the bark. These trees were older than the oldest post-war forestry trees.

We crossed a plain concrete bridge, switching to the other riverbank, and passed a grove of ghostly, feathery old larch covered in deep swathes of lichen. This old man's beard, or Usnea lichen, is an indicator of very clean air and thrives here in the damp, sheltered gloom.

As the light came on, we found each other in conversation, chatting about eagles we had seen, and about woodland restoration in Wild Nephin; Coillte would soon be finished here, leaving 5,000 hectares to the state to manage in the Wild Nephin National Park; in the meantime, logging was still going on as Coillte got out some of the best timber.

Our hike took us past other stands of lodgepole pine where the crop had failed, in forestry terms; after forty years the trees had a dwarfed, bonsai look, but they were festooned with mosses and lichens, and the ground was spread with a gentle cushion of purple moor grass: you could imagine its sibilance as your boots passed through it. As a fan of the future forest, I praised these new habitats to the ranger.

The track rose above the river, and then turned west; we now had a clearing view of the landscape, and of each other: one woman I knew to see from a café in Castlebar; a second lady I knew from other field trips. It seems that my hearing has sharpened as well as my vision: in the darkness at the start I had thought the lady with the bicycle spoke with a German accent, but now I'm sure she's a French speaker.

With the extra elevation and an opening in the forest we can see lakes and mountains around the Marine Institute at Burrishoole, and over to the east, a series of mountain ridges still draped with mist in thin drifts: Mount Eagle, the top of Leana, Bireencorragh. We get out our smartphones, and stand for a moment in silent wonder taking pictures. These are the calm conditions we have all hoped for, giving us the best chance of finding what we have come to see.

Then we are instructed to be quiet, and our voices fade off to an occasional whisper. Apart from the ticking calls of a robin in the pines, there is no other sound. The trail takes us round the end of a long ridge into open territory: the forestry was felled here about five years ago, and the replanted pines are like small Christmas trees in regular stands running up the slope above us. The ranger lifts his arm to signal that he has something; he points to the right, and we see three red deer hinds moving away, up the slope. They run at first, but are not panicked; they just want to get a safe distance away, out of range of a rifle perhaps.

There's a tiny calf following them up along a fence line; the first two jump the fence easily, the third hind does not attempt this and stays with her calf. I'm checking the colour of the rump and hind-quarters, to memorise these marks: pale rumps without a dark central tail-mark: biscuit-pale at the top, even white on the inner thighs; these tones edged with a darker shade at the back of the honeyed flanks.

Occasionally, an animal pauses to take us in, and our binoculars fix on the gleaming dark of a deer's stare; there's a bark, and another angry coughing noise in warning, but no sign of a stag, nor any sound of the rut: I'm told it's already late for this, and the activity may have ceased.

A little farther on, four more hinds emerge from the plantation onto the top of a knoll; here, for an instant, they strike a group pose with their heads turned back, the pale flashes and dark margins of their rumps adding a touch of early Picasso to this Wild Nephin dawn.

We can still pick out one or two animals from the first group moving across the open hillside. I manage to spot three more, including a young antlered male, on the other side of the valley, in a recently felled area. The rough terrain of forestry debris, of peaty trenches and old stools and dumped brash has come alive: our tally is eleven; we have seen all but the stag of the Letterkeen herd.

We are not ready to turn round yet and walk on towards a shelter built by Mountaineering Ireland; but, like children who have been set free by a teacher, our everyday chatter resumes.

The red deer at Letterkeen are descendants of a deliberate, unauthorised reintroduction over twenty years ago; a kind of unofficial rewilding using stock from a deer-farm. Several dozen animals were released in an area to the north of the national park; since then they have spread south, and a few have even reached Achill in the west. In some parts of the range they are persistently hunted, but they have managed to expand their range with the help of forestry cover. Because these deer are from farmed stock of east European ancestry, they don't qualify in the eyes of the scientific purist; but I have often gone out in the hope of catching a glimpse, and I am delighted every time I see one. Unlike the Killarney or Donegal deer roaming the hillsides freely, north Mayo's deer are still shy refugees that keep in cover during the day. The stags are particularly wary.

Seán Lysaght was born in 1957 and grew up in Limerick. He was educated at University College Dublin, where he studied French and English. He has published six collections of poetry and a biography of the naturalist Robert Llloyd Praeger (1865-1953), The Life of a Naturalist *(Four Courts Press, 1998). His recent collections include* The Mouth of a River *(2007), a celebration of the landscape of north Mayo, a volume of translations from Goethe,* Venetian Epigrams *(2008),* Selected Poems *(2010) and* Carnival Masks *(2014), all from Gallery Press. He teaches at Galway Mayo Institute of Technology, Castlebar and lives in Westport, Co Mayo.*

From BEN DORAIN:
A CONVERSATION WITH A MOUNTAIN

Garry MacKenzie

In the republic of red deer.

From PART EIGHT: EMERGENCE

Amergin, mythic bard who strode
from coracle to shore, chanting the Celtic earth,
its flowerings, fruitings, moultings,
entangle us in the present
of your song, the emergent world:

    I am the wind ranging over the sea
    I am wave and ocean, climate systems
    I am the charge in a circuit board

    I am elm and heather, aspen, alder
    I am hawkweed, hybridising
    I am the root and aril of the yew

    I am hookworms, pinworms,
    whipworms, rhizomes, spores
    I am herbivore and apex predator

    I am the subsoil superstrings
    of honey fungus, the wood's leviathan
    I am hazelnut and slow worm's scales

I am rust on pit wheels and dockyard cranes
I am peregrines perching on a towerblock roof
I am lace-workers stitching in air

I am the hunter downwind among the rocks
I am the hind fearing footsteps on the wind
fearing bullets and blood and terror and dogs

It takes skill to stalk a deer,
        a flair for patience
bordering on witchcraft
        (earache from the winter wind;
frozen hands that hold
        a gun for three hours
as you wait for her to stand).

                    I am the glacier of cloud flooding the glen
                    I am Pangea, Laurentia, Afro-Eurasia
                    I am the hyperobjectivity of the hill

She's alone —
        approach her at the pace
that eggshell thickens,
        that berries ripen
among the thorns.
        Work your way
through cover.
        If she's spooked, if she
raises her head
        and you're not invisibly
still, if she lowers
        her head again but out
of the corner of her eye
        she sees you breathe,
if she scents a single
        pheromone of you,
she's gone.

                Do you take the land into
                yourself, or does the land receive
                you further into it?

I am the world as sharp as an adder's tooth

Rethink knowledge:
    not information, not even
sense data.
    Knowing the hill
means prone legs drawn
    into the dampening earth.
It means peat in your hair,
    your boots, your lungs.
Negotiate each pit
    and fold, each clump,
each tuft of grass.
    Your knee
stiffens on cold stone.

Heraclitus: *each individual thing comes out of the one,*
and the one comes out of each thing

You open door
    after door until
you can go
    no further.
Taste of bilberry
    and bracken.
Memories of boulders,
    their angles
of concealment.
    Cartography
of clouds;
    shadows moving
over the earth.
    Body
and land, air
    and mind,
close on each other ...

(Pages 61-63, *from* Ben Dorain: a conversation with a mountain, *The Irish Pages Press, 2021.*)

SCOTLAND'S CALIFORNIA

The herring boom as environmental parable.

If you were to visit the Fife fishing town of Pittenweem in the 1850s and ask the way to California, you'd be told to row a little way offshore and shoot your nets. To an east coast fisherman, California meant the Treath, an underwater trench in the Firth of Forth and one of the richest fishing grounds in Scotland. It lay between Pittenweem and Elie, and gained its nickname from the gold rush: as with the rivers of gold flowing into San Francisco Bay, the Treath's riches gave rise to mid-century boom towns and grand infrastructure projects. And like gold panning in California, the heyday of the Fife fishing industry is now long over.

The fish that brought unprecedented wealth to the region was herring, which came here to spawn, attracting predators such as haddock, plaice and turbot. Anstruther, about a mile to the east of Pittenweem, was built on the herring trade. Its grand harbour was designed by the Stevensons – a teenage Robert Louis spent a summer in the town, ostensibly learning the family engineering trade whilst secretly aspiring to be a writer – and the arrival of the railway in 1863 meant that fish landed at Anstruther could be on the table in London the following day. The name of the adjoining village of Cellardyke alludes to the silver (or *siller*) scales which lined the streets near the harbour – mostly from herring, popularly known as the "silver darlings". In the early nineteenth century, migrating schools of herring would return to the Forth most years in late summer (around the time of the Lammas Fair) as well as in December or January. This seasonality meant that herring fishing was divided into two events, known as the Lammas Drave and the Winter Herrin'. But by the 1870s, the summer herring stocks had collapsed and catches were less than a tenth of their mid-century peak. Winter Herrin' catches held out, with significant annual fluctuations, until historic highs in the 1930s. However, by the end of the Second World War the herring catch was negligible, and has never recovered. Anstruther harbour, once packed with hundreds of fishing boats, is now a marina for pleasure boats, and the town's numerous fish and chip shops chiefly sell haddock, landed elsewhere. In Cellardyke, months can pass without a boat entering or leaving the harbour.

Herring gather together for safety. Predators are more easily detected when there are more eyes on the lookout, and can be overwhelmed when faced with a cluster of near-identical prey. There's evidence that in some fish species, including herring, larger individuals find their way to the middle of a school – a formation which is larger and more cohesive than a shoal – meaning the strongest are more likely to survive to pass on their genes. Travelling is also more efficient, as drag is reduced when large groups swim together in the same direction. The advantages of school-forming are turned into weakness, however, when faced with one of the oldest of human technologies: the net. The genius of the net is that a fish's instinct to congregate ensures an abundant harvest for the fisherman. Herring are always net-caught because their mouths are too soft to hold hooks.

Prior to the middle of the nineteenth century, the two main kinds of net fishing were seine-netting and drift-netting. Seine-netting involves staking a wall of net on the shore, and hoping that fish will be caught in it when the tide recedes. The intertidal zone of the upper Forth, and Loch Fyne on Scotland's west coast, were ideally suited to seine-netting. Drift-netting is done by boat, and requires nets to be suspended like curtains, with weights and floats ensuring that they hang perpendicular to the surface of the water. In Scotland, drift-netting was always done by night, when herring rose to feed. Laws were in place to prevent fishermen casting their nets by day, due to the fear that this would scare away the fish. Experienced crews would wait for signs that herring were near: gannets diving; a breaching whale. On a still night men would cup their ears and listen for the plips of surfacing fish, their eyes straining for glimmers of phosphorescence, caused by the phytoplankton which herring eat. In Gaelic this is called *a' losgadh*, the burning. Then they would shoot their net, wait, and hope.

Seine- and drift-netting are relatively passive forms of fishing. They ensure that younger, smaller fish, as well as spawn, remain in the sea. Entire schools are unlikely to be hauled ashore. These techniques would have been recognisable to fishers in many parts of the world. In 1777, for example, Captain Cook witnessed the indigenous inhabitants of Tonga seine-netting. In Australia, a form of seine-netting is likely to have been employed for millennia at the Brewarrina fish traps, a system of stone weirs on the Barwon River. Some historians argue that Brewarrina is the oldest extant human construction in the world, constructed by Aboriginal peoples perhaps 40,000 years ago. Drift-netting makes an appearance in the Bible – it's the method used by those of Christ's disciples who were fishermen. These included Andrew, whose kneecap, fingers and teeth were supposedly the relics which gave the town of St Andrews, ten miles north of Anstruther, its name. In Luke's gospel Andrew's brother, Simon Peter, tells Christ that "at your word I will let down my net". The phrase, in Latin, is the motto of the Fife fishing village of Crail: *in verbo tuo laxabo rete*.

In nineteenth-century Scotland, two innovations in net design changed the way herring were caught. As with many other banal-seeming technological changes, designs aimed at greater efficacy and convenience had unseen or conveniently overlooked environmental consequences (see tarmac, air conditioning, the plastic toothbrush, the disposable nappy). The first of these developments was ring-netting, developed on Loch Fyne. Instead of suspending a drift-net and hoping that herring would swim into it, ring-nets surrounded a shoal and dragged it onto the shore or into a boat. Ring-netting was far more efficient than drift-netting: by the end of the century, a ring-net boat on the Clyde would land four times as much herring as a drift-net boat. The second innovation was trawling, which involves dragging a net along the seabed behind a boat. Unlike drifting or seining, this disturbs an entire ecosystem. Young fish and spawn are caught; habitat is destroyed. Although there's some evidence of trawling in England from the fourteenth century onwards, the method only took hold there in the nineteenth century, and had spread north by the 1860s. This coincided with the rise of steam power, which enabled larger catches and quicker distribution.

These technological innovations coincided with increased demand. Railways and steamers created a near-inexhaustible market for fresh fish in Britain's cities, and faster transport to the continent ensured that exports of cured fish also grew. This fundamentally altered the nature of fishing. When fish are sold at local markets and support local communities, reasonably sustainable fishing is required in order that both human and herring populations thrive. If the former collapses, the latter will suffer. By the middle of the nineteenth century the expanding fishing industry was becoming locked into what we might nowadays call the logic of late capitalism: a race for short-term wealth accompanied by what a character in Thomas Pynchon's novel *Bleeding Edge* (2013) describes as the ideology of "getting the suckers to believe it's all gonna go on forever."

This wasn't an overnight transition. In fact, despite the resistance of the contemporary fishing industry to quotas, many nineteenth-century fishermen actively sought government regulation. When trawling first began in the Treath, vast amounts of spawn were hauled up, trodden underfoot, and shovelled overboard again. Some was sold as manure to farmers at a shilling a cartload. In 1861 the fishermen of Pittenweem and Cellardyke successfully lobbied for the industry regulator, the Scottish Fisheries Board, to halt all trawling in the Treath. The ban only lasted four years. In 1866 the Royal Commission on Sea Fisheries issued a statement chillingly prophetic of the environmental policies of Brexit Britain: fishermen should be allowed to fish "where you like, when you like and as you like".

The phrase belongs to Thomas Huxley, "Darwin's Bulldog", who would serve on a second Royal Commission on trawling in 1884-5, alongside William M'Intosh, Professor of Natural History at the University of St Andrews. After conducting many hours of interviews with local fishermen, and dozens of trips on a steam trawler in the Forth, M'Intosh concluded that fishermen's accounts of the damaging effects of trawling were vague and overly reliant upon tradition. Witnesses to the Commission consistently argued that since trawling had begun, catches were reduced and the size of fish caught was diminished. M'Intosh and Huxley insisted that spawn was unaffected by trawling, that fishermen exaggerated the numbers of young fish being discarded, and that a short rest period would allow stocks to recover. The fishermen of Fife were unimpressed by the Commission. In March 1885, as M'Intosh left his St Andrews home to attend a dinner of the university's Liberal society, he was met by a large, angry crowd carrying his effigy. As he fled inside, the protestors daubed the effigy with tar and set it alight at his gate.

Despite a halt on trawling within the Firth of Forth, the Commission's findings ultimately contributed to the terminal decline of the local fishing industry. Those fishermen resistant to trawling were faced with financial ruin if they didn't adopt the methods of their competitors. An arms race led to the building of longer boats, equipped with more nets, capable of carrying greater quantities of fish. The record catches of the 1930s were the swansong of East Neuk herring fishing, and today little is landed except crab and lobster. A different kind of net has come to dominate the local economy: the internet, which has facilitated a boom in short-term holiday lets overlooking picturesque harbours. As with the steam-age herring fishery, contemporary tourism appeals to a near-inexhaustible international market. Homes are the new resource to exploit, and the implications for affordable housing and community facilities have recently attracted the attention of the Scottish Government.

A similar story can be told in Argyll. In *The Ring-Net Fishermen*, a record of the industry's rise and fall, historian and poet Angus Martin notes that twentieth-century fishing technologies far outstrip those used in the preceding century, but the once-rich fishing grounds of Loch Fyne are quiet. The Argyll fishermen who foresaw the unsustainability of trawling have been proved right, and many of the villages and crofting communities where generations lived and worked are abandoned or converted to tourism. Martin demonstrates that ecological loss is accompanied by cultural loss, and this is a theme which also preoccupies his poetry. In his poem "Tonight the Fleets" he conjures a vision of all Argyll's historic fleet drifting on the phosphorescent loch. Like the ghostly birch wood in Sorley MacLean's "Hallaig", the boats are illusory. The poem ends with the stark truths that the fleet has long since been used for kindling, and that the community which fishing supported is no more: "[t] here was an end of culture, history, / an end to the burial of the dead."

Martin's *The Ring-Net Fishermen* was published in 1981, and it concludes with the statement that humanity "has brought itself to the edge of an ecological and moral crisis from which, without the exercise of immediate and unswerving restraint, there can be no withdrawal." Nearly four decades have passed, and identical pleas are dismissed by progressive politicians and conservatives alike, with environmental movements condemned as threats to "business as usual". On Scotland's east coast, as early as 1884, the Pittenweem fisherman James Marr told the Royal Commission that the Treath "was once termed California, but it is now like the walls of Jerusalem; it is nothing but desolation." In several East Neuk villages today it's easier to buy a wooden ornamental fish than a fresh fillet.

Garry MacKenzie is a poet and non-fiction writer based in Fife. His poetry has been published in journals and anthologies including Antlers of Water, The Clearing, The Compass Magazine *and* Dark Mountain. *He was awarded an Emerging Scottish Writer Residency at Cove Park in 2019, and is a recipient of a Scottish Book Trust New Writers Award. He has won the Robert McLellan Poetry Competition and the Wigtown Poetry Competition, and his book* Scotland: a Literary Guide for Travellers *is published by I.B. Tauris. He has a PhD in contemporary landscape poetry, and teaches creative writing and literature. His first collection of poetry,* Ben Dorain: a conversation with a mountain *(with Introductions by Kathleen Jamie and Meg Bateman) is published by The Irish Pages Press in January 2021.*

ON *PRAISE OF BEN DORAIN*
&
POEM

—

Meg Bateman

Mystery and potency.

Moladh Beinn Dòbhrain (Praise of Ben Dorain) by the eighteenth-century poet, Duncan Bàn MacIntyre, is one of the greatest marvels of Gaelic poetry – indeed it is one of the greatest marvels of the whole of Gaelic culture. It is hard to comprehend how without recourse to writing Donnchadh Bàn composed and remembered a poem of some 550 lines in a complex metre alternating, like a pibroch, between ground, variation and *crùnludh*. His minute observation of the deer and their habitat alone is marvel enough.

It is a mysterious poem with multiple ramifications. Donnchadh Bàn seems to have had an early understanding of the interrelatedness of different life forms long before the word "ecology" was coined. Thus, he is able to view the killing by the hunt of the deer that he has just so lovingly described without horror or sentimentality, because man and deer share the same environment and man eats the deer to survive. There are plenty other deer in the herd and the balance between life and death has been maintained. Man is part of nature, and as Iain Crichton Smith has pointed out, his gun and ingenuity at manufacturing and using it are praised by the poet as much as the agility of the deer. In understanding different species' adaptation to the environment, Donnchadh Bàn appears an early Darwinian too.

Ben Dorain's sustenance of various life forms – man, deer, birds, fish and vegetation – makes the hill a distinctly female presence in the poem. She is like a mother, dressed in the land's richly varied vegetation in the model of Gaelic mythology. It wasn't until the twentieth century that James Lovelock used the image of a woman again in his Gaia Hypothesis to communicate a sense of the Earth as an integrated living whole.

The richness of Donnchadh Bàn's language becomes a metaphor for the richness of nature, both seeming capable of endless variation and renewal. The poem is a song and the music itself becomes a metaphor for the co-existence of different forms of life. If there is some repetition in the poem describing the movement of the deer between their favourite pastures and their calling to one another as they ascend and descend the peaks, that is because there is repetition in nature.

Donnchadh Bàn says, *Tha an eilid anns an fhrìth/ mar bu chòir dhi bhith (The hind is in the forest / as she ought to be)*. He alludes often to the right of animals and humans to Ben Dorain, drawing again on Gaelic mythology in which land and man form a union, each prospering the other. Human culture is part of nature and their communal and balanced existence creates harmonies of rich complexities. It is how the world is meant to be.

In a later poem, *Òran nam Balgairean (The Song of the Foxes)*, he goads the foxes to destroy the sheep that have replaced the people. He complains that the absence of people resulting from the Clearances is an unnatural state for the Highlands. He received a terrible shock towards the end of his life when he returned to Ben Dorain after working for many years in the city guard in Edinburgh and found that the mountain that he had taken as a symbol of immutability had indeed changed. In his song *Cumha a' Choire Cheathaich (Lament for the Misty Corrie)* he notes how with bad management, the corrie's forests and waterways have become clogged and the deer population – those avatars of the land – have fled.

> How the corrie has gone to ruin,
> since now it has no deer,
> nor any man who loves them
> and is efficient on their trail.

Donnchadh Bàn's view of intermeshing life forms and man's stewardship of nature – which have enormous implications for our present ecological crisis – seem to have been overlooked by earlier commentators. Kurt Wittig, writing of eighteenth-century Gaelic nature poetry, said, "Nature is valued solely because of the aesthetic delight which it affords; there is no philosophical reflection on it, no pantheism" (*The Scottish Tradition in Literature*, 1958). Moreover, Donnchadh Bàn's editor, Angus Macleod, viewed him as naïve, albeit with a virtuosity for versification, stating, "If in poetry we require sublimity of thought, a philosophy of life or compelling emotion, we shall find Duncan Macintrye wanting" (*Orain Dhonnchaidh Bhain*, 1978).

Garry MacKenzie however is acutely aware of the implications of the poem for our times. (*Editor's Note:* see pp 65-67 and 79-80 of this issue.) He is also aware of the impossibility of a writer today not working intertextually.

MacKenzie is analytical and furthers his knowledge of the natural history of deer through study. If Donnchadh Bàn's stance is subsumed in the words, structure and music of the poem, MacKenzie's meaning literally appears intertextually, between his translation of Donnchadh Bàn and his own and other's writing. He has conversed with many aspects of the poem and has created another poem, I feel, of equal mystery and potency. Donnchadh's grounds have become MacKenzie's variations.

There are comparisons and contrasts to be made between MacIntyre and MacKenzie. While MacIntyre, following Alasdair mac Mhaighstir Alasdair (Alexander MacDonald), chose the form of the pibroch to mirror the variations and circularity of nature, MacKenzie has invented a new form: a conversation read from top to bottom of the page, but where left and right correspond to Donnchadh Bàn's translated lines and MacKenzie's reflections on them. We recognize the rhythms of the Gaelic in the translation but sometimes the columns blend as concrete poetry and the words scatter on the page like hinds and fawns on a hillside or like a burn tumbling down between a variety of mosses.

MacKenzie runs with the musical metaphor. The land plays the drones and the deer play the reed in a tune that is both ancient (because the deer have been on Ben Dorain since the end of the Ice Age) and new (because animal culture does not age like human civilisations). For MacIntyre and MacKenzie, the sounds made by the deer, birds, wind and burns, and even the hounds and the gun, sound together in harmony, and the whole is more than the sum of its parts.

Like Donnchadh Bàn, MacKenzie expresses the overwhelming fecundity of nature, the same force that Dylan Thomas sees in "The force that through the green fuse drives the flower". If Donnchadh Bàn expresses this through a wealth of plant and verse forms, MacKenzie expresses it in the vigour and sensuousness of the rutting of the deer. The stag ejaculating on the grass reminded me of the oak trees raining down acorns of which only one or two might become a tree in Lars von Trier's *Antichrist*.

In addition to MacKenzie's learned interjections (about deer eating bones when short of calcium, about Gaelic literature and details of Donnchadh Bàn's biography), there is another important subject raised in his poem. That is a longing for pure existence, for a perception of reality, not as a series of discrete objects perceived by the intellect but as experience perceived through the senses. The stag's perceptions are as far from the poet's as Jupiter in its ability to see things as they are: *The world / is its own / true self in him*. This philosophical strand sounds throughout the poem and we are wakened to it by quotations from Spinoza, Thomas A. Clark and Heraclitus. They recognise the interconnectedness of all things, the goal of many a school of mysticism including Neoplatonism, and part of Gaelic thinking too. It isn't only the deer who are one and the same with what they perceive. MacKenzie quotes at length from Amairgin, the mythic poet of the Milesians who came with the first Gaels to Ireland according to *Lebor Gabála*. Amairgin, in making peace with the sovereignty goddesses of Ireland, achieves an identity with the land, beasts, wind and waves.

In both MacKenzie's and MacIntyre's poems, music represents the union of nature. It is also suggested by MacKenzie's use of synesthesia, by which, for example, he "sees" the call of the hind like lace in the wind. Donnchadh Bàn speaks directly to the deer and to the mountain, for – like Amairgin and the Masai hunters of today – he would have to sense being a deer himself to be able to track them. By contrast, MacKenzie mostly addresses a reader: *look with me / ... listen!*

It is interesting that another early Gaelic text, Suibne Geilt or The Madness of Sweeney, led another poet, Rody Gorman, to create a new form of translation, *Sweeney: an Intertonguing (a Subversion from the Irish)*. Clearly, the formulation of the Gaels regarding their relationship with nature makes sense to us today, in the midst of an ecological crisis. Gorman speaks on behalf of a king who preferred the company of trees, deer and a river to the bustle of the court. We see too that nature, viewed by Augustine as a distraction from the spiritual, was considered an incitement to piety among early Gaelic Christians. Both MacKenzie and Gorman work intertextually with a mixture of translation and creative response. Rather than attempting to reproduce the thinking of our ancestors, is it not more honest to come to their texts with our contemporary intellectual armour and concerns? Both poets have found a place

> *where words and landscape fuse*
> *in an ecology of myth.*

MacKenzie wants to see reality. The deer and Ben Dorain belong in reality to each other. Ben Dorain is only owned temporarily by a landlord and that only in the imagination of society. On the cover of the book there is a photo of Ben Dorain, "the equal of any mountain under the sun", its tranquil shape recalling Fuji Yama. But today its covering is scree and lichen rather that the luxuriant growth described by Donnchadh Bàn. MacKenzie's poem comes to an end with fleeting images of various creatures rather than with the majestic *crùnluth* of the older poem. Ben Dorain is still beautiful but its ecosystems of vegetation, deer and human society are not sounding together as they used to.

August 2020, Isle of Skye, Scotland

This is the Introduction to Duncan Bàn MacIntyre's long Gaelic poem, Moladh Beinn Dòbhrain, *which is included as Part II of Garry MacKenzie's volume,* Ben Dorain: a conversation with a mountain, *published by The Irish Pages Press in January 2021.*

THE BUTTERFLIES

Homero Gómez Gonzalez made a sanctuary for Monarch butterflies in Mexico on one of the few mountain tops where they hibernate in the oyamel pines. His body was found hidden by loggers in a well in January 2020.

The loggers killed him for his mountain pines
where butterflies cluster winter long
ghostly below their sweeping boughs
    and they stuffed his body down a well.

"Souls of the ancestors", old women cried
when they'd rise in the spring in a golden haze;
this year they'll take you with them, Gómez,
    far far from your watery cell,

Flying in relays three thousand miles,
supping on milkweed, steered by the sun;
if we could but join them on their course
    we wouldn't so lightly let life unfurl.

One of Scotland's most distinguished poets, Meg Bateman was born in Edinburgh and grew up in the New Town area of the city. She studied Celtic at the University of Aberdeen and completed a PhD in medieval Scottish Gaelic religious poetry. She taught Scottish Gaelic at the University of Aberdeen between 1991 and 1998, before moving to the Isle of Skye to teach at the Gaelic college, Sabhal Mòr Ostaig, The University of Highlands and Islands. She has also taught Scottish Gaelic at the University of Edinburgh and is an Honorary Senior Lecturer at the University of St Andrews.

Bateman's first collection of poems, Òrain Ghaoil (Love Songs) *was published in 1990 and her second,* Aotromachd agus Dàin Eile (Lightness) *was published in 1997. Both her first and second collections focus on human relationships and the idealised idea of love. Her third collection,* Soirbheas (Air Wind), *was published in 2007. Her latest collection* Transparencies *was published in 2013 and was her first book to include both Scottish Gaelic and English poems. She is the Scottish Gaelic Editor of* Irish Pages.

A TIME FOR REAPPRAISALS

Kathleen Jamie

Have human beings ever known such a moment?

Ben Dorain: a conversation with a mountain is the first full-length work published by Scottish poet Garry MacKenzie. It appears in this handsome edition courtesy of The Irish Pages Press, which is a new presence in Scottish poetry publishing. The press is associated with the journal *Irish Pages* which for two decades has been an important and intelligent contributor to the cultural life of these islands.

When we say "these islands", we think we know what we mean, but *Irish Pages*, as journal, press and arts festival, is alert to an alternative map reading. It seeks to link what Editor Chris Agee calls the "dissident peripheries". Moving between the Republic of Ireland, Northern Ireland and Scotland, the journal is also concerned with wider Europe, the Balkans in particular, and North America. It considers ancient nations and languages, emerging ecologies and reconsidered identities.

We are alive at a time of sudden, necessary reappraisals, and changes of direction. History is far from over, the future struggles to find its shape. Change is happening, whether it be local, in the fracturing of the United Kingdom, or across the wide sweep of history, as revealed by the truths and hopes of the Black Lives Matter movement. It is happening on a planetary level, in the perils of climate change and species loss. Have human beings ever known such a moment?

When we may feel as though our species and our planet are cascading into a future unknown, and uncertainty is all about, it may seem odd to publish a book which is "a conversation" with a mountain, the very symbol of solidity. The mountain is Ben Dorain, which rises near Bridge of Orchy. It appears as a Fuji-esque cone from some angles. The conversation is also with a praise poem composed 250 years ago, by Duncan Bàn MacIntyre. MacIntyre's poem is a musical paean to this one particular Scottish mountain and its deer. The original poem is in Gaelic, a language no longer spoken on that mountainside. (There, in that one fact, you have your political and power shifts, your economic and cultural push and shove.) But what Garry MacKenzie has done, in this wonderful book, is to revivify that poem. He has created a new "inhabited music" which springs MacIntyre's work into the present day. It's not a translation, nor a modernised version, though there is that also. He has opened MacIntyre's mountain poem like a geode, to use a geological term, and he has created an environmentally-aware, science-informed poetic counterpoint in English, which he presents dancing along with MacIntyre's re-expressed eighteenth-century vision. Like the deer they so admire, the two poets' lines leap back and forth across the page, across times, across languages, across species and poetic forms. It is a new work which alerts us to the tradition, which is to say, to the consciousness of the past. It calls this consciousness into the present, so that its wisdom might strengthen us for the environmental challenges to come.

Who knows what future? Our times would have been unimaginable to Duncan Bàn MacIntyre. When he composed his poem, we were already on the way to species loss, to environmental degradation. His Ben Dorain deer may have known Scotland's last wolves, which are variously said to have been extirpated in the seventeenth century, or the eighteenth or maybe even the nineteenth. (MacIntyre was himself a gamekeeper.) But who knows if they might not one day be returned? Who would have thought, 50 years ago, that huge tracts of Scottish land, mountain ranges and moorland, their populations cleared, land held in a few private (wealthy) hands, might be taken into community ownership, and managed for nature? Who knows what the "dissident peripheries" will think of next?

But this is not primarily a political work. This is a work of love: of landscape and animals and poetry. Despite the shifting grounds which surround it, Ben Dorain the mountain remains true and centred, its marvellous creatures marvellously observed.

This is the Introduction to Ben Dorain: a conversation with a mountain, *by Garry MacKenzie, published by The Irish Pages Press / Cló An Mhíl Bhuí in January 2021.*

Kathleen Jamie was born in the West of Scotland in 1962. She is the author of ten collections of poems, most recently The Tree House *(Picador, 2004: winner of the Forward Prize and Scottish Book of the Year),* Mr and Mrs Scotland Are Dead: Poems 1980-94 *(Bloodaxe Books, 2002: shortlisted for the 2003 International Griffin Prize),* The Overhaul *(Picador, 2012: shortlisted for the 2012 T. S. Eliot Prize, winner of the 2012 Costa Poetry Award), and* The Bonniest Companie *(Picador, 2015). Her non-fiction work includes* Among Muslims

(Sort of Books, 2002), Findings *(Sort of Books, 2007),* Sightlines *(Sort of Books, 2012: joint winner with Robert McFarlane of the 2013 Dolman Travel Award, winner of 2014 John Burroughs Award and the 2014 Orion Book Award) and* Surfacing *(Sort of Books, 2019). In 2017, she received the Ness Award from the Royal Geographical Society for "outstanding creative writing at the confluence of travel, nature and culture." She is the Scottish Editor of* Irish Pages, *and lives with her family in Fife.*

OUR FRAGILE EARTH?
THE OBJECT OF OUR ENVIRONMENTAL ANXIETY

—

John Wilson Foster

The space-blue chalcedony.

*"We are indeed travellers bound to the earth's crust,
drawing life from the air and water of its thin and fragile envelope …".*

— Barbara Ward and René Dubos, *Only One Earth* (1972)

In 1971 Governor Ronald Reagan was of the opinion that "things like excessive population growth and decline have a way of balancing themselves out to avoid the Domesday predictions" (quoted by Robert J. Mayhew, "Politics and Flapdoodle", *Times Literary Supplement*, 2018). The "balance of nature" idea had long dominated many people's thoughts about Nature. Balance and harmony, preordained and default conditions, were imagined by way of structural metaphors of cosmic wheels and chains that were, for example, part of the Elizabethan world picture. Keith Thomas believes the idea of the balance of nature had a theological origin, by which he means Christian, especially Protestant theology, of which Reagan was an inheritor (Keith Thomas, *Man and the Natural World: Changing Attitudes in England 1500–1800,* 1983). Open-ended disruption or rupture of the natural order was not in the cosmic cards, save by divine intervention. Charles Mann attributes the idea of a secular and scientifically accountable balance in our environment to Frederic Clements, the Nebraskan author of the first ecology textbook, *Research Methods in Ecology* (1905), who believed that mature ecosystems achieved an equilibrium unless disturbed by natural calamities or human intervention. The acknowledgement that ecosystems can be imbalanced or even destroyed allowed for the notion of environmental crisis, but in Clements' day thoughts of a doomsday environmental crisis were in the future. The balance of nature idea was routed by Charles Elton, author of the pioneering *Animal Ecology* (published as early as 1927) and co-winner of the 1976 Tyler Ecology Award (Elton wrote his book when he was only 26). Ecosystems, he showed, do not form a stable

climax community when they reach maturity but exist in continuous turbulence – "the confusion is remarkable" (Charles C. Mann, *The Wizard and
the Prophet: Science and the Future of Our Planet*, 1983). James C. Malin called
Clements a spokesman for "Classical ecology" which studied succession, climax
(or disclimax), and uniformity in the environment, which Malin and others
rejected in favour of continuous change and endless diversity (James C. Malin,
The Grassland of North America: Prolegomena to Its History, 1947). Still, the idea
of balance or imbalance in Nature was a tenacious one and seemed justified
by the disproportionate and destabilizing depredations made upon Nature
by human activity; in the larger picture, the times were out of joint, to quote
Hamlet, when it came to the relationship between humanity and Nature.

The Tyler Award was predicated on this fear that there had indeed developed recently a serious and dangerous imbalance caused by human threats
to the environment. In March 1973, the President of Pepperdine University,
California, Dr Bill Banowsky, when announcing the creation of the Tyler
Award, said that human beings could no longer depend on Nature's balancing
out her credits and debits, hence the "desperate urgency" behind the new
Prize (*Los Angeles Herald-Examiner*, 1973). (*Editor's Note:* see concluding note
on the Tyler Award.)

Banowsky's sense of urgency, as it had been for many, was fuelled by one
of the collateral outcomes of the Apollo 17 mission. Having been a pastor, he
refers to "our fragile spaceship earth" with perhaps a Christian tenderness but
also a newly-motivated environmental anxiety. Dr Harrison Schmitt's address
to the first Tyler Ecology Award in February 1974 in Los Angeles was entitled
"The Fragile Blue Earth", a phrase recalled from what he said while aboard
the spaceship and photographing Earth: "If there ever was a fragile appearing
piece of blue in space, it's the earth right now". This was reproduced on the
first Award program in a section called "The Pale Blue Earth" describing a
gemstone on display at the banquet. This was a blue lace chalcedony donated
by the Swansons, an American family living in South Africa and mining a
deposit of chalcedony (microcrystalline quartz) on the Namibian side of the
Orange River, cobbed or trimmed at the mine, then finished at Swanson's
Yard, Springbok, South Africa. In colour, blue lace chalcedony varies from a
very pale blue to an intense sky blue. The latter hue provides the Schmitt and
Tyler connections. Blue lace chalcedony gained its fame after the last landing
on the moon by Apollo 17 in December 1972. Module pilot and geologist Dr
Harrison Schmitt claimed to have taken the world-famous NASA photograph
called "The Blue Marble" which showed a perfect, blue and white, illuminated

picture of Earth taken from the Moon. After seeing that photograph, George Swanson immediately noticed the similarity between spheres made from his blue lace, and "The Blue Marble" photograph. "His future marketing strategy was obvious, and he set off for his homeland of America with spheres and samples of the stone" (see online: "Blue Lace Chalcedony: Fascination with a Stone", and for a description of this stone, *Mining Africa Yearbook October 2009*). One he donated to the Tyler Award Committee once it had been cut and polished in Johannesburg and taken to California. George Swanson, founder and owner of the mine, attended the first Tyler Award dinner. Its program told the guests that "Because of this unique gemstone and its remarkable similarity to our earth as seen from outer space, the Tyler Ecology Award has adopted the stone as a symbol of world ecology – a constant reminder that the earth is a fragile blue form in space."

This literal perception of the Earth as fragile was sharpened by the images from spaceships of Earth as a discrete entity, suspended as if helplessly in space, unfellowed, unique, and in its uniqueness curiously vulnerable. These images fed back into earthbound perceptions of the environment, which had already begun to see Nature as terribly exposed in parts to damage and destruction. Until recently, less than a century ago indeed, Nature was regarded in the West, especially by Europeans after they "discovered" (i.e., for themselves), and settled, the New World, as a limitless source of plenty to be availed of and utilized, as their religion taught. The limitless bounty of Nature cohabited with the presumption of Nature's toughness and resilience, its perpetual replenishment, its indifference to man, its perpetual threat. The notion of Nature's vulnerability and even its companionability, was a rare one (John Wilson Foster, *Pilgrims of the Air: The Passing of the Passenger Pigeons*, 2017). In the late nineteenth century, the Scots-American naturalist and conservationist John Muir was a pioneering environmentalist who unusually saw wilderness as eminently habitable by humankind in a spiritual as well as physical sense (in Charles C. Mann, *The Wizard and the Prophet*). When in 1879 he imagined the Earth whole, a planet in space as Schmitt actually witnessed it from his spaceship, Muir attributed not frailty to it but strength, confidence, fellowship and beauty: "when we contemplate the whole globe as one great dewdrop, striped and dotted with continents and islands, flying through space with other stars all singing and shining together as one, the whole universe appears as an infinite storm of beauty" (John Muir, "Puget Sound and British Columbia", *The Wilderness Journeys*, 1996). The prevailing contemporary idea of the formidable, self-sustaining, and replenishing force of Nature was the source, of course, of a pervasive human anxiety, not despite, but because of, the belief that Nature was powerful and at best indifferent, at worst latently hostile, capable of visiting catastrophes and pestilence on the human and animal kingdoms. But it is probable that our new idea of Nature's frailty and of Earth's vulnerability, thereby transferring immense responsibility to humanity, is breeding its own pervasive anxiety. We have been reminded that "human actions, however minuscule their effects may seem when set against the total scale of the planet's energy system, may nonetheless trigger off one of those small but fateful changes which alter the balance of the seesaw" (Barbara Ward & René Dubos, *Only One Earth: The Care and Maintenance of a Small Planet*, 1972).

As late as the *Titanic* disaster in 1912, Nature, in the raw guise of rogue icebergs, was seen as menacing and hazardous in the extreme, and anti-human; Nature was thus something under normal circumstances to be challenged, subdued, harnessed and put to work, again as the religion taught. For atheists, Nature and humanity were locked into a Darwinian struggle for survival with the odds against humanity, even with the help of giant machines like *Titanic* (John Wilson Foster, *The Age of Titanic: Cross-Currents in Anglo-American Culture*, 2002). "Nineteenth-century Americans", writes Richard White in his remarkable study of the Columbia River, "gave contests between machines and nature an epic quality. They measured progress by the results. Machines stood as both the agents and the symbols of their conquest of nature" (Richard White, *The Organic Machine*, 1995).

This Industrial Revolutionary perception of Nature (now seen as a rival to humanity, not its master) attempted decisively to reverse a pervasive human trepidation that lasted through the ages when prayers, invocations, sacrifices, petitions, and magical expedients tried to influence or propitiate the gods (or God) who manipulated Nature and countenanced humanity on sufferance. Only lately did a century and a half of exploitation and utilization through machinery and colonial geographic spread become widely re-perceived as plunder. An early example of the change was the book by the New Jersey environmentalist, Fairfield Osborn Jr., *Our Plundered Planet* (1948); Nancy G. Slack believes that conservation became a popular concern after the publication of Osborn's book (Nancy G. Slack, *G. Evelyn Hutchinson and the Invention of Modern Ecology*, 2010). The history of the human translation of Nature into our vulnerable homeland and habitat is the history of the emergence of contemporary, post-Clements environmentalism. By 1987 a series of Darwin Lectures could be published under the title *The Fragile Environment* (1989).

The subtitle, *New Approaches to Global Problems*, intimates how seeing the earth in real space as a globe encouraged a "global" perspective when it came to ecology (and many other intellectual endeavours then and thereafter). One of the chapters is "Observing Earth's Environment from Space", zooming in, as it were, on Schmitt's whole-earth photographs to inspect details of this planet's frail environment (Laurie Friday & Ronald Laskey, *The Fragile Environment: New Approaches to Global Problems*, 1989).

In June 1972 Barbara Ward, Baroness Jackson, told an audience in Stockholm that "what our incredible scientific breakthroughs of the last century have taught us is that the ultimate energy of the universe both sustains or destroys life and that the mechanisms and balances by which it becomes life-enhancing are fragile and precious beyond our belief" (see Wade Rowland, *The Plot to Save the World: The Life and Times of the Stockholm Conference on the Human Environment*, 1973). The fragility she was identifying had become a staple premiss of what was starting to be seen as a rapidly deepening environmental crisis to which the Tyler Ecology Award, then in its conception, was a simultaneous reply. In the same year as her lecture, Ward co-edited with René Dubos *Only One Earth: The Care and Maintenance of a Small Planet*. The title suggests that the planet was in a sense being diminished and domesticated for tactical environmentalist reasons. (Four years later the French-born Dubos was co-recipient of the Tyler Ecology Award. He is credited with the memorable imperative: "Think globally, act locally", but had conducted pioneering research in the 1930s that led to the development of antibiotics. He was also a prolific author, among his books being the Pulitzer Prize-winning *So Human an Animal*, 1968.) Ward and Dubos in their Introduction thank Adlai Stevenson for his perception of earth as a little spaceship on which we travel together "dependent on its vulnerable supplies of air and spoil". The editors concur with their own through-the-other-end-of-the-telescope view: "We are indeed travellers bound to the earth's crust, drawing life from the air and water of its thin and fragile envelope, using and reusing its very limited supply of natural resources."

If the perception of Nature had changed, so had our self-perception, seeing ourselves no longer as "lodgers on the earth, but as its landlords", as Ward and Dubos put it, a second, truly era-defining power-role reversal in the developed western world. It is humankind that now has all the power, it seems; Nature has ceded rivalry, and we must wield our new power by becoming not merely the planet's landlords but its stewards, its custodians, even caregivers, and that role requires restraint, self-sacrifice and global altruism.

It is, of course, in our own vital interests, since we have caused the dangers that threaten the earth and therefore ourselves. Ward and Dubos enumerate those dangers as they saw them in 1972: food shortages, depletion of natural resources, accumulation of environmental pollutants, a worrying increase in human population, and the threat to certain human values derived from Nature and which transcend our bodily needs. They even saw the danger of what has now become a common cause of anxiety: climate change. Given humanity's technological activities, "It is perhaps ... unsurprising that the whole global climate can itself undergo profound modifications", one of them being "the so-called greenhouse effect" when carbon dioxide intercepts the earth's heat radiations and transmits them back to earth (Barbara Ward and René Dubos, *Only One Earth*). It all added up to a crisis and a tipping-point. "... As we enter the last decades of the twentieth century, there is a growing sense that something fundamental and possibly irrevocable is happening to man's relations with both his worlds [the biosphere and the technosphere]" (Barbara Ward and René Dubos, *Only One Earth*). Harmful human intervention in the natural order is happening at an unprecedented speed and depth and is a revolution in human experience. We are, as the authors tell us in a striking phrase, at a "hinge of history".

Only One Earth, a 225-page book, was in fact a report commissioned by the United Nations in advance of, and in active introduction to, the United Nations Conference on the Human Environment which took place in Stockholm, Sweden 5–16 June 1972. Ward and Dubos wrote it after perusing submissions and correspondence from a Committee of Corresponding Consultants, which included internationally prominent figures. The book's Preface was written by the man who, as Secretary-General of the Conference, had expertly stick-handled the conference to its successful beginning if not to its wholly satisfactory conclusion. Maurice Strong, the Canadian diplomat and oilman, was at first glance a surprising environmentalist. Soon to be a Tyler co-laureate (1974), and someone who was said to have had "an astonishing network" that connected diverse groups (Peter Frost's obituary of Strong, *The National Post 29 November 2015*), Strong was unable nevertheless to overcome the diplomatic obstacles to a consensual perception and interpretation of the global environmental crisis that had provoked the conference. The contemporary world political scene was inauspicious for collective agreements, intentions, and actions. The Cold War was still frigid, with the Soviet Union boycotting the conference because East Germany was not invited; the Vietnam War being waged; Third World discontent becoming incendiary; the Chinese leading the undeveloped

nations in assailing western colonialism not just for the environmental depredations of its past but also (with some vulnerable logic) for its alleged
attempt in the present to halt Third World development through specious
ecological concerns. The consequent Declaration, Principles, and Action Plan
were a confused and politically fraught and coded outcome. But nevertheless,
the perception of a crisis involving the environment survived when the dust
settled. Wade Rowland's *The Plot to Save the World* is a detailed contemporary
account of the Conference, though it is a rather Canadian account filtered
through the mild anti-Americanism of Pierre Elliott Trudeau's Canada. Its
Introduction is supplied by the Canadian Strong (datelined 1972), then in
New York working for the United Nations.

Rowland thought that the counter-conference mustered by the American
poets and eco-campaigners was naively apolitical and romantic-transcenden-
talist. He suggested that the official American delegation nevertheless allied
itself with it because the delegation also wished to de-politicize the UN Conference, separating politics from environmentalism in order to draw attention
away from contemporary American political and military involvements. Many
of the distinguished among the invited guests at the first Tyler Awards may
also have been willing to lend a sympathetic ear to the problems of resource
depletion and wildlife conservation as long as those problems were decoupled
from politics, thereby avoiding a link between environmental concern and
political liberalism (Wade Rowland, *The Plot to Save the World*).

Rowland reminds us that just weeks before the UN conference, a book
entitled *The Limits to Growth* appeared. It was co-authored by Dennis L. Meadows, an American scientist who while at the Massachusetts Institute of Technology directed the Club of Rome Project on the Predicament of Mankind,
an informal think-tank of scientists, economists, industrialists and other
assorted concerned figures from around the world who first convened in the
Italian capital in 1968. Their concern was the alarming problems caused by
a burgeoning human population battening on finite resources. Systems-anal-
ysis and computer models were used by the group and the book to show
that growth on the planet is limited by population, agricultural production,
industrial production, natural resources, and pollution. Only determined and
prompt action to halt population growth and freeze the current population
size could avoid a global calamity (Wade Rowland, *The Plot to Save the World*).
Despite its sophistication and gloom, *The Limits to Growth* sold 12 million copies
and was translated into 37 languages (Charles C. Mann, *The Wizard and the
Prophet*). A similar anxiety about overpopulation and its disastrous effect on

the environment exercised "Blueprint for Survival", a manifesto that appeared in the London-based journal, *The Ecologist*, six months before the Stockholm conference. The manifesto was signed by 36 scientists and intellectuals and warned that "if current trends are allowed to persist, the breakdown of society and the irreversible disruption of the life-support systems on this planet, possibly by the end of the century, certainly within the lifetimes of our children, are inevitable" (quoted by Wade Rowland, *The Plot to Save the World*). Seven essential stages of action were identified, from anti-pollution technology through alternative technologies of long-lived material goods to greater decentralization and education of the public. The manifesto's call for the United Kingdom to become self-supporting in food and to halve its population to 30 million people dates the "Blueprint for Survival" to an era preceding mass migration, multiculturalism, the United Kingdom's membership of the European Economic Community (later European Union), and the emergence of India and China as global economic powerhouses increasingly beyond western influence and injunction and with colossal populations.

The year 1972, when *Only One Earth*, *The Limits to Growth*, and "Blueprint for Survival" appeared, and when the international delegates arrived in Stockholm, was a signal year for global attention to the environment. So too was 1968, when the UN General Assembly decided to convene a major gathering on the human environment and the Club of Rome first mustered. That of all the environmental anxieties, human overpopulation was in those years felt to be the most urgent was demonstrated by the explosive success, one might say, of *The Population Bomb* (1968) which sold two million copies in its first two years. (It is almost a shock, therefore, to be told, as G. Evelyn Hutchinson tells us, that there were those who were worried by *under*population due to the downward trend of women's fertility: see Hutchinson, *The Kindly Frutis of the Earth: Recollections of an Embryo Ecologist*, 1979). Paul Ehrlich, a Stanford University entomologist, predicted famines because "the battle to feed humanity is already lost" and prescribed drastic expansion of contraception, abortion and voluntary sterilization (see Patrick Allitt, *A Climate of Crisis: America in the Age of Environmentalism*, 2015). Perhaps the metaphor of detonation in Ehrlich's title derived unconsciously from the pervasive worry caused by Cold War tensions, lending an apocalyptic note not only to his ecological picture but to the picture offered by the most prominent environmentalists of the time. Understandably, perhaps, since one of the environmental hazards was radioactive debris left in the atmosphere by nuclear tests conducted above ground. Barry Commoner, a biologist at Washington University, St Louis, campaigned against nuclear tests in the late 1950s and in 1966 published *Science and Survival*, a book that identified that and other threats to the environment and to humanity itself, warned of the danger of science and technology themselves, and allied the need for environmental activism with social justice activism, thereby giving quasi-political coloration to concern over the human despoliation of Nature (Patrick Allitt, *A Climate of Crisis*).

To the list of foremost human impositions on Nature that he warned were hazards to human as well as environmental health – nuclear fallout, detergents, and phosphates – Commoner added DDT because he had read and been convinced by Rachel Carson's *Silent Spring* that had appeared four years before his own book. The promiscuous employment of DDT (dichloro-di-phenyl-trichloro-ethane) was the major culprit in her alarming indictment. *Silent Spring*, the product of six years' research, was serialized in *The New Yorker* the summer before its fall publication and initiated a vigorous new phase of environmentalism. Carson identified a particular crisis (the negative effect of insecticides) inside a larger environmental crisis, and did so for at least 40,000 contemporaries who bought *Silent Spring* and propelled it on to the *New York Times* best-seller list for almost a year.

Silent Spring indicted the chemical industry and governments (from municipal to federal) for the development and use of pesticides in ignorance, wilful or innocent, of the devastating reality that they were in fact ecocides. Carson's book is in part a detective story, as she describes the symptoms in nature that have appeared discretely and have to be explained: dead birds, withered roadside vegetation, dying fish, polluted streams. She identifies what has most immediately and culpably transpired as a result of humanity's wish to conquer Nature: "The most alarming of all man's assaults upon the environment is the contamination of air, earth, rivers, and sea with dangerous and even lethal materials" (Rachel Carson, *Silent Spring*, 1962). The insidi-ousness of the chemical contamination, its dark invisible energies, its biotic legacies over generations and across species, can be pursued, brought to light, only by a biologist who, because she is an ecologist, is also an environmental investigator. The resulting picture as a whole was deeply worrying to Carson. Firstly, through invention, discovery, and application, the human chemical contamination of Nature had accelerated since World War II. Secondly, *Homo sapiens* had become the first species able consciously to drastically alter its own environment. (She was not the first, of course, to point out the ways in which mankind had impacted radically on Nature: see *Man and Nature, Or Physical Geography as Modified by Human Action*, by George Perkins Marsh,

1864. However, although he wrote in the wake of Darwin, Marsh did not see humanity itself as a biological species as did Carson). Thirdly, the ecologist in the light of human violations of Nature had to become a social activist. The third anxiety was vindicated when Carson was attacked by chemical corporations. (One of Carson's supporters was René Dubos: see Sharon E. Kingsland, *The Evolution of American Ecology*, 1890–2000, 2005). But although her book changed environmentalism by energizing it, it was attacked also by some biologists for apparently cleaving to the outmoded notion of the balance of nature, the idea that until late human intervention, Nature had maintained a happy equilibrium. More advanced ecologists had by then discarded the balance of Nature in favour of the environment as in perpetual flux, of flows of energy, of equilibria more complex than the balance of Nature implied. Yet Carson was alert to Nature's rhythms of injury and remedy, insult and recovery, being an ecologist of her time, but thought that the scale and speed of human tamperings with Nature had interrupted, sometimes lethally, those natural rhythms to the extent that not only Nature but human health were threatened.

Attention to a grave environmental crisis that was both local and global sharpened between 1962 and when the Tyler Ecology Award was projected a decade later. Before *Silent Spring*, there had been those whom Mann calls prophets, those naturalists after the Second World War who sounded the alarm about threats to species, to habitat, to human-nature relations, to humans themselves. The same historian of environmentalism tells us that Carson had been inspired by William Vogt's *Road to Survival* (1948), published the same year as Osborn's *Our Plundered Planet* (Charles C. Mann, *The Wizard and the Prophet*). Vogt, a New York State ornithologist and ecologist, organized the Inter-American Conference on Conservation of Renewable Natural Resources in Denver in September 1948. Two days after that conference, a UNESCO conference in Paris (at which Vogt was an observer) opened and ended with the founding of the International Union for the Protection of Nature. Chiefly through the efforts of the British zoologist Julian Huxley, this was a self-starting network which, much later, would connect the Sierra Club, the Nature Conservancy, Greenpeace, the Rainforest Alliance and the World Wildlife Fund among other organisations (Charles C. Mann, *The Wizard and the Prophet*). The notions of the network and of networking, which mimicked the essential dynamic interconnections in Nature, would become important in environmental activism. Yet despite these early warnings and responses, the former outstripped the latter in urgency and effectiveness during the environmental crisis of the 1960s and 1970s. What was to be done and how ought it to be done?

A medievalist at the University of California, Los Angeles, Lynn White Jr., gave his answer in what was regarded as a landmark essay in *Science* in March 1967: "The Historical Roots of Our Ecologic Crisis". He traced those roots to the second half of the nineteenth century when scientific knowledge in the West generated technological power over Nature which included the combustion of fossil fuels during the Industrial Revolution. Now things have reached crisis-point. "As we enter the last third of the 20th century … concern for the problem of ecologic backlash is mounting feverishly" (Lynn White Jr., "The Historical Roots of Our Ecologic Crisis", *Science*, 1967). Fittingly for an historian with a long rearview perspective, White saw the crisis as a result of a reckless and spiritless view of Nature. He expressed some fellow-feeling with west-coast beatniks who were then adopting a Buddhist and pacifist environmental posture but thought that a posture more firmly grounded culturally and therefore more productive would come from the West's native Judaeo-Christian tradition and he nominated St Francis of Assisi as the patron saint of a new ecological awareness.

Despite the milestone status of his essay, White's solution to the crisis, a wholesale cultural paradigm shift, was hardly likely to appear urgent or practical enough to those of a scientific bent. (Nevertheless, 50 years after the essay appeared, two ecologists called it an "intellectual bomb" in its time, an enduring "classic", and affirmed its continuing relevance: see online Michael Paul Nelson and Thomas J. Sauer, "The Long Reach of Lynn White Jr.'s 'The Historic Roots of Our Ecologic Crisis", Nature Research Ecology & Community, 2016). What was needed in the eyes of those at the coalface, as it were, of environmental problems, which most ecologists agreed by 1967 had become dangerously critical, was first of all greater knowledge of how the environment actually worked. And this required seeing Nature, "in the round", to borrow a phrase from a 1973 book by a British science writer, Nigel Calder (Nigel Calder, *Nature in the Round: A Guide to Environmental Science*, 1973). In his 1964 Introduction to *Silent Spring*, Lord Shackleton reminded readers that "The science of ecology teaches us that we have to understand the inter-action of all living things in the environment in which we live", which includes the relationship between species, between species (their physiology and behaviour) and their environment (including that between plant life and animal life), between wildlife and humanity, and even between individuals and species. We should remember, however, that in 1947, Aldo Leopold, author of the venerated *Sand County Almanac* (1949), recalled that it was in northern Mexico in the 1930s that he "first clearly realized that land is an organism", that land or a biota could be sick or healthy. The environmental historian Roderick Nash saw that ecology enabled Leopold "to conceive of nature as an intricate web of interdependent parts, a myriad of cogs and wheels each essential to the healthy operation of the whole" (Roderick Nash, *Wilderness and the American Mind*, 1967). It is, however, G. Evelyn Hutchinson (Tyler co-laureate with Maurice Strong and Arie Haagen-Smit in 1974) who has been called the "father of modern ecology" though he modestly refused acknowledgement of his paternity in favour of a more avuncular role. (Darwin was the father, Hutchinson said.) The extraordinarily versatile Hutchinson began in England as a limnologist, a naturalist who studies inland aquatic ecosystems, and in that field he pioneered "the coordination of the chemistry and biology of lakes into theories concerning the functioning and structure of ecosystems" (Ruth Patrick, "George Evelyn Hutchinson: 1903 − 1991", *Proceedings of the American Philosophical Society*, 1994. Stephen Jay Gould calls Hutchinson "the world's greatest ecologist" in *Dinosaur in a Haystack*, 1996). He tells us that this coordination seemed possible after he read Elton's *Animal Ecology* when it appeared in 1927 (*Kindly Fruits of the Earth*). Elton's concentrated study established, among other things, the importance of food chains and cycles, food item size, the ecological niche, ecological succession, and animal populations in relation to ecosystemic structure.

Animal Ecology could be regarded as ushering in what Edward O. Wilson (famous student of ants, sociobiologist, island biogeographer, environmentalist, and co-recipient of the Tyler Award in 1984) called "the golden age" of ecology which lasted, "very roughly, five decades, from the 1930s into the 1970s" (Foreword to Nancy G. Slack, *G. Evelyn Hutchinson and the Invention of Modern Ecology*). In other words, the awakening of naturalists and the general public in the 1960s to the scale of the environmental crisis happily coincided with the latest flowering of ecological knowledge and awareness, nourished by the work of Hutchinson and Wilson themselves. When Wilson calls Hutchinson the founder of modern ecology, he means that he credits Hutchinson with turning ecology into a fundamental science. Hutchinson introduced mathematics and chemistry into ecology and more or less created the field of biogeochemistry. In addition, and as a result, Hutchinson revealed new layers and dimensions in organic life and this enriched our ecological understanding. In her obituary of Hutchinson, Ruth Patrick (herself a winner of the second Tyler Ecology Award in 1975) said he led the transformation of ecology from a fact-finding branch of natural history into a coherent branch of science. The Tyler Ecology Award, in so far as it was created partly because there was no Nobel Prize for Ecology, was in 1974 recognising Hutchinson as a major scientist as well an environmentalist.

Out of the many anxieties shared by ecologists over the decades and then by the populace, one has emerged to trump, symbolize and incorporate all the others and at the same time divide the scientists. Tyler laureates' concerns about greenhouse gases were voiced as early as *Only One Earth* in 1972 and, a little later, in the 1992 laureate Robert White's World Climate Conference of 1979, and Bert Bolin's service from 1985 on the Advisory Group of Greenhouse Gases, assembled by the International Council of Scientific Unions (ICSU). (It was, however, the Canadian geophysicist, Gilbert Plass of Johns Hopkins University, who as early as May 1953 warned in the pages of the *Washington Post* and *Time Magazine* that releases of carbon dioxide from burning coals and oils blanket the Earth's surface "like glass in a greenhouse" and that the Earth is warming [see online "Environmental History Timeline: 1940-1960", Radford University, Virginia].) Bolin of Stockholm University was a meteorologist who won the Tyler Prize in 1988; he had seen the need for international cooperation on climate research back in the early 1960s. His work led to the ICSU's Committee on Atmospheric Sciences in 1964; this Committee in turn initiated the Global Atmospheric Research Programme in 1980. Michael Mann supplies a demonstration of the diplomatic skill with which Bolin as chair sought consensus at the Intergovernmental Panel on Climate Change in Madrid in 1995, caught as he was between his climatology colleagues and the oil powers of Saudi Arabia, Kuwait, and the United States (Michael E. Mann, *The Hockey Stick and the Climate Wars: Dispatches from the Front Lines*, 2014).

In the past two decades there has been a radical shift in the choreography of the ecological stage, and global warming presently outranks extinction and deforestation (and other habitat degradation) as the public ecological subject of our time and is firmly centre stage. Scientists have brought global warming to the public as an ecological topic to an unprecedented degree but have incited more response than they can perhaps handle as scientists. One can see why. Veerabhadran Ramanathan (winner of the Tyler Prize, 2009) told his TEDx talk audience that it had been necessary to change the term "global warming" to "climate change" because of the droughts, floods, species extinctions, and glaciers melting that all signified something even larger than mere change of temperature ("Bending the Climate Change Curve", TEDx Talk, You Tube, 2016). The 19 Tyler Prize laureates between 2008 and 2019 have included 11 scientists who are involved in studying what they regard as dangerous climate change: Ramanathan, Richard Alley, Kirk Smith, John Seinfeld, Diana Wall, Jane Lubchenco, Partha Dasgupta, Paul Falkowski, James McCarthy, Michael Mann and Warren Washington.

There are scientists, including climatologists, who deny that global warming is catastrophic, unnatural, or anthropogenic. The language of environmental debate even among scientists has escalated and become emotive and judgemental. Charles Mann's "prophets" are now called "alarmists" by those who in turn are called "contrarians". These include Professors John Christy, Judith Curry, Will Happer, Richard Lindzen, and Tim Ball. Christy, a climate scientist and winner of NASA's Medal for Exceptional Scientific Achievement, declares himself "a strong critic of scientists who make catastrophic predictions of huge increases in global temperatures and tremendous rises in sea levels" (John Christy, interview on National Public Radio, 2003). Global warming occurs but it is neither human-made (there is no "smoking gun" of human culpability) nor catastrophic (see John Christy, editorial in *Wall Street Journal*, Wikipedia). But for those on the more crowded side of the heated climate change debate, the danger is clear and present: our climate change is happening and worsening, it is human-caused, and it will issue in the sixth mass extinction, destroying not just the animal kingdom but also the human race. The latter consider that human intervention, since human behaviour has caused the climatic crisis, is essential. (Mann's "wizards" must muster now and take decisive action.)

Paul Falkowski of Rutgers University and McCarthy of Harvard shared the 2018 Tyler Prize and both are biological oceanographers. McCarthy studies primary production (the synthesis of organic compounds from aqueous carbon dioxide) and nutrient supply in the upper oceans of the North Atlantic, equatorial Pacific, and Arabian Sea. His work on phytoplankton (microscopic algae that are the basis of food for all other forms of aquatic life) has allowed him to gauge the impact of climate change. He won the Tyler Prize for both his biology and his policy-influence, having co-chaired the Intergovernmental Panel on Climate Change in 2001. Refreshingly, McCarthy believes that his undergraduate training in art history, philosophy, and literature "have proven instrumental in articulating climate change" (Peter Tormey, "James McCarthy: Scientist for Others", *News-Events*, Gonzaga University, 2018). Falkowski has also studied phytoplankton and Earth's geochemical processes; when asked what the next big question is in his field, he answered: "Over the next 50 years, as greenhouse gases increasingly alter climate and more natural resources become depleted by humans, scientists will be increasingly called upon to help steer the Earth's systems back towards a more stable state" ("Q & A: Paul Falkowski", *Current Biology*, 2017). Falkowski alludes here to geoengineering. An example in his field would be the fertilising with iron of regions in the Pacific Ocean to induce plankton blooms which draw carbon dioxide out of the air and into the ocean, which would (it is believed) reduce the effects of global warming (see Emma Young, "Can 'fertilising' the ocean combat climate change?", *New Scientist*, 2007). But others have in mind more drastic action.

Geoengineering presupposes a certain attitude to Earth that alters the concept of a "fragile Earth". One of Richard Alley's books is *Earth: The Operators' Manual* (2011), a survey of the energy problem for human beings and their possible solutions, including geoengineering. The title's tacit metaphor, and succeeding the more familiar one of Earth as a fragile ecosystem or vulnerable organism (the space-blue chalcedony), is of Earth as a mechanism which humankind must learn to operate safely and efficiently. I think here of Richard White's approval in *The Organic Machine* of machine-Nature synergies, of science applied to Earth's dynamics, not in a clash of opposites but in a meeting of collaterals. Humanity is now to be Earth's engineer in the American sense of train-driver. If geoengineering, altering natural processes to halt or lessen global warming, were to involve hardware, then the term would suggest a hybrid science of engineering and geophysics.

Alley's interest in climate modification was anticipated by Wallace Broecker of Columbia University and Arizona State University who shared the Tyler Prize in 2002. He is credited with popularizing the specific term "global warming", having published his 1975 paper in *Science*: "Climatic Change: Are We on the Brink of a Pronounced Global Warming?" Aware of his own impending mortality, and demonstrating the passion some ecologists bring to the subject of climate change, the ailing 87 year-old laureate sat in front of a video camera in February 2019 a week before his death to record a farewell message. It was live-streamed via a large screen to forty of his colleagues gathered at ASU to discuss untested solutions to the global warming he had warned of. It was as close as he could come to participating in the university's first Planetary Management Symposium on Climate Engineering. Of the climate challenge, he told his colleagues and posterity with grim decisiveness: "We are going to have to go to geoengineering" (see James Rainey, "Wallace Smith Broecker, the 'grandfather' of climate science, leaves a final warning for Earth", *Green Energy Times*, 2019).

Geoengineering on the scale Broecker envisaged has about it the whiff of Wellsian science fiction and, as in science fiction and indeed at times in science, risk (and human hubris) play a crucial role. (Edward Teller in 1958 championed the detonation of a chain of five thermonuclear devices to create an artificial harbour in Alaska as a demonstration of "the great art of geographic engineering, to reshape the earth to your pleasure". The project was halted by the opposition of Alaskan conservationists [see online "Environmental History Timeline: 1940–1960", Radford University, Virginia].) The possible side-effects of geoengineering have worried some climatologists, for example the unforeseen consequences of shortwave climate engineering aimed at reducing incoming solar radiation. If the solution focuses too greatly on the problem of warming, it has been claimed, critical risks will not be evaluated appropriately. Proposed solutions such as "increasing the number of atmospheric reflecting particles in the stratosphere or by placing reflecting 'mirrors' outside the atmosphere", neglecting patterns of precipitation, could have detrimental unforeseen consequences, such as droughts (see Gabriele Hegerl and Susan Solomon, "Risks of Climate Engineering", *Science*, 2009). In any event, we may be in process of returning at least partially to the frontier, Victorian, and modernist concepts of Nature as something resilient enough to bear strenuous human intervention and re-making, a post-fragile Earth. To transpose Philip Larkin's wilfully unhelpful words, "Well, we shall find out".

The essay above is a shaped extract (two extracts coupled) from Foster's new book, The Space-Blue Chalcedony: Earth's Crises and the Tyler Bounty *(Alice C. Tyler Perpetual Trust, 2020). The book is a bio of the annual Tyler Prize for Environmental Achievement and the Tylers who founded it — the writing of which translated into a history of ecology.*

John Wilson Foster was born in 1942, grew up in Belfast and was educated at Annadale Grammar School. He won a scholarship to Queen's University Belfast where he graduated with a BA (1963) in English, Philosophy and Social Anthropology, and MA (1965) in English and Philosophy. His graduate teachers and mentors were the philosopher W.B. Gallie and the critic and poet Philip Hobsbaum, who had been taught by F.R. Leavis and William Empson.

On a Fulbright Travelling Scholarship he was accepted into the PhD program of the University of Oregon (Department of English) and received his doctorate in 1970 with a dissertation on the Irish fiction writers Brian Moore, Michael MacLaverty and Benedict Kiely. Before being appointed in 1974 to the Department of English, University of British Columbia, he expanded his dissertation for his first book, Forces and Themes in Ulster Fiction *(Gill & Macmillan, 1974), the first charting of Northern Irish fiction.*

Since then, he has authored and edited 17 books of literary criticism and cultural history, most recently Pilgrims of the Air *(Notting Hill Editions, 2014) and* Titanic: Culture and Calamity *(Belcouver, 2016). He is Professor Emeritus at the University of British Columbia and Visiitng Research Fellow at Queen's University Belfast, and now lives in Portaferry, Co Down.*

ON SEA AND LAND

—

André Gumuchdjian

From entrepreneur to activist.

I have always loved the sea. I first stepped on a boat when I was one-year-old and every youthful year spent long summers living on our small family cruiser. At 15, I discovered the world of sailing, the virus bit me and never left. Sailing is addictive, you get a sense of freedom that is hard to find on land.

At 19, I did my first transatlantic crossing, from Bermuda to the Mediterranean. 30 years later, the call of the sea and the desire to sail to faraway lands rose again in me. I decided to sail around the world. When I was back in the Atlantic, the vastness of the ocean hit me. It really takes an ocean crossing on a sailboat to comprehend the immensity of the body of waters on our planet.

When land disappears over the horizon, after a few days the wildness of the ocean reveals itself. When the wind picks up, a fascinating show begins. The huge mass of water we are moving on builds up into ever-stronger movements. The waves seem to become enchanted, they boil up into white crests and the waves break all around our vessel. One never tires of watching them. I am fascinated that just as they are about to break, the water below the bright white foam takes on a light-green colour, then the water becomes translucent, almost diaphanous, as if to suggest that all that force is an illusion. I am fascinated and cannot take my eyes off it. The spectacle can continue for days and nights and each moment is different from the other. As I continue watching, the wild becomes familiar and the waves become companions.

I am just as comfortable sitting on a boat many days from the closest land as someone sitting in his living room in the city. Yet my attitude to the sea has always been guided by humility. We have to be mindful that we are nothing compared to the force of the oceans. Never dare the sea; we are merely tolerated there. If it becomes furious, do not attempt to defy it. On the contrary, be humble, respect its might and if the winds and waves turn against us, we need to adapt and alter course.

As big as oceans are, though, I slowly became aware that human activity is destroying them. From over-fishing by ever more numerous and efficient ships to the millions of tons of plastic being dumped into the seas each year and from the consequences of climate change. Oceans absorb about half of the CO_2 we are emitting. This has two direct consequences: they are warming up and they are acidifying, both leading to a cascading chain of events, both dire for the future of life on the planet.

Over the years, this love and respect of the sea has made me keenly aware that we need to protect Nature in general.

About two years ago, I made a startling discovery. This finding was all the more striking, as it is central to what everyone is talking about these days, but very few know. It is a number: *2.3*. Kilograms to be precise.

That number is key to understanding the scale of the climate crisis the world faces today. 2.3 kilogram is the amount of carbon dioxide that is emitted when one uses just one litre of petrol in a combustion engine.

2.3 kg for one litre of petrol? I first thought that this was not possible. It's enormous! 100 litres is thus 230 kg of CO_2. Two stops at the gas station.

Suddenly everything started to make sense. I understood now why the CO_2 issue was such a big problem. Why all the environmentalists, scientists and activists were so worried and ringing the alarm bells. If indeed that number was correct, it is not difficult to arrive at the many Gigatons of CO_2 that are emitted each year when considering the millions of cars, planes, ships, industries, farming, housing, etc., that the whole world is recklessly using.

I wanted to check how much CO_2 I was emitting in a year. For the year 2018, I was startled to discover that the figure was 77 tons of CO_2. It was much more than the average European, more even than the average American. This figure was 20 times the world average and about 30 times what is considered sustainable for the planet. And this despite being environmentally conscious, having rooftop solar panels on my house and my garage, an electric car, not eating meat, etc.

As this reality was sinking in, I could not help but think: "We all need to act now." Indeed, I had to act.

The biggest culprit in my carbon footprint was flying, so I decided to reduce flying. But, as an active entrepreneur, it was impossible to stop altogether. Hopefully one day there will be other fuels but for the moment there is no alternative.

At the same time, I also felt a tremendous amount of guilt. I became conscious of the fact that over many years I have been polluting our beautiful planet carelessly. Sure, most of us were not aware of it, but now that we are, what right do I have to leave to future generations the chore of cleaning up my own pollution?

I decided to plant trees. Planting trees to offset the carbon footprint seemed the easiest and most natural option. 10 trees will offset about 1 ton of carbon in 8 years after they have grown about 10 to 20 years. I started studying the topic and learned much in the process.

However, rather than donating money, I decided to create an association myself, hoping that if I can convince others to join, the impact will be greater. I chose Armenia because of cultural ties and the fact that there is a lot of empty space. The initial objective is to plant 400,000 trees per year. It sounds like a lot but actually this represents offsetting carbon emissions of about 500 individuals like me.

As I learned more on the subject, I started to realise that trees, and in particular when they are part of a forest, are incredible organisms. Forests are much more than just individual trees together; they function as a holistic entity. The more I read, the more I realised the incredible benefits that forests are providing. In fact, like Alice in Wonderland, I felt that I had passed through a mirror to discover a magical new world that seemed so familiar yet so much misunderstood and ignored.

Forests are indispensable for life on earth. Consider all these benefits: besides the carbon they capture, they release three times more oxygen in the atmosphere; they lower temperatures, increase humidity, prevent soil erosion, avert desertification, increase water retention, increase flora and fauna, preserve and enrich bio-diversity, are a major source of medications, provide food and income for people – and many, many more. To be honest, I was so amazed at all the benefits that I forgot the reason why I became interested in forests in the first place!

One advantage that is crucially important is the role of forests in increasing humidity. By releasing humidity forests help themselves survive. Tropical forests are called "rain forests" for a reason, the increased humidity increases rainfall, which in turns help forests sustain themselves. It is a virtuous cycle. If we destroy the Amazon forest, a dry savannah will replace it. Where will the water come from to recreate it?

The discovery of the importance and the beauty of forests echoed my love of oceans. They are often similarly huge expanses of wild nature, which are essential for human life on earth. We need to respect them because our very lives depend on them.

As important as these realisations were, it was only the beginning. More was yet to be discovered.

The organisation I started, *My Forest Armenia*, had to solve many challenges.

We created two nurseries from scratch. We gather, sow and grow local seeds collected in nearby forests. We are intent on creating rich forests that preserve biodiversity, which means we use only local species. After one year, most of these species are re-planted in the reforestation areas.

During our first year, we monitored closely the evolution of the small plants and I soon realised that one of my original premises was plainly wrong. Planting trees is anything but easy. Many hazards loom and threaten the saplings. To begin with, not all seeds will germinate. Just like having a baby for a human, that miracle of nature should not be taken for granted. Depending on the species, success varies between 10 and 50%.

After seeds germinate, more dangers loom. Frost is the first one. In our first year of operation, a week after germination, temperatures dropped below freezing point for a few days – and 90% of our maple seedlings, which are the first to germinate, were lost. Then there are different types of fungi that damage the young seedlings. Mice ate the roots of yet others. Another threat is heat and dryness. Add the wind in the summer and it's as if someone is blow-drying the land. You water every day but the young plant is using so much energy to survive – absorbing water to compensate for evaporation – that there is little energy left for growing.

As I was sitting down with the staff pondering all these threats, a thought dawned on me that would change my perspective forever. I said, "Actually, building a forest is ten times more difficult than building a ten-story building!"

They were surprised but I noticed the nursery manager nodding silently in approval.

To fully understand nature, a word of explanation about ecosystems is required. What is an ecosystem and what does it mean really? In fact, a forest is composed of hundreds if not thousands of living forms. All the different species of trees, shrubs, fungi, birds, insects, worms, even fallen branches, leaves, soil, etc., all play a role. Each one of them provides a service to the whole and each one contributes to making the whole stronger. The richer the ecosystem, the stronger the forest.

It is easy now to understand an important consideration. Sure, we are planting seedlings with maximum care to ensure their survival and we are confident of our future success. Still, these are very small plants. It will take years before they grow and reach some height. It might take a hundred years before the whole becomes a fully-fledged forest.

It is therefore of enormous importance that we protect all the existing forests that remain. Nature took hundreds, often thousands of years to arrive at the perfect equilibrium that we find in earth's lush forests. We, homo sapiens, need to realise that destroying them is destroying ourselves. Unlike constructions that one can demolish and reconstruct in the space of a couple of months, building a forest involves an extremely long process. A process that is, at its core, not fully under our control because we are dealing with Nature.

This journey has been – and still is – every bit as fascinating as sailing around the world.

I come back full circle to the oceans. And sailing made me realise one thing. Homo sapiens has learned to conquer the seas but we are a land species, this commands us to be careful when sailing on the oceans. However, on land, because we are more confident, we are behaving irresponsibly. Yet, just as we need to respect the oceans, we need to respect, protect and (now) restore our forests.

Throughout this journey, my conviction has become that each one of us would not think of visiting a friend's house and leaving a bag of trash in their living room before going away. Similarly, are we not but passing by on this planet? Should not each one of us clean up what we have sullied, before leaving?

We are part of Nature not separate from it. We depend on Nature and urgently need to restore what we have destroyed. Our very own survival as a species depends on it.

This essay was written in English.

André Gumuchdjian is a Francophone Belgian-born entrepreneur and philanthropist of Armenian ancestry. After graduating from Harvard University in 1979, he joined the family business of wholesale diamond trading at the Antwerp Diamond Bourse. Over the years he has been active in various non-profit organizations. He was the president of the Belgian Association of Diamond Traders, President and Founder of the Armenian Cultural Centre in Brussels, and the Founding President of the French School in Antwerp (for which France decorated him as a Knight of the Legion of Honour). He founded My Armenia Forest in 2019, and to date 150,000 trees have been planted in the Lori region of Armenia.

A SONG AT IMBOLC

—

Moya Cannon

Now at spring's wakening, short days are lengthening
and after St. Bridget's Day, I'll raise my sail.

A blind man, on a stone bridge in Galway
or the road to Loughrea, felt the sun's rays
in his bones again and praised the sycamore and oak,
crops still drowsy in the seed, wheat, flax and oats.
His song rising, he praised Achill's eagle, Erne's hawk
and in beloved Mayo, young lambs, kids, foals,
and little babies turning towards birth.

Blind Raftery invoked Bridget, Ceres of the north,
born into slavery at Faughart, near Dundalk
to an Irish chieftain and a foreign slave.
Why, of all small girls in so distant a century born
is she honoured, still, in place-names, constant wells,
new rushes plaited to protect hearth, home and herd?

Bridget, goddess, druidess of oak, or saint – a girl
who gifted her father's sword to a beggar for bread,
we, who have wounded the engendering seas and earth,
beg you to teach us again, before it grows too late,
your neglected, painstaking arts of nurture and care.

Moya Cannon was born in 1956 in Dunfanaghy, Co Donegal and now lives in Dublin. She holds degrees in History and Politics and in International Relations from, respectively, University College, Dublin and Corpus Christi College, Cambridge. She is the author of seven collections of poetry, most recently Keats Lives *(2015) and* Donegal Tarantella *(2019), both from Carcanet. She is a member of Aosdána.*

TWO POEMS

Ciarán O'Rourke

JOHN CLARE ENCLOSED

John Clare, your eagle's nose
grows wise and flat

on the else unsmelt
suppressions of the earth.

You knew the world particulate
and true – and here you sit,

demure in inky water-colours,
bright-berry-eyed and stately,

a water-jug at rest
in elbow-distance down the tray.

A boyish elder-look, like light,
breaks across your face; you stare

as if an age of plenty, long ago begun
in green delight and common-song,

had all dissolved, a memory,
to noise and nothingness,

some bleak *beyond*
that slips your faded, folding

fist of bones, for now –
though the groan (or grin)

that's surfacing, the watch you keep,
would make a merry mix.

My own un-peasant hunger
knows no muck or grass,

the sodden *thing like bread*
you supped for miles

that kept your famine-fingers clean,
but longs, in indolence, sweet-bitterly,

for you yourself, restored:
a five-foot shadow,

lit by wind and all at large
a-down the ringing heath —

when time, like verse,
was gentle, coarse and full.

I've heard the very sun
would touch the earthen rim, far-off,

and lead you on ... perhaps to this,
(my wisp of want, a lark's desire),

to hale the air of once, and ever,
meeting no enemy & fearing none.

THE COMMONS

Sean, our common earth's in smoke,
the shadow-rule

of feasting, famine-fed conspirators
(a sleek elite) extends

to every nook
where gladness one-time grew.

'Tis like a sunbeam
in the mist, said some other

loss-eyed wilder-man
of love, like you

a grey-sky-sodden
hierophant

of dirt in bloom
and revelry: John Clare,

whose digger's life
and empty-bellied sorrowing

you praised as *permanent*
and *true* —

in this, our age
of wilting seas

and homesick, lock-out blues.
With quick largesse,

your bursting blend
of magnanimity and vim,

in a liquor-flux of inspiration,
you reeled his verse

from memory, and pictured
peasant-crowds alit

with world-transforming rage.
I trod home across

the mossy, rain-
bewintered city's wreck

in quietness, alive
and less alone.

To feel at all: an act
of intimate dissent,

as gentle-hearted heretics
have ever felt and known.

Is this, then, our one inheritance,
the ache where voices grow?

My poem's a lifted echoing,
as if they might continue.

Ciarán O'Rourke was born in 1991 and took a degree English and History at Trinity College, Dublin. He received a Masters in English and American Studies from Oxford in 2014, as well as a doctorate on William Carlos Williams at his alma mater in Dublin in 2019. A winner of the Lena Maguire / Cúirt New Irish Writing Award, the Westport Poetry Prize, and the Fish Poetry Prize, his first collection of poems, The Buried Breath, *was published by The Irish Pages Press in late 2018. His next collection, in preparation, is* Phantom Gang, *He currently lives in Carrick-on-Shannon, Co Leitrim.*

AFTER A FASHION

—

Muireann Charleton

In the graveyard of things.

Paris was freezing that January day I queued for eight hours outside the Musée des Arts Décoratifs to catch a glimpse of the lavish exhibition about Christian Dior and his legendary House of Dior. Finally, when I made my way through the exhibits of haute couture, I was in awe of the craftsmanship and beauty of design that his deep and intelligent connection with materials created. Shape, stitching, colour, silhouette, form and textures: all combined in a display of mini-architectures. I marvelled in particular at Dior's iconic 1947 "New Look" collection that featured a dream of extravagant draperies and voluminous A-line full skirts. This look was a liberation from the previous war-period of frugal and austere attire. Inside the spacious Dior exhibition, I took in the rich atmosphere of sensuous fantasy. It was a reverie that for a moment I belonged in. I followed up the museum visit with another cathedral of consumption in Paris: the Gucci store on rue du Fauborg St. Honoré. That pilgrimage was for the experience, and to purchase a small black leather belt. If Gucci was virtuous enough for Samuel Beckett (photographed in 1971 with a Gucci bag), then it would do fine for me. Yet, in recent years I have become disenchanted with this make-believe. I am more conscious of our unbridled emotional and psychological needs that give rise to our complex relationship with objects, things and fashion. Perhaps, it is now time we return to an austere and humble vestiary to help mitigate fashion's role as one of the worst contributors to the climate crisis in the Anthropocene?

Our relationship with objects and clothes has come along way since the imagined first pot was crafted on the banks of the Euphrates in Mesopotamia. The rise of department stores in the late nineteenth-century in Europe as formidable theatres of consumer craving enabled a sleek process of identity commodification to take place with relative ease. They facilitated in a practical way a bringing together of consumer habits among the different social classes under one architecturally impressive roof. Another big change was the practice, spawned in the twentieth century, of styled obsolescence. This was the dubious practice of intentionally reducing the shelf-life of products in order to boost sales in pursuit of an endless upwards curve of economic growth. Both of these developments have led to mass consumption, which has contributed to the loss of our material intelligence and appreciation of the tacit knowledge that goes with it. Now, we live in a culture in which making has become largely separated from consuming. This has obscured the importance of making. But, as writer and curator Glenn Adamson has written in *Fewer Better Things* (2019), the relationship we have with materials "determines much about the way we live on earth".

According to the United Nations, the fashion industry now consumes more energy than the aviation and shipping industries combined. Its special report found that due to its high energy production and long supply chains, the fashion industry contributes 10% of global greenhouse gas emissions. If that's not bad enough, over-production of textiles leads to more than 85% ending up in landfill or being incinerated. The fashion industry is now one of the most environmentally dangerous industries in the world. And, this highly damaging sector is also the most manipulative.

One of the features of our psychology is the way we use fashion to express our identity whether as a member of a group, or to imply our uniqueness and sense of personality. As late nineteenth-century Dandyism exemplified (a chief proponent of which was Oscar Wilde) we still use dress codes to project a sense of aesthetic taste, authority, class and professional membership. The history of fashion also makes clear that we use dress especially to appear attractive to others. However, we are now in the era of fast fashion, with all the extra harm that implies for the environment. Closely associated with fast fashion is the new profession of "influencer", an online role to peddle or endorse products in a 24-hour cycle of the new. Coupled with the vanity-appealing digital platform Instagram, influencers have helped develop a *see it, buy it* culture that stormed a whole new generation. "Shop the look" has become a norm for millennials who are digitally seduced into endless purchases from cheap high-street fast fashion stores. Superficially, yet understandably, at the heart of this activity is a longing for visibility and connection to a congregation for both the influencers and the influenced. In his book *Taste* (2017), writer and founding director of the London Design Museum Stephen Bayley showed how fashion is primitive in its insistence on exhibitionism. It cannot survive isolation from the gaze of others. Remove the stage, and it ceases to perform.

Fast fashion has also perpetuated the myth that buying something new is the same as attaining worth. In addition, a critical factor is how fast fashion producers make garments so cheap to manufacture that there is a strong incentive for consumers to buy frequently in spite of increasing awareness about the impact this has on damaging the environment. Many of us who work in design were horrified at two shattering events. One was the 2013 Rana Plaza disaster in Bangladesh in which an unsafe garment factory collapsed killing over a thousand workers. The second in 2018 was the fashion house Burberry destroying millions of pounds of stock in order to preserve its brand exclusivity. Fashion is the monster that feeds on its own skin.

But, fashion designers *know* how things are made; they work with raw materials, factories, production. They know how to cost items of clothing. They understand the price of fabrics, embellishments, packaging. They are acutely aware of the economic principles of supply and demand. So, they work with marketing teams and social media influencers to conjure up advertising campaigns with the sole purpose of creating a desire in us to consume their products. Some of these campaigns use multiple artists: talented photographers, stylists, copy writers. The results are often akin to magical stories. The late *Vogue* magazine stylist Isabella Blow was particularly famous for extravagant fashion features, often obscuring the narrative away from tawdry consumption and towards artistic expression. And there is real and fulfilling art to good fashion design. Nevertheless, the goal is still to sell fashion and to use the earth's limited resources for this purpose. No wonder, then, that fashion designers often talk in codes, communicating that their work is pushing artistic boundaries, committed to ideals of beauty and innovation. But many are trapped in a system not of their own making but one they are sustaining; a harlequin masquerade pushing a re-worked *new* while the climate declines.

The author and activist Naomi Klein saw all of this trouble coming when she was researching her ground-breaking 1999 book *No Logo*. Decades earlier Vance Packard warned us in his compelling in 1952 book *The Hidden Persuaders* on the ways we were being manipulated by advertisers. Designer and pioneer Victor Papanek's 1970 guidebook, *Design for the Real World*, was one of the first brave voices of protest from inside design itself, as he encouraged designers to create only for positive environmental and social change. I often try to imagine a world where designers in training and practice adhere faithfully to Papanek's words. He wrote, "As socially- and morally-involved designers, we must address ourselves to the needs of a world with its back to the wall …" Environmental and social responsibility has to be integral to design education. We need to do more to educate the next generation to be these socially- and morally-involved designers that can solve the complex, global challenges of our time.

Today, there are a few leaders in the fashion industry who try to connect sustainable principles with creative enterprise. Leading the charge is Stella McCartney, one of the rare fashion designers to work by a code of ethics. For example, declining to work with leather, McCartney explores technology and innovative processes to create products made from recycled plastic (e.g., recycled fishing nets). There is also the former punk, designer Dame Vivienne Westwood, who has in recent times pleaded with consumers to buy less and to "choose well, make it last". The time has come to reconnect with the concept of slowness and slow fashion, which will require us to buy garments that are designed for long-term use. Quality of materials and construction for longevity, combined with an enthusiastic culture for fixing and repairing, can become a seductive proposition again. Much like the pastoral in poetry and art, perhaps a nostalgia for a making and mending way of life can be marketed to us. I often reflect that perhaps buying fast fashion in the future will be viewed in the same way as smoking: unhealthy and no longer cool. But we do need to develop an intelligent relationship to the fabrics we wear and the way our clothes are produced. Well-designed, well-made and long-lasting clothes such as a Studio Donegal tweed waistcoat, or a battered Barbour re-waxed jacket, can give us an enhanced and deeper *connection* with the fabrics we inhabit. We can sense they are not shallow things.

Since there is no scientific or philosophical evidence that we are what we wear (or don't wear, as the case may be), we should be able to embrace releasing ourselves from the relentless pursuit of the new, and pivot our desires towards the imperfect and the serviceable. Perhaps we can embrace the ancient Japanese philosophy of *wasi sabi*, discovering the beauty in the imperfect, the worn, the already used. This is as much a battle-cry for the persistence of craft, as it is a Gregorian chant for behavioural change. And, what of my black Gucci belt, once so beloved and desired? It is stored away for now in a dresser drawer, in a graveyard of things.

Muireann Charleton is a Lecturer in Design at the Yeats Academy, IT Sligo. She co-curated a design and craft exhibition entitled Generation *for the National Design & Craft Gallery, Kilkenny, scheduled to open on 12 March 2020, but postponed due to the Pandemic.*

MILLENNIAL GUILT

Niamh Moritt

A last parachute?

Red for paper and plastic, green for glass. Red for last week's box of bran flakes, green for the weekends bottle of wine (red). Dinner's onion peel in the compost, Malteser packet in the black bin. No, is that right? Coffee into my reusable takeaway cup, water into my brand-new, all the works, "will keep your liquids hot or cold", lifetime warranty steel bottle. I open today's post, a parcel from eBay, a Levi jacket, it smells fusty. My water tastes like metal. As I leave the house one of the five trillion single use plastics bags that are used every year greets me at my front door. I couldn't tell you the last time I bought one of these 5p suffocation chambers but on my walk to work I notice them in the hands of half the people I see. Is the future of the planet in my hands alone? No, but it's in the hands of the twenty-some-things, the teenagers and the toddlers that will be sheltering from the acid rain, putting bags of sand in front of the doors of their used-to-be-idyllic-not-so-idyllic-now seaside cottages and puffing on inhalers through their pollution filled lungs.

Growing up my mum always said she had Catholic guilt. A born-again atheist she still can't walk past a cemetery without crossing herself. Still awash with original sin I've never experienced this phenomenon, I'm not opposed to fish and chip Friday, but swapping it for a curry wouldn't keep me awake at night. Yet this inherent guilt isn't something that is alien to me. I seem to have found my own version of it in the water I drink and the food I eat. My metal water bottle, my daily recycling filing system, my stagnant smelling new clothes are my penance. Single use plastic is my sin and the destruction of the Earth is my eternal damnation. The metaphor stands: millennial guilt. It's not just me that feels this way, a quick survey of close acquaintances unearths several stories of £50 shirts made from recycled tyres, catching a 12-hour bus/ferry/train journey to save on carbon footprint and spending three hours on the phone to the council trying to second recycling bin. With the future of the planet on our organically sourced, naturally dyed, ethically made, cotton clad backs it's no wonder this sentiment is shared.

On 8 October 2030 my mum will be 64, I'll be 33 and it will be 12 years since the UN released their report stating that we have 12 years to prevent catastrophic climate change. The 8th of October 2018 was my mum's birthday, so I was home for the weekend. We ate chocolate cake and didn't talk about the demise of the planet; or how every good birthday should be. The millenials don't seem too phased by the news, but I vow never to use one of those plastic bags that you put your onions in to stop them rolling around your trolley ever again. The environment isn't my niche. As a politics student and a life-long Kate Bush fan I've never been particularly drawn to nuances of the ecosystem. However, the photo of the turtle with the straw up its nose and the condemning consequences detailed in the UN report haunted me into a paperless bank statement lifestyle. The report found that the temperature of the planet is set to rise by 0.5 degrees Celsius, 2 degrees hotter than the pre-industrialisation temperature of the planet. This will lead to intense droughts, hurricanes, a 90% loss of coral world-wide, the list goes on. Unrelenting millennial guilt.

Yet it wasn't me that did this, my single-use straws did not raise the temperature of the planet by 1.5 degrees. I didn't start this, but I must finish it. 2019 and beyond will be shaped by the twenty-somethings and the teenagers that stop buying plastic bottles, and new t-shirts, and plastic bags. Meanwhile, 100 companies make up 71% of global emissions. Knowing this makes drinking out of a soggy paper straw that little bit harder, but that seems to be the last parachute on a quickly descending plane. Avocado toast aside, helping the environment seems to be one of the few things millennials should be commended for. The sinking ship that is being left behind by the generations before us can't be patched up by bamboo toothbrushes alone — but we will certainly try.

Niamh Morritt was born in Nottingham in 1997 to an Anglo-Irish family. She studied History as an undergraduate before receiving an MA in Politics in December 2019, both from Queen's University Belfast. She is a self-defined Socialist, having witnessed the introduction of Universal Credit and the rise of food banks in her teenage years. She currently works for a Labour MP in her hometown.

THREE STORIES
From INVISIBLE WOMAN

—

Slavenka Drakulić

COFFEE NO LONGER TASTES THE SAME

Coffee no longer tastes the same since my husband died three months ago. True, the smell is still rich and opulent, but not the taste. Something is missing – in fact, after a sip I sense bitterness, as though the beans are too roasted. And it cannot be that I've chanced upon such coffee several times in a row. Therefore it thrilled me to find a new brand on the shelf in my supermarket, one they never had before, also an espresso blend, pure Arabica. I decided to try it.

When we were getting to know each other, he drank filter coffee. I found that out, of course, only when I first stayed the night at his place. In the morning he made an excellent breakfast, with soft-boiled eggs and croissants, butter and marmalade, all served in silver bowls and with silver cutlery. But the coffee was a horrendous, brown liquid that barely even reminded of the taste of coffee – and it didn't smell good either. If I had known I was going to stay overnight, I would have brought my espresso machine, the little one for two cups. It would have fit in my handbag. Although it would have been of no use, because it takes a different blend of coffee. And I wasn't that enterprising.

The thought that the man who swept me off my feet drank filter coffee was as agonizing as telling me he had some infectious disease. It was a bad habit that needed to be uprooted. It proved easier than I thought. He didn't resist, he even found a cafetière in the kitchen, the kind in which hot water is poured onto the coffee which, and after standing a little while, is pushed down almost to the bottom by a perforated metal ring. This coffee was much better, stronger, more flavourful. A decent replacement, but only a replacement, for espresso, for which I had to wait for us to start living together, so as not to strike him as too meddling. Then I bought two espresso machines, of two different sizes. And for his birthday, the first we celebrated together, I got him a real Gaggia machine, a retro model, with a handle like those in coffee shops (except, of course, for home use). To me it was a sort of test of a good relationship, not to mention marriage. I don't mean so much a love for coffee, but more adaptability, sensitivity, listening attentively to the other person's needs. From then on we began our days with a cup of coffee together, one from a larger *cafetière* or *moka pot* — whatever you call this little appliance — for six persons, served in mugs to which we added some milk to make a *macchiato*. But a strong one, to carry us through the day.

He quickly forgot filter coffee and came to love this morning ritual, so much so that he even would be the first to get up and put on the coffee, and I would join him only when the seductive smell would creep up on me in the bedroom and wake me up. He continued to make breakfast, though I have to say not as grand and without silverware (except on my birthday). More than the coffee itself, it made us happy to drink it together, as this was our morning ritual to start the day. So much had kept us together through the years, but the shared drinking of coffee was like a glue. That's why I still drink it now, although I'm alone. In fact, it is precisely because I don't want to be alone that I drink coffee; when I drink it, I think of him, and in a way it feels like we're still together. They say that people live as long as somebody remembers them. Now I think about him intensively every morning, and quite often something in connection to him crosses my mind later on too. When I listen to the news I think about how he would comment, or when I cook a meal he liked, such as beef soup, I always make too much. Getting used to living alone is hard for me, it takes time. Half an hour in the morning belongs to us, the way we liked it to be. To me it was beautiful to watch this vigorous man bring the cup to his lips and look at me over the rim with a smile. Listening to his voice while he tried to bring my attention to the book he'd just been reading, even though I didn't always listen attentively to his words. We're together and still going strong, I would think. Sometimes I would ask myself how much time we had left, but I'd chase away the idea like a pestering fly. Why think about that which we cannot influence, while we're sitting by the open window that looks out on the garden, with already-blossoming primroses, and while I'm pouring us another cup of coffee?

It was precisely with coffee that his illness began, with the word *coffee*. I can never forget this. One morning, exactly seven years ago, he seemed to me somehow strange. He was looking at the cup, frowning. What do you call this, he asked, confusedly. Which, you mean the cup or the coffee? Coffee, yes, thank you, for a moment I lost the word. Lost the word? How is it possible that a man living off words — loses a word? He didn't say "I forgot it", which seemed even stranger. Did he also forget the word "to forget"? I didn't imme- diately take it as an omen. I attributed the loss of the word to fatigue — the last few days he had been spending too much time staring at his computer, translating. But it happens to everyone, I said: the other day at the shop I couldn't remember what I had come in for. And my Mum, as you remember, she couldn't remember words like flour or milk, things she used every day. We even laughed at her. This comforted him. But soon he began to lose more and more words or, even worse to me, he replaced them with what came to his mind that very moment. For salt he'd say bread – at least the same category, food – but if for book he said shoe – for example, could you please pass me the shoe from my desk – I found it hard to cope. Moreover, the desk was covered in books. Should I perhaps ask him which "shoe" he needs? The very next moment, unconscious of the mistake, he would say the right word. The new phase followed when he began repeating himself. Whatever he would tell me about, some event from his youth – and he returned more and more often to youth and childhood– he would repeat a minute later, almost word for word. It was hard for me to listen to him, although at the beginning I found it odd that he recalled older episodes but couldn't remember what had happened yesterday, or that very morning. For example, the fear of a maths test. If you only knew how much I was scared by this maths test. We had an old teacher, one who'd pull a schoolboy's ear if he suspected him of whispering: everyone was afraid of him. When he gave us a test, he would walk between the benches ensuring we weren't copying. For years after I dreamt that I didn't pass the test, I still today don't know how I managed to graduate from high school. And then, not five minutes later, he would say: Have I told you how much I was scared by a maths test? I adapted myself, I got used to not listening to him talk – just a voice.

But still it happened sufficiently rarely that we didn't worry. I started sticking post-its wherever I could, so that the book said "book" and the shoe said "shoe", but at first he removed them. The idea that he needed help made him angry. It's like learning a foreign language, only that now you're relearning your own, I would say to him. But the words did not entrench themselves in his memory, and would fall again out of his vocabulary, which lessened all the more. As if trying to keep coins in a torn pocket, the journey to deep illness was sprinkled with lost word-coins. Mostly the ordinary ones, the names of things surrounding us. Stairs and door, soap, newspaper, chair, all vanished. For some time he still went to the shop with a list. What would happen is that he would read, for example, dough, but would have forgotten what it was and wouldn't ask a shop girl to show him, so he would come back home with cookies or the first thing he laid his hands on. Or he would leave his wallet at the till. At the market, while he could still walk, he would pay for lettuce with a large banknote and walk off. I say while he could still walk, since soon he started to fall down. Out of the blue. He did not trip — rather his legs would simply fail him. I was with him when it happened. He just clung to my sleeve and crumbled down on the sidewalk. Slowly, like when they shoot an actor in a movie and he falls and falls and it takes him ages to reach the ground. He got some medication, but it was a sedative from which he dozed. It was of course easier for me, since before that I had to be on standby all the time to make sure he didn't get out of the house in his pyjamas or get burned. But still he was more dear to me awake, though his behaviour started to physically wear me out. I didn't have the strength to make sure he didn't find the matchbox because he loved to watch how they burn, or shove crunched-up newspapers down the toilet or rummage in the dustbin in search of a little car he had lost seventy years before.

Then the nightmares followed. He was already sleeping alone in the bedroom — I had moved to our son's room, but the door had to be open. At first he would talk in his sleep and wake up in cold sweats, not knowing where he was. I would sit by his side and calm him down until he fell asleep again.

When he came around, he was sad to be sleeping alone. He promised me he would sleep quite calmly, that he would neither squirm nor wake me up ... I only want to touch you in the night, to know that I'm alive and you're by my side. I cried when he couldn't see me. I knew I was losing him. The worst thing was that in between the fits he was completely conscious of what was happening to him, that he was losing his own self. His pain could not be compared with mine. I'm begging you, put me in a home. I don't want you to see me like this. This isn't me, you understand? I nodded with my head. I couldn't tell him I didn't want to leave him alone.

After he started to cry for Mum at night, he didn't come around to himself anymore. He moaned, like a baby in heavy pain, and cried: Mum, Mummy, it hurts, come, it really hurts. When I appeared at the door, he would stretch out his arms towards me. You came, he hugged me and squeezed me tightly. I let him call me Mum, there was no point in explaining. For he was indeed nothing more than a little boy lost, very sick, who needed his Mum to stroke his hair and comfort him. Fortunately, he contracted pneumonia and his torture was ended. Fortunately, because I believe he wanted it that way. When I entered the room after one peaceful night, quietly, so as not to wake him up, he was lying on his back and his still-striking face made it all serene. I found comfort in the thought that he died in sleep because I would emotionally break down from the thought of him fully conscious and alone at that moment. Yes, he died in his sleep — otherwise he would have called me. But sometimes I think he didn't want to call me, he wanted to spare me his dying, it was his farewell gift and his way of showing me how much he loved me. Although it is completely certain that he had lost the word love long before.

Mum, go back to your room, you can't live in a museum consecrated to Dad and me, said my son after the funeral. He came for three days from Canada. I was content that he didn't see his father in that state. But this is not a museum, I just don't have the strength to change anything, clean up, rearrange, paint, but I will move, I lied to him on his departure. I did not return to the bedroom. I'd have to sleep alone in the bed I had never slept alone in. And wake up in the night listening closely for if he is breathing — and hearing that he is not breathing. What does our son know of loneliness, of the emptiness in me after the death? Or of how it cannot be mended, like holes in socks long ago?

New coffee happily announced itself to the kitchen. The pleasant smell filled the room — and I already knew by the smell that he'd like it. I thought of the resilience of the organism; of my own obstinate cells that keep on living as if nothing has happened; of the lust for life that has nothing to do with my will. I took a sip of the hot liquid. He'd like it, I concluded contentedly — but this new brew still does not taste like when we took coffee together.

CLEARING UP

Mum died on Monday, 4 March, early in the morning. She died in the hospital, exactly where she didn't want to die. Please, don't let me die in the hospital, she used to say. Promise me. I promised, of course. She hated this hospital and avoided it for as many years as she could. Because every one of hers died there: father and mother and husband and son. It was the only hospital in town. I let her down, but there was no way I could stop it.

On Friday evening the ambulance took her from the nursing home to the hospital. She had trouble breathing, a nurse later told me, but she was fully conscious. They probably didn't want her to die in the clinic in the nursing home where she had lain the past few weeks. A cousin, who lives hear the hospital, came to see her straight away. A doctor, a young woman, told her that the test results were ok for her age and condition, and that they would probably send her back to the nursing home the following day. But they still kept her in the pulmonary ward for a specialist examination. On Saturday she said that Mum looked exhausted and had barely spoken. A nurse told her that she had had soup for lunch, which had comforted her. We spoke on the phone. Mum murmured indistinctly. Later I found out that she had an oxygen mask on her face. I was nervous, as I always was when we spoke. I can't understand you at all! – I said angrily. It was the last thing I ever said to her.

On Sunday my cousin again informed me of her condition – Mum was weak, she couldn't get out of the bed, but she was composed. They were awaiting a pulmonary specialist, who would come on Monday. She had eaten a fruit yoghurt and drunk a bit of juice. No, the nurse on call whom I spoke with that day told me, the situation is not alarming, you don't need to travel down, everything will be ok.

Everything will be ok? With a patient with chronic lung emphysema, on oxygen and with a barely-beating heart? Weren't these very words supposed to sound alarming? Why, instead of believing a nurse who wanted to get rid of me as soon as possible so she could sit before a TV screen and watch her favourite series, did I not pack straight away and set off to see my Mum? I must have known the end was near. But I didn't want to accept it.

On Monday the phone rang at about 7.30 in the morning. My cousin again. I no longer remember what exactly she said, how she said it – how do you even tell someone their mother died? Even though it was too early in the morning for a phone call, I didn't suspect it even for a second, I wasn't startled – I didn't sense death coming. Was it just self-defence?

The hospital had just called to tell her that "madam died". I remember only these words because, from her mouth – even though she was obviously quoting the doctor – they sounded too formal.

I didn't react. The meaning of these words at that moment somehow missed me. I lived in another city, in another state. I saw Mum every few months. I didn't immediately comprehend how I would never see her again. I didn't cry. I dreamt of her almost every night. Only a few nights after her death I dreamt of her lying on a couch. She was sleeping on her side, uncovered. She was naked. I remember how it astonished me, even in my sleep. I touched her, her skin was warm and unbelievably tender, like a child's. I must have remembered it because Mum was already dead, yet still was warm to touch.

I travelled, although I don't remember how. Those few days before the funeral are as if erased from memory.

In the morgue my cousin placed on the bier a black and white photograph of Mum I hadn't seen in a long time. In it she is about 30, it could have been 1960. Her hair is up and her face symmetric, open, smiling. Around her neck is a pearl necklace. Her head is slightly inclined, the way they used to take portraits in the photo studios. I remember the dress she's wearing, dark blue silk with three buttons on the collar, a kind you couldn't find in shops those days – gilded, with an inserted crystal that glittered like a diamond. In the picture Mum looked classy and elegant. I was grateful that she chose this very photo, because if there ever was a single photo that was supposed to portray my Mum in her best light, the way she saw her own self – then this was it.

Not even the funeral convinced me she was dead. I couldn't watch them lower the coffin into the tomb, but perhaps I should have. There is, distinctly stored in my memory, a small cemetery lit by the stingy sun peeking under clouds, and the moist clumps of earth which fell on the wooden coffin. And then, the empty village square in front of the church and a small group of friends and relatives. The square is flagged in white stone and we are all in black, almost like giant birds slowly and unskilfully massing towards the inn.

I tried to postpose clearing up her suite at the nursing home as much as possible. After two months, though, I finally made the trip. The day was sombre and the journey took longer than usual. I figured I would need a few hours to clear up her things. Two people would be helping me – I didn't dare enter that space alone, rummage through her clothes, feel her smell.

I mustered up courage only when I remembered how it was Mum herself who packed for the nursing home. She was used to migrations, because of father's work she had already moved five or six times in life, not counting the move to the nursing home. She spared me then. But the last clearing up awaited me.

How much could a person living in a nursing home suite leave behind? It should have been easy, but still, when I opened the wardrobe – first one, then the other – the task seemed all at once enormous and indescribably difficult. Two closets full of clothes! Clearing up the kitchen and the living room was easy. Some dishes and documents, jewellery and pictures. Nothing too personal, I thought, no letters or notes … How few of these intimate remnants left behind her. But what was I expecting to find? A diary? Love letters? In fact, the most intimate thing she possessed was her wardrobe.

With strange nimbleness and determination I dug into the first closet. The smell of her overwhelmed me. Like some women leave letters, a lock of children's or lover's hair, these clothes were the personal, the most personal, possession my Mum left behind to me. How beautifully they were hung and lined up, sorted by type and colour, these garments of hers. Coats, jackets, skirts, trousers, pullovers, t-shirts, blouses, nightgowns. At the nursing home she would have put on something different for lunch and sometimes for dinner, too.

That was her, the neatly arranged closet with the clothes she loved and which made her what she was. She would spend so much time washing, ironing and matching them, enjoying her wardrobe and taking care of it.

When I stretched out my arm to take the first garment, I felt a sudden pain in my chest. But nevertheless I roughly, almost brutally, started to take things out, paying no attention to how and what. I brusquely selected what to leave at the home and what to donate, throwing them to the left or right pile. I wanted to get this torturous duty over and done with as soon as possible.

Her long mink coat was already at my place in a closet, wrapped in a sheet, as she had instructed me. You must take the coat, she said quietly, confidentially, so as not to be overheard by the clinic's nurse. As if she was talking about gold or diamonds. It's not safe here! What do you mean, Mum? – I asked her in wonder. You know that the key to the suite is not with me, it's in the infirmary, anyone can go upstairs and take it. I saw she was seriously worried, the mink coat was something of great value to her, something she cared about.

First put it on the balcony, for a good airing, then put it away. Take a clean sheet from the drawer and wrap it carefully, and by no means put it in something plastic! That was as far as her instructions went. She didn't say something like "it'll do you good", because she knew I don't wear coats of real fur. Pity, she said when I had turned down another of her fur coats, earlier. Although she had expected it, it was a shame to her all the same. I hope she sold it later. The fur coat for which I had gotten the instructions was expensive, a sign of prestige. She had bought it on credit, of that I'm certain, although she didn't actually need the coat – in our littoral town it never really got that cold. But she wore it, she wore all clothes with natural grace and style.

Maybe she then remembered the fur coat she had bought me a long time ago, after I had spent my first winter in Zagreb shuddering in a thin little coat of brown corduroy. That autumn of 1966 I visited a friend who was already studying. I slept at her dorm. I had intended to return home quickly, but I stayed a bit longer, without clothes, without anything. I remember I was standing at a tram stop when the first snow found me. Back home on the sea it rarely fell and as a child I rejoiced in the fluffy flakes, speeding through the yard and catching them with my open mouth before they melted. That day snow swept me over in dense drifts, accumulating on my hair and shoulders. I returned to the dorm freezing and soaking wet.

The next winter, when she had gotten it through her head that I was staying in Zagreb, she brought me a brown sheepskin jacket lined with fur, visible only on the edge of the sleeves, around the neck and along the buckling fold. It was warm and simple. I remember how her face was beaming when she took it out of the suitcase. It was a symbol of her victory over father, who disapproved of my decision to move to Zagreb. She must have considered buying something that expensive a true success of her own and undoubtedly kept this loan a secret from father. To be sure, she paid the instalments out of her own salary as a state official, which was not low. She knew how winters in Zagreb are humid and cold and she was proud she could at least ensure I had a coat to keep me warm. That was as much as she could do for me, every now and then secretly slip me a good garment or a little money. It was her way of showing she cared despite the fact that father thought I didn't deserve it.

I didn't thank her. I couldn't accept this gift simply as warm clothing. To me this fur coat was a reminder. I couldn't forgive Mum for not defending me from father's enraged attacks. Why was she so powerless? When I once later asked her about it, she replied in wonder: What was I supposed to do, divorce him because of you?! What she meant was "because of your stupidity and stubbornness", but she never said it.

This lambskin jacket could not substitute for her care, although this was – as I later grew aware – exactly what it was, a sign of her true care. I constantly kept rediscovering this anger of mine, kept coming back to it uncontrollably on almost every visit. We would start talking, and my voice would suddenly change, become of a higher tone, tense, full of suppressed feelings.

Nevertheless, I wore it as long as I was a student – I had nothing else, not one other coat. When I graduated, I left it at the cafeteria, on purpose, hoping that it would serve someone else. In fact, it was as though I threw it off me, at the same time throwing off all the other things it reminded me of. Years later I met a young man, I can no longer remember his name, who told me that this fur coat saved him and that he later gave it to someone else who also needed it. Perhaps someone is still wearing it?

Mum would have been happy if I even just occasionally put on her mink coat. But later it was too late for any mending.

On the top shelf of Mum's wardrobe stood a box. At the bottom, beneath felt and straw hats was a black tulle veil. Already frayed, creased, as though it had gotten there by mistake. I recognised it immediately and an image of her appeared before my eyes. Mum is standing on the edge of a grave, father is holding her, she is leaning dangerously close to the vault into which my brother's coffin has just been lowered. Her face is hidden beneath that thick black veil, the one I'm holding in my hand. I'm standing next to her and all I can hear is her sobbing, muffled by her hand in a black lace glove held firmly against her mouth. I still cannot comprehend how she coped with it, standing there while moist lumps of soil fell on the wooden coffin of my 35-year-old brother, echoing dully like distant thunder. And before that sitting in a cool chapel listening to the sermon, and earlier still kissing his face in the morgue by the hospital.

Then, only a month later, my father died, crushed by grief for his son. And the same scene repeated itself, her face covered by this very veil, on the edge of the tomb.

She lost them both in a month, the two men who she lived with and to whom she meant everything. Only I remained for her, distant, bitter, poor support in her old age. But I did take on her care, I've always been good at fulfilling duties.

I dropped the veil in the black rubbish bag, together with her old slippers, newspapers, leftovers from the fridge and two dirty kitchen cloths. After my brother died, more than 20 years ago, Mum wore only black. But a few years ago, when I paid her a visit, she was wearing a long summer dress, a kaftan actually, of live colours. She saw my astonished face. Well, my girl-friends here at the nursing home told me that it is enough mourning, so I'm wearing something of lively colour – so she justified her new clothing. I think I laughed, but I'm not sure. I guess I couldn't believe Mum would listen to anyone's advice regarding clothes and fashion. There, she's found an excuse to shop for more clothes, I thought, but immediately knew how unjust this was to her, how cynical. To redeem myself, next time I brought her a set of light grey angora t-shirts.

Underwear was neatly arranged on the bottom shelf. In two piles, by colour. Black and white. My Mum's generation experienced not only the post-war shortages, when both food and clothes were rationed and bought with coupons, but also the subsequent shortage of anything beautiful. Of course, there was underwear (manufactured by Galeb of Omiš and Tvornica Rublja of Duga Resa), but there was no choice. Ladies' underwear, like men's, were cotton, high-waisted and only available in white. That's why Mum all her life longed for lace underwear. Luckily, we had an aunt who lived in Italy who Mum visited relatively often. The most important thing for her was to buy underwear and shoes.

In the closet I found an outfit from the fifties, a skirt and a blouse. A purple and black combination, light satin, today again in fashion. I didn't throw it away. I couldn't, not after Mum had kept it for decades, only not to wear it for the two decades in mourning, only to start wearing it again towards the end of her life, proud that she could still fit into the clothes of her youth, that she had kept her figure.

Her bras, even the orthopaedic one, had to be lace, black lace, no less. When she had her breast cancer surgery (of which we were not allowed to speak, no one was allowed to know), the protective bras covered by her health insurance weren't good enough for her. Back then it was incomprehensible to me that she wore fine underwear exclusively for herself, for her own satisfaction, because no one else saw it except her. But looks were what were eternal to her.

Did I throw all that underwear away, both the black and the white pile, simply because I couldn't stand her vanity? I threw it in the black bag somehow too quickly, too decisively, more decisively than with other clothes ... But without her these were only remnants, simple rags.

She used to tell me: look at how you're dressed, those trousers don't fit you, you've gained weight again, these colours don't match ... I endured her criticism because I knew she was never satisfied anyway. Once I tried on one of her jackets and of course it didn't fit me like it fit her, although we were built the same way. It's not about what you wear, but how you wear it – I remembered that comment of hers.

Ruthlessly and perfunctorily, without stopping much, I was clearing up through that day all these carefully ordered garments that she held so dear. I penetrated into her most intimate world and demolished it like they demolish a painstakingly-constructed structure. Mum was disappearing before my eyes, but not the body that had betrayed her, whether heart or lungs. The real Mum. Clearing up was an undiluted destruction of her identity. I destroyed that which had made her unique. People leave behind paintings, compositions, money, houses – she left her second skin, the one in my hands and made of fabric, without which she would not be – herself. She didn't leave it to anyone in particular – it is simply what she left behind as proof of what she was.

I had a dream about her the first night after the clear-up. Mum didn't like escalators, once she fell on one and broke her leg on the sharp edge.

After that she used them only if someone held her. We were in some large space, maybe a department store. At the top of the very steep stairs she took the first step and tumbled down. She was lying lifelessly at the foot of the stairs. I saw people coming towards her. I was standing at the top, paralysed, and I heard my own sobbing, the sound that woke me up.

I only saw her a few times in my life without make-up. Even when she came to visit me she'd wake up early to put make-up on before the rest of us woke up. She considered it polite to look your best.

In the drawer of the clinic table she had a cosmetic bag and as soon as she had the strength she would take out a mirror, and first put on some cream, then foundation: then she would place a magnifying mirror on the table and start drawing her eyebrows and eyelids with a liner-pencil. After she became too weak to go to town, to the pharmacy, we brought her all the cosmetics she needed. Her instructions were precise, and this was the most important order of all. Not long before her death, when we went to the pharmacy together, she bought three eyeliners! Why three, Mum? Because I don't know when I'll get to the shop again, I need to have a stock. She didn't even finish one. It didn't occur to her that soon she might not need so many eyeliners, kohls, lipsticks and creams. You know, she said, I somehow can't believe I'm 85, I don't feel that way at all. If it weren't for these breathing problems and weak legs … Mum was indeed much younger than me – I felt old even before my body started to fail me. She had well-groomed hands and nails. She could no longer get up to go to the hairdresser's to get her hair dyed, her hand trembled too much to put make-up around her eyes, but the last time I saw her she had lipstick on. Only now I know that in clearing up I buried her a second time around: she died only at the moment when she was left without clothes and cosmetics.

But the problem wasn't just her vanity. She had an innate sense of beauty she hadn't acquired by upbringing or education. She had style, and it took more than mere vanity, more even than knowledge. It took talent.

Perhaps because of that she was not widely popular – she stood out too much, not only by her looks. Sometimes she was known to complain a little flirtingly of how both her sisters had envied her. And indeed, both younger sisters, who had died before her, were like their mother. My grandmother was a short plump little thing of plain features who secretly smoked in the toilet. She used to send us granddaughters to buy her cigarettes, which were then still sold by piece. Mum resembled her father, a tall well-built man of symmetric features. From him she inherited something more important than looks: an upright posture (which could strike as arrogant at first glance). Such posture cannot be taught – it is something you're born with. This is precisely what caused her to stand out from the crowd. And the two little chubby girls, her sisters, had to learn to live with it from very early on. But she tried to make everything around her beautiful as well – on the old Minerva sewing machine she made summer dresses for her sisters. With the same passion she redecorated the rundown apartments we moved into, as well as the furniture (which looked shabbier with every move). She wouldn't accept the dreariness surrounding her.

The price she paid for looking different and making everything around her that way was loneliness and misunderstanding. Her talent for beautification was like some sort of sin, pretentious behaviour considered inappropriate in post-war *provincia*.

When she moved to the nursing home suite, she behaved exactly the same way. On one occasion when I visited her, I was surprised to see a new painting on the wall, among several old ones she brought from her apartment. An oil painting of an olive tree. What do you think?, she asked me, anticipating my appraisal. Because of my education she thought I was more competent than her. I didn't respond well. So-so, I said, casting a superficial glance, with an obvious intention of avoiding an answer. It reminds me of our olives, of my childhood. She said it, it seemed to me then, as though she were justifying the money she had spent on this pleasure of hers. The same way in which she, in defence against an anticipated accusation of extravagance, would speak to my father. I didn't call the painting ugly or pretty. I didn't comment on its value – I simply didn't say a single word about it and this hurt her feelings. Her aesthetic, her need for beauty, the important resolve to not begrudge something that would make her life beautiful or at least rekindle memories – was of no interest to me at all.

Today when I remember this scene, her reproachful look, I think of how she in fact did not want to justify herself anymore. Mum wanted me to finally accept this need of hers. She tried to endear me to her reasons, appealing to sentimentality, to memories, hoping I would understand her better. Perhaps the olive tree did indeed remind her of childhood, perhaps that was why she decided to purchase it. But the crucial thing was the fact that she couldn't endure the suite into which she had moved unless she tried to refine it somehow. Before the move I had had to have it redecorated only for this reason, which I then saw as trivial, although to her it was most important.

When she moved to the nursing home, she let her own apartment out. She did it so as not to be a burden to me, as the rent covered her accommodation costs. It was a reasonable solution. An older married couple moved into her apartment, completely void of her belongings. She went over a few months afterwards for the signing of some documents, for bills, mail and the like. And came back in a state of complete shock. She couldn't believe what the place looked like. No, they hadn't destroyed anything or stained the walls, nothing of the sort. They just had decorated it according to their own taste. Nothing of her, of her personality, remained in it.

While I was clearing up the last things from the closet like a stranger, I came to the purple t-shirt, the very last garment she ever bought. Still today it hurts me the most that I didn't, when we were then at the shop, buy her the long white cardigan that she had found on sale. It doesn't comfort me that I did not know that this was our last visit to a clothes shop. She was like a child in a toy store, she was feeling and trying on the clothes, undressing was not a problem for her. Finally she chose a cyclamen-coloured wool shirt. But then she saw the long white cardigan on the sales rack, almost a coat, made from the kind of wool that sheds. Even on it, there was a written warning: this garment sheds. Mum, I said, don't buy that. Your clothes are mostly dark, and you'll look messy, like having a molting cat. But it's so beautiful and warm, who cares if it sheds, she said looking longingly.

She wore the purple t-shirt often. But I keep thinking of the white cardigan we never bought, and my wish that at least once in life I could take her shopping and buy her everything, everything she wanted. I imagined how it should be somewhere in Italy, maybe in Rome, she loved Italian fashion. Or at least in Trieste. Like in the old days, when she would stop before a luxury boutique and enthusiastically point to a dress in the window. Or shoes. We would go inside. She would try the dress on and it would fit her perfectly. For a moment she would see herself somewhere else, at a ball or a première, with a glass of champagne in hand, happy. Then she would return to reality and take leave of the dress, actually of herself in this dress. She would sadly shake her head while returning the dress to the saleswoman, who was trying to persuade her to buy it because it fit her like a glove.

She had that same longing look on her face the day we went shopping for the last time. She had trouble breathing and was puffing heavily while we were climbing up the small slope towards the street with the boutiques. Nevertheless, she had no trouble, no matter how weak she was, in undressing and trying on the clothes in the changing rooms.

I could have assumed this was her last shopping trip. But I didn't want to think about it. Her insistence on buying the white cardigan irritated me. I did not succeed in granting her even this simplest of wishes, although I wanted to buy her everything.

I am the one who abandoned her when it was the hardest for her. I betrayed her, and not the other way around.

One of my earliest memories is of me standing by the entrance to my grandmother's apartment, crying. I am three or four. I'm looking at the shiny, yellow brass door handle; I feel the smell of Sidol cleaning paste that my grandmother used to polish all the handles in the apartment. I cannot reach it to open the door and look for my Mum. I don't want to move away from the door. I am inconsolable. Mum, Mummy, why did you leave me? — I sobbed. Mum didn't leave you, she just went to town for a short while, said my grandfather trying to console me. It did not help. There were no words to alleviate the pain of our separation. Mum, Mummy, why did you leave me? — I repeat standing by the door until she finally appears. This childhood cry crept through, through my entire life. I never forgave her for leaving me. I never grew up and that was the reason why I was unjust to her to the very end.

INVISIBLE WOMAN

YOU ASK WHAT DISTURBED ME SO MUCH.

How would I describe it . . .? One day in my own apartment I met a person I didn't know. I was heading out but stopped. Before me stood a grey-haired woman with blue eyes. She was looking at me, aghast, un-blinking. A strange woman, and yet somehow known, surrounded by greyish haze. It seemed to me that I had seen a ghost.

I didn't immediately recognize myself. First of all, my hair is not grey — look! I neatly dye it every month with L'Oréal light blond. And there are many other hues too, some sounding crazily appealing: *champagne, strawberry, cognac*, like something you'd eat or drink: but this one is the most dear to me, I've always used it. I dye my hair myself, I've gotten used to it over the years since retirement. But it's not so much about the hair, for this colour is sufficiently light to look grey in half-light. In fact, it was the face that scared me. You see, this was the wrinkled face of an old woman. It was as though I had seen in the mirror my own older sister, who's been dead for at least ten years. We were quite alike. I couldn't possibly have seen my dead sister! It took me a moment or two to collect myself and get it through my head that this woman staring at me was not an apparition, but my own reflection in the mirror. And the realisation that this was I shocked me further still.

Why did I figure that an apparition stood before me?

Well, it was already late, it was dusk, and only the contours of this person were visible. She somehow seemed to be ... fading away? Like when you look at yourself in a very old mirror, dimmed by brown discolouration. The stains spread and entire parts become hazed, the rest of the image hovers, the edges are unclear, evanescent. A bit frightening. It's easy to say that this is not the real image of a person, and yet, it seems it is. That is how others see you, or don't see you. As if you are a ghost. And the real person too — I have experienced it personally — becomes somehow paler, increasingly transparent. I thought that this unknown person, this strange woman, had somehow entered the apartment, perhaps because I'd forgotten to lock the door. I know this happens with me, more and more often I forget to lock. Or I leave the key in the outside lock. And then it dawned on me that it was I, as others see me. My own image.

The mirror has always been there, in the lobby, right by the front door. A big, old mirror from my late mother, from their old apartment. With a worm-eaten baroque frame. I had already forgotten that it was there; so many useless things have piled up over the years. I keep planning to clear up thoroughly, throw out the junk, but I haven't got the strength. I am tired. I might have removed the coat from the hanger or the curtain from the window and thus rediscovered the screened-off mirror. But I noticed it only when I saw in it this strange person — myself.

After this encounter, all mirrors became a real nightmare. I'm always looking anew at this person standing before me. I ask myself how it is possible for a person not to see, not to recognise themselves immediately. Is it possible to see oneself so differently? True, my glance in the direction of this person is usually hurried, quick, nonchalant, superficial, the way you look at a passer-by. But, for the love of God, I almost crashed into my own self! I was walking straight towards this woman approaching without showing the slightest intention of moving aside for me. I stopped at a distance of only a few feet and it was only then that in this woman I saw myself. The way in which others see me. If they see me at all.

This encounter with myself, the way others see me, disturbed me for another reason, too. It reminded me of something else that I hadn't seen for a long time. Of the gaze of a man. No, not of some particular man! Something similar sometimes happens when I walk the pavements and see an unknown man walking towards me. The pavement is narrow and you must inevitably pass each other by. When two people pass by, they usually instinctively look one another in the eyes. Unless they really want to avoid it, but why should they? Their glances meet, it's inescapable, so I believed. Perhaps because I was used to this. He is, let's say, middle-aged; his temples are already grey, but still he couldn't be your son, though he is younger. And then you notice his glance. He's looking at you, and you can tell he doesn't see you. He's looking through you, as if you're made of glass. You see how his gaze passes through you. Of course, your first thought is that he's some madman, a somnambulist about to crash into you. He's moving like you're not even there, as if his whole body will cross through you, not just his gaze. Still, at the very last moment he detours round you as though an indefinite object has blocked his way on the road, a disturbance, a living obstacle. I didn't recognise myself, and this is already terrible enough: but now others don't see me either!

I became an obstacle, nothing more. And that's only the beginning.

The beginning of what?

Well ... of people looking through me. Or, if their gaze does rest on me, of feeling their sympathy, sometimes I might even say repulsion. I feel more and more invisible, as if I'm fading away. Yes, of course I certainly exist, but what does this mean if I'm not receiving acknowledgment of my existence from others? If they act like they don't even see me?

I live near a big crossroads. Sometimes, if the traffic is light and there is daylight, I dare to cross the street without waiting for the green light.

I shouldn't be doing this because the cars drive fast and they could easily run someone over if they are crossing the street with the red light on for pedestrians. It happened that a driver just didn't see me, didn't slow down. This experience frightened me. Naturally, I can't run anymore, nor do I want to. Sometimes I stand at this crossroads and watch drivers braking when they see a mother with a stroller crossing the street, a woman with a child, young people. I am the same weight as the girl who, right before me at the same spot, crossed the street with the red light on. But all the same, the driver acted as though I wasn't there. He was driving so fast that I had to step back onto the curb. Of course, it was not the same driver that had slowed down for the girl. But still …

Ask how I explain this to myself.

I seem to be discovering a new dimension of existence. I simultaneously exist and don't exist, because I'm … paling. Maybe in society there is some sort of custom that prohibits telling older women that they are in fact turning into glass? First the blurred kind, then the completely transparent. Their size means nothing, their weight and height are irrelevant. Their clothes too.

It's not exactly like you don't exist, more like you're living in some other dimension. Everything is the same, and yet – it's not the same. People behave differently towards you, and it is you, as the invisible woman, who must adapt yourself to it. It's just that it's not all easy to do it. On the contrary, it took me quite some time to comprehend at all that I'm becoming invisible. In the shop, in the bank, at any counter, on the street …

It took me enough time to notice how I'm disappearing; I first saw it in the eyes of others. In fact, somehow the hardest part was that I see myself just as clearly as before. I'm conscious of the change, but I'm still a visible, real and living person, although I've grown old.

I thought to myself: if I now exist in this invisible form, maybe this transparent thing I'm turning into is – pure ghost?

Yes, I'm asking, even though I know you don't have the answer.

You may have noticed that I don't use the word "aging". It is a process, at first quite a slow and imperceptible one. At a certain moment it begins to hasten, and you only notice it then (perhaps because someone else is already noticing it), and suddenly you have become – old.

You say I'm fostering a negative image of myself?

No, no! The problem is that I don't have such a negative self-image, I simply see myself differently than others. Certainly not as some unknown woman in a mirror. Or as an apparition. Or a transparent ghost. It's the others, it's their perception. When other people stop noticing you, soon you no longer see your own self.

Are you interested in knowing when I started to feel that I was changing, that I was growing old?

First it was my body that changed. I first noticed it when buying new clothes. All of a sudden nothing seemed to fit. Or better put, I felt as though I was trying on someone else's clothes. And it was only yesterday that tailored dresses and tight-fitting t-shirts fitted me quite well. How come there's nothing left anymore that might suit me? Everything had become too tight and too short, somehow unsuitable. I no longer had the strength to try anything on. It became boring to me, pointless. Spending hours going through stacks of clothes to get to something you like. Furthermore, I shuddered at the changing rooms, at the neon light and the tight space in which you have to undress while trying not to look at your tired, dejected body, at the surplus kilograms, at the saggy skin. No, no, this was not just because of my current state of mind. The exact reverse: I'd be unnerved by the fact that nothing seems to fit me. I started to hesitate at the entrances to shops whose salesgirls until yesterday would greet me warmly, since I spent a lot on myself and it showed.

Now, if I do resolve to enter, the young saleswoman scans me from head to heels to assess if I'm just going to take up her time. These too-beautiful girls are not kind. They are brusque; they make me painfully aware of my age. At my age I'm supposed to be more self-confident, I say to myself. Don't let some whippersnapper stop you from shopping. As long as you have money, you're the lady. But it doesn't help. I feel worse; I no longer shop.

I used to find pleasure in a beautiful pair of shoes. But when I could no longer walk in high heels, I found out that elegant low-heel pumps are quite a rarity. Previously I had never noticed this; it had seemed to me that there were all sorts of shoes and they were all stylish. When my soles started to hurt — madam, your arches are falling, as the orthopaedist explained — I started wearing trainers. I remember when a friend of mine showed me her bunions one summer. Back then she was only 56. Your arches are falling, I told her, and she looked at me in bewilderment. It'll pass; she just waved her hand. It didn't pass, and the pain became stronger and stronger, until she too started wearing comfortable flats.

But you asked when my invisibility, as I call it, began.

Until recently I'd have said that it began with the encounter with the unknown woman in the mirror, with the non-recognition of the self. Thinking about it today, I'd say it was a longer process. I would call this process the dis*appearance chronicles*. It is strange how particular parts of a person gradually disappear.

Is the face the first to disappear?

No way, it's not the face first! From today's vantage, I know that the face is the last to disappear. You don't stare at it, but you see it, you meet with it daily. And the people around you, they still look only at your face.

The first symptoms of invisibility begin in bed, not on the street. In the conjugal bed. My husband and my invisibility are close-knit. It began on my 63rd birthday.

He had had a few. Later, in the bedroom, while I was undressing, he said I was fat. Just like that, fat! He had never said this before, never used the word.

Nor was he himself skinny. He said this as if he'd just then – after a long time – looked at this body, my aging body. And as if it had seemed unknown to him. When he did then recognise it, it was as though with these words he both acknowledged and simultaneously dismissed it. Dismissed, that's how I felt at that moment. I still remember the horrific feeling of shame that overwhelmed me as I was standing naked before him, he who saw me that way. I remember, it was during my menopause and I'd gotten a little belly that I could easily camouflage with clothes. It happens to all women. I couldn't have had more than 10 pounds extra, but I looked a lot better than him, with that beer belly of his.

I know, I should have been on a diet, lost the damn kilograms. Gone to the gym or yoga ... I should have taken better care of myself. But I didn't have the time back then: I was still working, I had an interesting job and friends. Anyway, was he taking care of himself? No. He found it normal that I was taking care of myself and he wasn't. It was as though he'd suddenly slapped my face, though that never actually happened.

I felt more and more like a piece of furniture, a useful piece, which only occasionally speaks, and more often listens, cooks, saves him from loneliness and depression. My husband was a good man, but books interested him most, not people. He didn't completely live in this world. I was his only link with reality until he died from dementia.

And so, that night I withdrew to my side of the conjugal bed. He stretched out his arm to draw me in and embrace me like he always did before sleep. He knew he'd said something bad. I didn't mean it, he whispered. He didn't mean it, but he said it because that was how he'd just seen me.

I remained lying on my side of the bed. Don't despair because of him, it's not worth it, I told myself.

But there also comes a time when we are too old and too wise to suffer over such words. At that point I found myself very rational and calm. But the pain I felt remained, and today it's still there, I can almost find it by feeling around, like a small lump in my chest. Yes, on the left side, of course. Here, in the heart area. Like a chafing pebble.

I no longer wished to be intimate with him. We tried, yes, several times. He occasionally showed a slight interest, though more from habit. And I responded, also out of habit. But I no longer changed in the bedroom, but in the bathroom; I traded lace and silk underwear for high-waist cotton ones – this sort of intimacy was over for me. Somewhere around the age of 65. And it was no longer pleasant for me, either. At a certain point, intercourse became painful. When my gynaecologist gave me a lubricant ("the epithelia seems very dry"), it was already too late: I no longer needed it.

We lived together out of a love that turned into solidarity, out of a habit that became an obligation and out of a fear of being alone. But it tortures me that we didn't know better how to help each other. He could no longer protect me from fear, from pain. Can anyone?

No one touches me anymore, except the hands of doctors, hairdressers, dentists, but these are not gentle touches: they're all only here to fix things.

Recently I waited in hospital for hours for my turn for a standard examination, an ordinary eye check-up necessary due to my cataracts. I remember, I was sitting completely hopeless among an equally hopeless crowd. Our charts were in doctors' offices, in the hands of nurses who came out every now and then and called out people loudly. I was already glued to the seat when they called me. The check-up was short and only confirmed what I felt anyway, some sort of crawling blindness. After so much sitting and waiting and the loudly-uttered confirmation that a part of my body was failing me, I felt half-dead. I could hardly wait to get home.

I need more and more time to shake off depression and I sometimes cannot do it alone. I need a human being to whom I can tell that I'm afraid of blindness, that I'm tired and that I can no longer waste time in waiting rooms to have confirmed what I already know, that there is no cure.

I called a friend. She listened to my not-too-long lament, my attempt at describing this feeling of sinking, suffocating, vanishing … After that I felt even worse. What did I expect? What could anyone tell me to make me feel better? I thought a hot tub full of scented bubble-bath might relieve the cramping I was feeling in every part of my body, but turning on the tap and waiting for the tub to fill seemed simply too strenuous. Instead I lay down on the couch, covered my head and cried. There was no one even just to sit and hold my hand even though I know there's no consolation. The experience of choking in fear isn't transferrable, anyway.

When my husband died, I spent days washing the curtains. Not only washing, but starching and ironing them as well. I had never done that before. Never washed curtains in my life! It was like a cleansing ritual. I was burying the past, my youth. With slow movements of the iron I crossed over these curtains of thin cotton linen with lace trimmings. But I never hung them back up on the windows.

It has already been a long time since, instead of going out with friends to a café or a concert, or sometimes to the theatre, I started watching evening TV. And no, I don't read like I used to, either. My sight is deteriorating. I don't go out, especially at night, the darkness bothers me. I'm somehow more interested now in the lives of others, but not of real people, but of those in TV shows or films. When I transport myself out of this dull goggling at the screen, I feel how hollow I am, and this hollowness in my head is filled with beneficent gauzy contents which put me to sleep and don't prompt me to think.

I wonder why I'm telling you all this.

This encounter with my own self in the mirror disturbed me. My friend took me to you, for you to calm me down, supposedly. But how could you even help me at all? Yes, the only way is by listening to me … Or could you perhaps write me a prescription?

Translated, from the Croatian, by Jacob Agee.

One of Croatia's most distinguished and celebrated writers, Slavenka Drakulić was born in Rijeka, Yugoslavia in 1949. She graduated in Comparative Literature and Sociology from the University of Zagreb in 1976, and from 1982 to 1992 was a staff writer on the bi-weekly Start *and the news weekly* Danas *(both based in Zagreb), writing mainly on feminist issues. Her subsequent books on feminism, communism and post-communism have been translated into many languages. She is the author of five works of fiction and eight of non-fiction, the latter including* How We Survived Communism and Even Laughed *(Hutchinson, 1991),* Café Europa: Life After Communism *(Abacus, 1996),* They Would Never Hurt a Fly: War Criminals on Trial in The Hague *(Abacus, 2004), and* A Guided Tour through the Museum of Communism: Fables from a Mouse, a Parrot, a Bear, a Cat, a Mole, a Pig, a Dog and a Raven *(Penguin, 2011). She lives in Stockholm and Zagreb.*

POEM

Benjamin Keatinge

THE PERSISTENCE OF RAIN

One cannot speak of soft rain here
among mosques, among churches. Rain
doesn't cross in squalls, nor drift,
nor darken to a flood. It gathers
and grows to unspeakable clouds,
ending where it starts, in sudden drops,
like the film *Pred doždot*. Or it is leaden,
as Kadare's General found, sodden,
a swelling wound. And, drenched,
he digs in rain that will not stop
on mountains that cannot tell
or grant the restitution of the dead.

Benjamin Keatinge is a Visiting Research Fellow at the School of English, Trinity College Dublin. His poems have been published in The Stony Thursday Book, Orbis, Eborakon, The Galway Review, Agenda, Cassandra Voices, Flare *and in* Writing Home: The "New Irish" Poets *(The Dedalus Press, 2019). He taught English literature for nine years at South East European University, North Macedonia and he has travelled widely in the Balkans. He is the editor of* Making Integral: Critical Essays on Richard Murphy *(Cork University Press, 2019).*

THE IDENTITARIAN DELUSION

Gerry Cambridge

Pugnacious certainty.

In July 2018 *The Nation* published an apology/retraction by its poetry editors for printing what I thought a modestly interesting poem by the young poet Anders Carlson-Wee; an apology not because the poem wasn't better, but because it was written in the voice of an American panhandler speaking in what its critics interpreted as African-American Vernacular English (AAVE) and using the "ableist" verb "crippled". The poetry editors wrote: "[…] we hold ourselves responsible for the ways in which the work we select is received." They then apologised for the "pain caused to the many communities affected by this poem." Anders Carlson-Wee, who seems an interesting writer, and has a first book appearing from W. W. Norton in March 2019, issued a public apology on Twitter, and stated that he was "re-evaluating what it means to make art in this world from a place of privilege." An African-American linguistics professor at Columbia University, John McWhorter, writing in *The Atlantic Monthly*, put up a defence of the poem's use of AAVE, but to no avail. The poetry community, or at least one segment of it, had censoriously spoken.

In November's *Poetry* magazine, Don Share published "From 'Titan / All is Still" by Toby Martinez de las Rivas, a seven-page excerpt which ended with a graphic featuring an image of a black sun (also the title of Martinez's second collection from Faber), superimposed over a text block composed of the repeated word "Judgement" in italics. *Poetry,* as it does frequently with work published in its pages, tweeted, all innocently, a brief extract with a link to the poem online on 23 November 2018. Shortly after, outraged Twitterati descended like a bunch of starlings on a field of cast grain. The black sun was latched onto as a fascist symbol; the poem itself was portrayed as fascist in intent. Individuals with PTSD claimed they were "triggered" by the poem. Demands were made for the editors to explain themselves. On 27 November *Poetry* tweeted, somewhat worthily, "To our readers: We have been listening" with a link to an explanatory statement by Martinez on the magazine's website. The concession seemed to backfire spectacularly. The poet was criticised for not stating outright that he was not a fascist, even though he had linked to an essay in *PN Review* which made this very point. Calls for the editors to explain Martinez's inclusion were repeated. Don Share, *Poetry*'s editor-in-chief, and usually a daily, prolific tweeter, as of this writing (11 January 2019) has made no posts on his Twitter timeline since 24 November 2018.

I am not an habitual Twitter user, but the little I have noticed in regard to this matter has been, frankly, astonishing. The Martinez excerpt in *Poetry* has had sections quoted out of context: a comfortless and in some ways horrifying image such as "the white irradiate city" has been taken in the most literal terms as a valorisation of white supremacy when, to my reading and in context, confirmed by Martinez's own account, it is an image of terrible sterility. Some commenters' tweets dropped the "Young" from the title of the Martinez poem "Elegy for the Young Hitler" and then convicted the poet in the easy court of Twitter on the basis of this new, imagined title. Recently I noticed that the Dave Coates blogpost, which Rob A. Mackenzie responds to in his essay in this issue [of *The Dark Horse*], has had a link appended to it; clicking through brings up a photograph of a white supremacist, wielding a placard featuring the image from the floor of Himmler's castle discussed in Mackenzie's essay, as if this were proof of something. In reality it reveals only a notable lack of similarity between the image and the Martinez black sun that would be plain to an average seven-year-old. What is one to make of all this? Poetry, an art once considered a free space for intellectual, emotional and spiritual enquiry and exploration, seems increasingly an arena governed and to some degree imperilled by thought-police. The ability to invent, or re-imagine, such as would be extended to any novelist, is being constricted. Only the personal, autobiographical lyric, preferably dealing with trauma which has, naturally enough, a sort of guarantee of authenticity, can be thought – perhaps – to be risk-free.

In regard to *Poetry* magazine, seeing an editor who has been instrumental in opening up this major venue in American letters to manifold voices, orientations and ethnic diversities reflective of the great cultural mix of America, even if that may be seen by some as at the expense of quality, has been both instructive and deeply ironic. Even a trendsetter such as *Poetry* has felt it had to make a response to reader reaction. The atmosphere is one of nervy compliance to the dictated mores of outraged opinion; a wariness of stirring up offence-culture. Yet one cannot keep everyone who decides to open themselves up to the art of poetry, as a reader, happy – not even some of the time. In that sense *The Nation*'s editors' statement that they are responsible for the "ways" in which their readers receive a poem strikes me as not only extraordinary but unachievable. The implication, taken in the context of their apologia for the Anders Carlson-Wee poem, is that they are accountable for the unforeseen "negative" reaction, on whatever grounds, to any poem published under their editorship. Well, good luck with that. Editors of poetry are certainly responsible for what they publish. And they may well make mistakes. Beyond well-defined and obvious limits, however, such as evident provocations or devil's advocacy, they cannot be responsible for reader reaction. How can you be responsible for something you have no control over, particularly with an art such as poetry which utilises as part of its substance the indeterminacy and ambiguities of language, symbol and image? How, beyond the limits above, can you control how the words are received? And, why would you want to? To avoid Twitter outrages – which, presumably, are considered important by those at whom they are directed only when they reach a level as to make them uncomfortable? Poetry editors, no matter how distinguished or experienced, are not omniscient. Are they now custodians of readers' psychological health? Has poetry now become an insipid branch of the wellbeing industry?

The result will be, initially, a closing down of the possibilities of the art to something cowed, tamed and neutered such that it will never risk causing offence, except in the most current, politically correct of ways of course.

Poetry is not a vessel for virtue signalling, for the display of what a good person one is. Any mature artist knows this. What I find breathtaking in the contemporary poetry climate, characterised by the critique of Martinez's poem in *Poetry*, is the conviction of rightness, indeed righteousness, by the commenters. There is little looking to the mote in one's own eye there. But if the practice of poetry as an art teaches one anything it is that everything is singular; everything is complicated. One must refuse, as Robert Frost said, to falsify the ambiguities, and such refusal takes courage and steadiness. The singularity of a genuine artist is of course a threat to ideologues of whatever stripe, whether of the Left or of the Right, who would try to subsume everything into one encompassing identity. As C. H. Sisson, quoted in an introduction by David Wright to a Penguin selection of Edward Thomas's poems said, "All desire for the truth is revolutionary." That is to be found in the workings out of one's own thought processes and character, at the most intimate levels. It does not lend itself happily to easy and simplistic denunciations which are more remarkable for their pugnacious certainty than for any insight they may contain.

From the editorial of Issue 40 of The Dark Horse *(Winter / Spring 2019).*

The Editor of The Dark Horse, *Scotland's leading poetry journal, Gerry Cambridge is also an essayist, print designer and typographer, with a background in natural history photography. He lived in an Ayrshire caravan for twenty-five years before leaving to become a Brownsbank Fellow in Hugh MacDiarmid's former home for 1997–1999. His most recent book is* The Light Acknowledgers & Other Poems *(HappenStance Press, 2019). In his early twenties he was, as far as he knows, one of the youngest ever regular freelancers, specialising in nature articles, for the UK* Reader's Digest, *which at the time (the 1980s) had a monthly circulation of 1.5 million copies.*

THE SILICON SIX

—

Sacha Baron Cohen

Freedom of speech is not *freedom of reach.*

*Sacha Baron Cohen was the recipient of the Anti-Defamation League's
2019 International Leadership Award*

Thank you, Jonathan, for your very kind words. Thank you, ADL, for this recognition and your work in fighting racism, hate and bigotry. And to be clear, when I say "racism, hate and bigotry" I'm not referring to the names of Stephen Miller's Labradoodles.

Now, I realize that some of you may be thinking, what the hell is a comedian doing speaking at a conference like this! I certainly am. I've spent most of the past two decades in character. In fact, this is the first time that I have ever stood up and given a speech as my least popular character, Sacha Baron Cohen. And I have to confess, it is terrifying.

I realize that my presence here may also be unexpected for another reason. At times, some critics have said my comedy risks reinforcing old stereotypes.

The truth is, I've been passionate about challenging bigotry and intolerance throughout my life. As a teenager in the UK, I marched against the fascist National Front and to abolish Apartheid. As an undergraduate, I traveled around America and wrote my thesis about the Civil Rights Movement, with the help of the archives of the ADL. And as a comedian, I've tried to use my characters to get people to let down their guard and reveal what they actually believe, including their own prejudice.

Now, I'm not going to claim that everything I've done has been for a higher purpose. Yes, some of my comedy, OK probably half my comedy, has been absolutely juvenile and the other half completely puerile. I admit, there was nothing particularly enlightening about me – as Borat from Kazakhstan, the first fake news journalist – running through a conference of mortgage brokers when I was completely naked.

But when Borat was able to get an entire bar in Arizona to sing "Throw the Jew down the well," it did reveal people's indifference to anti-Semitism.

When – as Bruno, the gay fashion reporter from Austria – I started kissing a man in a cage fight in Arkansas, nearly starting a riot, it showed the violent potential of homophobia. And when – disguised as an ultra-woke developer – I proposed building a mosque in one rural community, prompting a resident to proudly admit, "I am racist, against Muslims" – it showed the acceptance of Islamophobia.

That's why I appreciate the opportunity to be here with you. Today around the world, demagogues appeal to our worst instincts. Conspiracy theories once confined to the fringe are going mainstream. It's as if the Age of Reason – the era of evidential argument – is ending, and now knowledge is delegitimized and scientific consensus is dismissed. Democracy, which depends on shared truths, is in retreat, and autocracy, which depends on shared lies, is on the march. Hate crimes are surging, as are murderous attacks on religious and ethnic minorities.

What do all these dangerous trends have in common? I'm just a comedian and an actor, not a scholar. But one thing is pretty clear to me. All this hate and violence is being facilitated by a handful of internet companies that amount to the greatest propaganda machine in history.

The greatest propaganda machine in history.

Think about it. Facebook, YouTube and Google, Twitter and others – they reach billions of people. The algorithms these platforms depend on deliberately amplify the type of content that keeps users engaged – stories that appeal to our baser instincts and that trigger outrage and fear. It's why YouTube recommended videos by the conspiracist Alex Jones billions of times. It's why fake news outperforms real news, because studies show that lies spread faster than truth. And it's no surprise that the greatest propaganda machine in history has spread the oldest conspiracy theory in history – the lie that Jews are somehow dangerous. As one headline put it, "Just Think What Goebbels Could Have Done with Facebook."

On the internet, everything can appear equally legitimate. Breitbart resembles the BBC. The fictitious Protocols of the Elders of Zion look as valid as an ADL report. And the rantings of a lunatic seem as credible as the findings of a Nobel Prize winner. We have lost, it seems, a shared sense of the basic facts upon which democracy depends.

When I, as the wanna-be-gansta Ali G, asked the astronaut Buzz Aldrin "what woz it like to walk on de sun?" the joke worked, because we, the audience,

(Continues after "Portfolio")

shared the same facts. If you believe the moon landing was a hoax, the joke was not funny.

When Borat got that bar in Arizona to agree that "Jews control everybody's money and never give it back", the joke worked because the audience shared the fact that the depiction of Jews as miserly is a conspiracy theory originating in the Middle Ages.

But when, thanks to social media, conspiracies take hold, it's easier for hate groups to recruit, easier for foreign intelligence agencies to interfere in our elections, and easier for a country like Myanmar to commit genocide against the Rohingya.

It's actually quite shocking how easy it is to turn conspiracy thinking into violence. In my last show *Who is America?*, I found an educated, normal guy who had held down a good job, but who, on social media, repeated many of the conspiracy theories that President Trump, using Twitter, has spread more than 1,700 times to his 67 million followers. The President even tweeted that he was considering designating Antifa – anti-fascists who march against the far right – as a terror organization.

So, disguised as an Israel anti-terrorism expert, Colonel Erran Morad, I told my interviewee that, at the Women's March in San Francisco, Antifa were plotting to put hormones into babies' diapers in order to "make them transgender". And he believed it.

I instructed him to plant small devices on three innocent people at the march and explained that when he pushed a button, he'd trigger an explosion that would kill them all. They weren't real explosives, of course, but he thought they were. I wanted to see – would he actually do it?

The answer was yes. He pushed the button and thought he had actually killed three human beings. Voltaire was right, "those who can make you believe absurdities, can make you commit atrocities." And social media lets authoritarians push absurdities to billions of people.

In their defense, these social media companies have taken some steps to reduce hate and conspiracies on their platforms, but these steps have been mostly superficial.

I'm speaking up today because I believe that our pluralistic democracies are on a precipice and that the next twelve months, and the role of social media, could be determinant. British voters will go to the polls while online conspiracists promote the despicable theory of "great replacement" that white Christians are being deliberately replaced by Muslim immigrants. Americans will vote for president while trolls and bots perpetuate the disgusting lie of a

"Hispanic invasion". And after years of YouTube videos calling climate change a "hoax", the United States is on track, a year from now, to formally withdraw from the Paris Accords. A sewer of bigotry and vile conspiracy theories that threatens democracy and our planet – this cannot possibly be what the creators of the internet had in mind.

I believe it's time for a fundamental rethink of social media and how it spreads hate, conspiracies and lies. Last month, however, Mark Zuckerberg of Facebook delivered a major speech that, not surprisingly, warned against new laws and regulations on companies like his. Well, some of these arguments are simply absurd. Let's count the ways.

First, Zuckerberg tried to portray this whole issue as "choices . . . around free expression". That is ludicrous. This is not about limiting anyone's free speech. This is about giving people, including some of the most reprehensible people on earth, the biggest platform in history to reach a third of the planet. Freedom of speech is not freedom of reach. Sadly, there will always be racists, misogynists, anti-Semites and child abusers. But I think we could all agree that we should not be giving bigots and pedophiles a free platform to amplify their views and target their victims.

Second, Zuckerberg claimed that new limits on what's posted on social media would be to "pull back on free expression". This is utter nonsense. The First Amendment says that "Congress shall make no law" abridging freedom of speech, however, this does not apply to private businesses like Facebook. We're not asking these companies to determine the boundaries of free speech across society. We just want them to be responsible on their platforms.

If a neo-Nazi comes goose-stepping into a restaurant and starts threatening other customers and saying he wants to kill Jews, would the owner of the restaurant be required to serve him an elegant eight-course meal? Of course not! The restaurant owner has every legal right and a moral obligation to kick the Nazi out, and so do these internet companies.

Third, Zuckerberg seemed to equate regulation of companies like his to the actions of "the most repressive societies". Incredible. This, from one of the six people who decide what information so much of the world sees. Zuckerberg at Facebook, Sundar Pichai at Google, at its parent company Alphabet, Larry Page and Sergey Brin, Brin's ex-sister-in-law, Susan Wojcicki at YouTube and Jack Dorsey at Twitter.

The Silicon Six – all billionaires, all Americans – who care more about boosting their share price than about protecting democracy. This is ideological imperialism – six unelected individuals in Silicon Valley imposing their vision on the rest of the world, unaccountable to any government and acting like they're above the reach of law. It's like we're living in the Roman Empire, and Mark Zuckerberg is Caesar. At least that would explain his haircut.

Here's an idea. Instead of letting the Silicon Six decide the fate of the world, let our elected representatives, voted for by the people, of every democracy in the world, have at least some say.

Fourth, Zuckerberg speaks of welcoming a "diversity of ideas", and last year he gave us an example. He said that he found posts denying the Holocaust "deeply offensive", but he didn't think Facebook should take them down "because I think there are things that different people get wrong". At this very moment, there are still Holocaust deniers on Facebook, and Google still takes you to the most repulsive Holocaust denial sites with a simple click. One of the heads of Google once told me, incredibly, that these sites just show "both sides" of the issue. This is madness.

To quote Edward R. Murrow, one "cannot accept that there are, on every story, two equal and logical sides to an argument." We have millions of pieces of evidence for the Holocaust – it is an historical fact. And denying it is not some random opinion. Those who deny the Holocaust aim to encourage another one.

Still, Zuckerberg says that "people should decide what is credible, not tech companies." But at a time when two-thirds of millennials say they haven't even heard of Auschwitz, how are they supposed to know what's "credible"? How are they supposed to know that the lie is a lie?

There is such a thing as objective truth. Facts do exist. And if these internet companies really want to make a difference, they should hire enough monitors to actually monitor, work closely with groups like the ADL, insist on facts and purge these lies and conspiracies from their platforms.

Fifth, when discussing the difficulty of removing content, Zuckerberg asked "where do you draw the line"? Yes, drawing the line can be difficult. But here's what he's really saying: removing more of these lies and conspiracies is just too expensive.

These are the richest companies in the world, and they have the best engineers in the world. They could fix these problems if they wanted to. Twitter could deploy an algorithm to remove more white supremacist hate speech, but they reportedly haven't because it would eject some very prominent politicians from their platform. Maybe that's not a bad thing! The truth is, these companies won't fundamentally change because their entire business model relies on generating more engagement, and nothing generates more engagement than lies, fear and outrage.

It's time to finally call these companies what they really are – the largest publishers in history. And here's an idea for them: abide by basic standards and practices just like newspapers, magazines and TV news do every day. We have standards and practices in television and the movies; there are certain things we cannot say or do. In England, I was told that Ali G could not curse when he appeared before 9 pm. Here in the US, the Motion Picture Association of America regulates and rates what we see. I've had scenes in my movies cut or reduced to abide by those standards. If there are standards and practices for what cinemas and television channels can show, then surely companies that publish material to billions of people should have to abide by basic standards and practices too.

Take the issue of political ads. Fortunately, Twitter finally banned them, and Google is making changes, too. But if you pay them, Facebook will run any "political" ad you want, even if it's a lie. And they'll even help you micro-target those lies to their users for maximum effect. Under this twisted logic, if Facebook were around in the 1930s, it would have allowed Hitler to post 30-second ads on his "solution" to the "Jewish problem". So here's a good standard and practice: Facebook, start fact-checking political ads before you run them, stop micro-targeted lies immediately, and when the ads are false, give back the money and don't publish them.

Here's another good practice: *slow down*. Every single post doesn't need to be published immediately. Oscar Wilde once said that "we live in an age when unnecessary things are our only necessities." But is having every thought or video posted instantly online, even if it is racist or criminal or murderous, really a necessity? Of course not!

The shooter who massacred Muslims in New Zealand live streamed his atrocity on Facebook where it then spread across the internet and was viewed likely millions of times. It was a snuff film, brought to you by social media. Why can't we have more of a delay so this trauma-inducing filth can be caught and stopped before it's posted in the first place?

Finally, Zuckerberg said that social media companies should "live up to their responsibilities", but he's totally silent about what should happen when they don't. By now it's pretty clear, they cannot be trusted to regulate themselves. As with the Industrial Revolution, it's time for regulation and legislation to curb the greed of these high-tech robber barons.

In every other industry, a company can be held liable when their product is defective. When engines explode or seatbelts malfunction, car companies recall tens of thousands of vehicles, at a cost of billions of dollars. It only seems fair to say to Facebook, YouTube and Twitter: your product is defective, you are obliged to fix it, no matter how much it costs and no matter how many moderators you need to employ.

In every other industry, you can be sued for the harm you cause. Publishers can be sued for libel, people can be sued for defamation. I've been sued many times! I'm being sued right now by someone whose name I won't mention because he might sue me again! But social media companies are largely protected from liability for the content their users post – no matter how indecent it is – by Section 230 of, get ready for it, the Communications Decency Act. Absurd!

Fortunately, internet companies can now be held responsible for pedophiles who use their sites to target children. I say, let's also hold these companies responsible for those who use their sites to advocate for the mass murder of children because of their race or religion. And maybe fines are not enough. Maybe it's time to tell Mark Zuckerberg and the CEOs of these companies: you already allowed one foreign power to interfere in our elections, you already facilitated one genocide in Myanmar, do it again and you go to jail.

In the end, it all comes down to what kind of world we want. In his speech, Zuckerberg said that one of his main goals is to "uphold as wide a definition of freedom of expression as possible." Yet our freedoms are not only an end in themselves, they're also the means to another end – as you say here in the US, the right to life, liberty and the pursuit of happiness. But today these rights are threatened by hate, conspiracies and lies.

Allow me to leave you with a suggestion for a different aim for society. The ultimate aim of society should be to make sure that people are not targeted, not harassed and not murdered because of who they are, where they come from, who they love or how they pray.

If we make that our aim – if we prioritize truth over lies, tolerance over prejudice, empathy over indifference and experts over ignoramuses – then maybe, just maybe, we can stop the greatest propaganda machine in history, we can save democracy, we can still have a place for free speech and free expression, and, most importantly, my jokes will still work.

Thank you all very much.

Sacha Noam Baron Cohen (born 1971) is an English comedian, actor, writer, director and film producer. He is known for his creation and portrayal of several fictional satirical characters, including Ali G, Borat Sagdiyev, Bruno Gehard, Admiral General Aladeen and Colonel

Erran Morad. Like his idol Peter Sellers, Baron Cohen adopts a variety of accents and guises for his characters. He interacts with unsuspecting subjects, who do not realise they have been set up for self-revealing ridicule. On these interactions, The Observer *remarks, "his career has been built on winding people up, while keeping a deadpan face." Since his first rise to prominence in Da Ali G Show in 2000, his various characterizations have had a distinctly prescient and predictive atmosphere.*

FOUR POEMS

Matt Kirkham

BECAUSE POETRY SHOULD BE GOOD FOR SOMETHING I HAVE WRITTEN YOU THIS LOVE POEM COMPLETE WITH FOOD HACKS

After a recipe article by Dale Berning Sawa

1

Like the blackbird sat atop our cherry tree,
red ripe cherry in beak, I stare at you,
and wonder what you're going to do about me.

2

Summertime Sir Blackbird and I
equally fantasise about making our own ways,
me with my lover, he with his own brown-feathered love,
into the abandoned golf course at one-thirty in the morning.
If my love and I were to bring pistachios,
we would know to *use an empty pistachio shell.*
It is thin enough to slide into any gap,
however slim, and hard enough for you
to be able to lever it and prise
the closed nut open. Think of this analogy,
setting out why I am now like the blackbird,
as an as yet closed pistachio.
We will know the tricks, me and my pistachios,
he and his stolen cherries, and we
will get it right. *A revelation.*

151

3

The golf course is the very golf course
where the security alert was last month,
the momentary helicopter blocking out the sun
so that both our kids and the blackbirds' looked up
and asked what's happening, what's that, what's it doing
making the branches of the cherry tree bounce,
and both blackbird and I had to answer
that we don't quite know.

4

See how he balances, the cheeky acrobat, on the branch,
right down to the end, to get the ripe cherry?
We both know the hacks, the blackbird and I.
The grass will be closely cropped, and dry beneath us.
The moon will be touching its fullness.
We will bring an avocado and a big knife,
so we can *whack the stone head-on with the sharp edge* …
Just be careful you don't end up in hospital.
How careful we shall be,
with our one-thirty in the morning,
upon the metallic grey grass.

5

Because he has been working hard to feed his young, and so

6

because his plumage, you pointed out, is a bit faded,
and he looks somewhat rough around the eyes and

7

because his stare seems to point out that
I too am a thief, an interloper,
and I don't just mean the food hacks,
and I don't just mean the American poets,
I am going to say that we've been told
of fathers and brothers, sisters and mothers,
not yours, not mine, who should be on the golf course

by day, blocking out the sun, and are not,
and I am going to mention you running in to ask your mother
what the soldier meant when he said come here,
come here, darling, come here and

8

How careful he is, holding the cherry
in his claw now to manipulate it
into a beak grip, the better to fly off.
How careful I'll be with our pomegranates,
as you lie on the moonlit close-cropped grass,
as *I cut around the calyx —*
that spiky protrusion on one end —
until you can pull it out,
as under the trees' silhouettes
we *score the skin of the pomegranate on the outside,*
from top to bottom, following those membranes.
If you know the tricks and get it right
the fruit will then fall open like a flower.

9

We both wonder, blackbird and I,
about the somehow unsatisfactory spelling of *complete*,
and both wonder about what you hear
when you hear our accents.

10

I wake you just before daybreak, as does he

11

Hold one of the halves, skin side down,
in your palm and work a glass
between the flesh and skin from one end
all the way to the other. I'll memorise this,
only to re-make myself as the maker
of a music improvised with glass and mango.
He is sweet and ringing, just before daybreak.
You end up with a satisfyingly solid piece

of mango in your glass and a pip
you can still suck on, because — let's face it —
that is part of the fun.

    12
Look at the branch of the cherry tree,
bouncing for a second after he has flown

AUTUMN

I am so grateful for all you have given me.
We stand by a river in a beech forest,
and I know that on waking I will have to unlock
what the trees mean, the light on the leaves
on the forest floor, the sleek river,
and you, and the meaning of this gratitude whose fullness
will persist even after our skin
turns to scales, and the scales turn to leaves.

FOX IN SNOW

When I saw him cross the deserted ring road
I knew him by the white tip of his tail
and I knew his paw prints would be like buttons on a blouse,
how he'd vanish up the bank and into the young oaks
to leave his road revealed for once on ours,
and I knew how your footprints would be walking towards me
from your abandoned car as mine walked towards you,
and I knew how I would be showing you this.

PEEKABOO

On the twenty-seventh I dropped you back.
You'd hoped for snow. Of course we saw no snow
so you'd hoped for frost, masked eyes with your hands,
lifted them with a flourish to reveal
the morning sun as it glared off tarmac
and just after the bad bend a red Renault
that had blindsided the hedge and landed
monolithic there in its sodden field.
I knew and resented that I would find
a way to put these thoughts into order,
written down neatly, the car and the sun,
with the hook formed at the back of my mind
that a decade and still more of stories
waited behind your fingers and your thumbs.

Matt Kirkham was in born in 1966, lives in Belfast, and works as a teacher. His two poetry collections are The Lost Museums *(Lagan Press, 2006) and* The Dumbo Octopus *(Templar, 2016). He was raised in Luton, England; attended Cambridge University; came to Ireland in his twenties; and has now lived in the North for most of his life.*

SECULAR PROPHESIES

———

Chris Agee

Our vulnerable plateau.

———

There it is

splendiferous London
lit bridges
girded over
the serpentine Thames
jewelled honeycomb
of hope
and joys and love
misery and power
this century's
high plateau
vulnerable before
the plagues and epidemics
that will surely come

Flight from Vienna
16 February 2013

(from Blue Sandbar Moon: a micro-epic, *by Chris Agee, The Irish Pages Press, 2018)*

This micropoem was broadcast nationally on "The Poetry Programme", RTÉ Radio 1, on 20 May 2020, in the midst of the Pandemic.

AUTHOR'S GLOSS

This little poem is about as clear a prediction of this pandemic as would be possible — seven years in advance and with a London setting (subtext: capitalism's splendiferous capital.)

Not, in fact, hard to prophesy — more of an emotional-visual epiphany that came upon me as I flew into London ... so that the poem was written more or less *in situ* on the plane ...

Of course *foresight*, instead of hindsight, has a certain compelling quality when it comes to poetry — one of those ancient poetic claims — and the fact that it *predicts historically* (that the poem took that risk) cannot be gainsaid, even if it is small and bijou ...

Yet, in a way, the poem illustrates the *opposite* ethical point: *that this pandemic was not, in fact, difficult to predict ...*

But where were our political leaders?

I notice and like especially that two words in the poem are being used continually in the political discourse on the crisis: *plateau* and *vulnerable*. That somehow (for me) further "vouchsafes" (to use some Seamus Heaney words) the "in-place" verisimilitude of the poem.

The small, it turns out again, is often good for the big.

Or put another way, "microcosm" — and I have long used this imaginatively — is good for clarifications of "macrocosm", in that the big picture at any one historical point is often obscured by itself.

So amidst the legions of poems now being written on the advent of the pandemic, you might say this one was the bijou mouse that saw it coming ... it has that historical watermark ...

April 2020

SECULAR PROPHESIES
(2018)

Some of these things will happen — more or less.

*Will all of these things happen? Probably, unless the technology
and social conditions that create them are curbed, suborned or halted.*

*Or, at least, some with certainty; with others, probability;
with the rest, possibility.*

———

Ebola breaks out in a major war zone — and, because of the collapse of the
social structure in the general mayhem, it spreads rapidly and uncontrollably
across the globe, especially in the great megapolises of poverty.

———

Cells of native-born American jihadis enter, say, ten gun shops in ten states at
the same time and buy a small arsenal in each. Then they launch huge planned
massacres simultaneously.

———

Drones with bombs, poisons and other nasties are clearly already in the offing
— underwater drones too will proliferate, with the clear advantage of silence
and relative invisibility.

———

The robot-car-bomb is inevitable — imagine dozens and dozens programmed
or guided to converge on a city centre with gigantic payloads.

———

If jihadis get hold of a nuclear weapon, deterrence will have finally failed – it will not work with them.

———

A modified virus – or some other biotech mistake – becomes a rampant and rabid killer, racing swiftly through the global population of humans and animals.

———

Sudden catastrophic climate change, and the resultant tidal waves of migrations, leads to the partial collapse of the nation state system, even the nation state itself, and the complete collapse of the global international system.

———

Something like Zika (perhaps in the sperm) spreads to all of humanity, interrupting the healthy generation of the species.

———

Satellite drones become the ultimate invisible killer, destabilizing all mutual security.

———

The relentless spread of the weapons trade, gun culture and violent technology generally spreads to all corners of the world, igniting every sort of tribal conflict and ethnic hatred, especially in remote areas – indeed, this is already well-advanced.

———

As resistance to the capitalist global economic system deepens and spreads, the left-wing assassinations (both senses) begin.

———

Chips embedded in the head are used as passports first, then as every manner of state control-and-surveillance technique.

———

Drones patrol and weaponize every inch of every border.

May 2018

Chris Agee is a poet, essayist, photographer and editor. He was born in San Francisco on a US Navy hospital ship and grew up in Massachusetts, New York and Rhode Island. After high school at Phillips Academy Andover and a year in Aix-en-Provence, France, he attended Harvard University and since graduation has lived in Ireland. His third collection of poems, Next to Nothing, *was shortlisted in Britain for the 2009 Ted Hughes Award for New Work in Poetry, and its sequel,* Blue Sandbar Moon *(The Irish Pages Press), appeared in 2018. His "poetic work",* Trump Rant *(The Irish Pages Press, 2021), has just been published. He is Editor of* Irish Pages, *and edited* Balkan Essays *(The Irish Pages Press, 2016), the sixth volume of Hubert Butler's essays, published simultaneously in Croatian by the leading Zagreb publishing house Fraktura. He lives in Belfast, and divides his time between Ireland, Scotland and Croatia.*

THE BUTTERFLY DEFECT

—

Ian Goldin

The next pandemic: not if but when.

An infected passenger flies from Wuhan to Milan, a computer virus invades an internet connection, subprime defaults in the US Midwest trigger a global economic crisis. The super-spreaders of the goods of globalization – airport hubs, fiber-optic cables, global financial centers – are also the super-spreaders of the bads. This is the "butterfly defect" of globalization, the systemic risk endemic to our hyperconnected world, in which small actions in one place can spread rapidly to have global effects.

My book *The Butterfly Defect* (2014) shows why globalization creates systemic risks. It also shows why stopping globalization will not stop global threats but rather will amplify them. There is no wall high enough to keep out climate change, pandemics, and other catastrophic risks. But high walls undermine the potential for cooperation required to manage our shared risks. Protectionism reduces investment, trade, tourism, and technological advances, which create jobs and higher incomes, reducing the capacity of countries to build resilience. The solution is in working together to make globalization safe and sustainable, not in working against each other.

Leadership is required to manage the negative dimensions of globalization and harvest the positive, to ensure progress is not overwhelmed by common threats. Resilient systems are only as strong as their weakest links. Stopping the next pandemic, which could be even worse than COVID-19, must be a priority. This requires reinforcing and reforming the World Health Organization (WHO) to give it the governance, staff, and capacity it needs to be the world's rapid-response fighting force on global health.

In recent decades, globalization has led to revolutionary changes that have outstripped the slower evolution of institutions, causing a widening gap between our increasingly complex systems and our methods for managing their risks. As we saw with the financial crisis and now with COVID-19, systemic risks can quickly overwhelm processes that previously appeared robust. While there is no doubting the pandemic threat, the slower-moving but accumulating dangers posed by climate change require equally concerted action.

The pandemic has highlighted our lack of immunity to natural threats, but also created an opportunity to reset our economies. There is no shortage of ideas regarding green stimulus policies, which offer the potential to build back better and accelerate the transition from fossil fuels. Global protests, from climate to race, have demonstrated the appetite for fresh thinking. And COVID-19 has also demonstrated that citizens are prepared to change their behavior when required to do so. All that remains is for governments to act.

Networked Solutions Are Needed

COVID-19 has highlighted the pressing need for better global risk management. So too has escalating climate change. As did the financial crisis. Urgent reform is required to tame the butterfly defect of globalization.

These networked threats require changes in all parts of the system. Action must begin with us as individuals changing our behavior – for example by wearing masks and weaning ourselves off fossil fuels. Resilience cannot be delegated to others. It is everyone's responsibility. Firms should value a prudent level of spare working capital as a valuable investment in resilience, not just as excess fat to be trimmed to maximize leverage. Minimizing the amount of capital or spare capacity tied up through just-in-time or lean management systems can undermine resilience. Regulators should note the lessons from the Eyjafjallajökull volcano, the Tohoku tsunami, Hurricanes Katrina to Maria, and now COVID-19 – that widespread leanness can multiply into systemic fragility.

Our financial, digital, trade, and other systems are intertwined through complex networks. The intersecting nodes and hubs are concentrated in specific locations, such as global financial centers and major ports and airports. The concentration of logistic or other nodes in one location makes them vulnerable, as does the concentration of key personnel and information in headquarters buildings. Resilience can be enhanced by greater geographic diversification, but its benefits have not yet found their way into competition policy or risk management strategies.

A growing number of shareholders and managers of forward-looking firms have expressed their desire to improve their companies' resilience to systemic shocks. And politicians are similarly keen to improve the resilience of the public sector. Although welcome, this requires deeper analysis, including to determine how much resilience, and to what; firms and governments do not have the financial or other resources to insulate themselves totally from all possible shocks.

Resilience can be improved by decentralization, so that individuals, businesses, and countries are empowered to make their own decisions. The principle of subsidiarity is, however, a complement not a substitute for higher levels of authority. Overarching principles are necessary for risk management, and for global systemic risks. This requires that countries yield some autonomy to supranational institutions. Countries that have assiduously followed the guidelines of the WHO have done best, whether they are relatively poor, such as Vietnam, or richer, such as Canada. Stark differences in the management of COVID-19 have demonstrated the importance of operating at multiple levels to contain risk and that robust international, national, subnational, and local actions are required.

Multilateral institutions should be at the apex of this layered approach. Yet there remains a set of orphan issues with no institutional home. A number of international agencies provide analysis and information on climate change, such as the International Panel on Climate Change. But there is no global institution with decision-making and enforcement power to coordinate responses. There also is no major global organization working on cybercrime, even though a single computer virus, such as WannaCry or NotPetya – whether produced by organized state agencies or lone-wolf individuals – can spread globally and cause billions of dollars of damage within days. This threat, like that of extremist ideologies and the subversion of democracy or vaccination campaigns through fake news, is spread opportunistically through the digital networks of globalization. While these threats transcend national borders, as do the threats posed by climate change, pandemics, and terrorism, current responses are predominantly national (or regional, in the case of the European Union).

Significant progress can still be made using the Pareto principle (which states that 80 percent of consequences come from 20 percent of causes), since a small set of actors can usually resolve a large part of any problem. And those that contribute the greatest share of the problem have the greatest responsibility to resolve it. A small number of countries and companies account for well over two-thirds of carbon emissions. New York state accounts for more carbon emissions than 45 African countries. It also consumes more antibiotics than all these nations combined. As the Oxford Martin Commission for Future Generations report "Now for the Long Term" argues, a C20-C30-C40 partnership of the largest countries, companies, and cities would include enough key players to make a significant difference in addressing climate change. The success of coalitions that emerged to tackle ozone depletion or reverse the tide of HIV/AIDS provides inspiring insight into the ability of coalitions of committed citizens, companies, and countries to make a difference, bolstering the efforts of the United Nations and multilateral institutions.

Global Governance in the Twenty-first Century

Multilateral institutions can only be as effective as their shareholders allow. In response to the COVID-19 crisis, the IMF has streamlined its processes and provided unprecedented support for its members. But not all institutions have been able to rise to the challenge, and developing economies remain in dire need of additional multilateral support. The WHO should be the world's rapid-response force on global health but has been undermined just when it is needed most. And while global trade could use a shot in the arm, the effectiveness of the World Trade Organization is stymied by trade wars and the blocking of much-needed appointments and reforms.

China-centered institutions are becoming increasingly important, including the Asian Infrastructure Investment Bank and the constellation of bilateral agreements forming the Belt and Road Initiative. Working with these institutions, rather than against them, is essential, as solving global problems requires more firepower and coordination. More diverse personnel also bring greater effectiveness and legitimacy, with broader engagement providing a source of strength rather than anxiety.

In addition to the rise of new powers and the inclusion of more diverse government views, the growing role of private companies needs to be factored into the global architecture. Amazon Web Services and Google Cloud are now systemically important financial infrastructure, while Amazon Marketplace is critical for commerce. Facebook has emerged as a dominant distribution system for public health information, and Alibaba for personal protective equipment; Apple and Google lead Western attempts at app-based contact tracing.

As ever, the next crisis will not conform to our old mental maps; establishing partnerships with those who understand the new landscape is vital to prepare for it. But the private sector is not always benign, and we require independent regulators who are able to control the rising power of superstar firms. A constant renewal of technical expertise is also necessary to ensure that the experience of the financial crisis, when experts and regulators failed to understand credit derivatives, is not repeated with newly emergent threats.

The Four Meta-Horsemen

What are the biggest barriers to reform of global institutions? We can fight pestilence, war, famine, and death—and we have in the past—but to do so we must confront the four meta-horsemen: short-termism, nationalism, cost, and capture. Electorates can prevent governments taking long-term actions and may support protectionist policies, while governments themselves have only limited finances and feel the need to prioritize the urgent issues of the day rather than vitally important looming issues.

COVID-19 shows that where there is a will, all four meta-horsemen can be overcome. Politicians have a limited attention span and focus on the issues of the day, but electorates shaken by COVID-19 will demand long-term solutions. Leaders in the United States, the United Kingdom, Russia, Brazil, and beyond are facing growing criticism over their responses to the pandemic; voters will not forgive governments caught unprepared a second time. Nor will history forgive a generation of leaders who fail to prevent catastrophic climate change. As the inspiring leaders who forged a new world order while fighting World War II taught us, it is possible to focus on both short-term and longer-term challenges simultaneously. The shareholders of global institutions, and of private companies, need to do the same thing.

The COVID-19 health and economic emergencies demonstrate that coordinated global efforts are required. To stop boomerang infections takes international cooperation on vaccines. To overcome chronic shortages of skilled doctors and nurses we need immigrants. And to address climate change, stop future financial crises, and overcome poverty we must harvest the benefits of globalization while resolutely remedying its weaknesses, not least the butterfly defect of systemic risk.

Resources are available in high-income countries – governments and electorates simply need to reorder their priorities. Governments around the world allocate an average six percent of their expenditures to the military but less than one one-hundredth of this amount to the prevention of pandemics, despite their much greater threat to the population than war. At the international level, the budget of the WHO is less than that of a single major hospital in the United States. Rapid growth in response to the COVID-19 crisis shows that when the national interest is at stake the resources can be found. These lessons need to be carried forward.

The financial crisis highlighted the risks arising from groupthink and capture of regulatory agencies by lobbies. Ensuring that gamekeepers have the knowledge and independence to keep increasingly agile and well-resourced poachers at bay is essential for resilient systems.

Inertia bedevils institutional reform. Overcoming the capture of organizations by vested interests is vital to ensure that their governance, staff, and activities reflect the needs of the future rather than those of the past. The institutional landscape is littered with well-intentioned reforms that have not been implemented.

Progress is possible, as is evident in the radical changes that many institutions have undertaken. Once a limited technical organization, the European Coal and Steel Community grew into the European Union, which has taken on a wide range of national responsibilities. Crisis can be a catalyst. The United Nations, IMF, World Bank, Marshall Plan, and welfare state were all forged in the fires of World War II. In recent months the IMF has approved a record number of loans in record time, with fewer conditions attached, while its staff was working remotely. National governments have torn up the old rulebooks to provide direct support to workers and firms. What once seemed impossible has been done. The devastation caused by COVID-19 compels us to redouble our efforts to create a fairer and more inclusive world. This requires that we address the threats that endanger our lives and exacerbate inequality, poverty, and climate change. Building a resilient and sustainable future requires action by all of us, from the individual level up to the global level. International cooperation is vital not only between governments, but through civil society, business, and professional collaboration. The networked problems of our time are amenable to networked solutions. We must use this crisis to build new and stronger bonds, in our communities, in our countries, and globally.

This piece first appeared in the 2020 Fall Issue of the Finance and Development Magazine *on the International Monetary Fund website, under the title "Rethinking Global Resilience".*

Born and raised in South Africa, Ian Goldin is Professor of Globalization and Development at Oxford University. He presented the BBC Series "The Pandemic That Changed the World" in the autumn of 2020, and is co-author (with Robert Muggah) of Terra Incognita: 100 Maps to Survive the Next 100 Years *(Penguin, 2020), as well as the author of 21 other books, including* The Butterfly Defect: How Globalization Creates Systemic Risk, and What To Do About It *(Princeton University Press, 2014). In this book, he clearly predicts that the next financial crash would be caused by a pandemic similar to that in 2020 — according to the principle that "pandemics are the spill-overs of globalization".*

[UNTITLED]

—

John Glenday

There's not a moment to lose.
    Speak now if you have something to say and sing
if there is nothing more that can be said.

Recite the names of the dead in no particular order.
    Talk in your sleep; talk while everyone else is sleeping.
Tell the one you love they're the one you love,

then tell the world you have been loved by them.
    I am saying this to you out loud because each moment
is granted us only to be lost, and because it's lost

there's never a moment to lose. Nothing
    goes without saying. So go ahead, say it now,
but not just to yourself. The great silence is coming.

John Glenday was born in Broughty Ferry, near Dundee, in 1952. He studied English at the University of Edinburgh, and after graduating worked as psychiatric nurse and an addictions counsellor in the NHS. He has published four collections of poetry: The Apple Ghost *(Peterloo Poets, 1989),* Undark *(Peterloo Poets, 1995: Poetry Book Society Recommendation),* Grain *(Picador, 2009: shortlisted for both the Ted Hughes Award and the Griffin International Poetry Prize); and* The Golden Mean *(Picador, 2015: shortlisted for the Saltire Scottish Poetry Book of the Year and Winner of the 2015 Roehampton Poetry Prize). He now lives in Carnoustie, Scotland, with his wife Erika.*

From PLAGUE CLOTHES

Robert Alan Jamieson

Poems from the Covid-recovery love-stream.
(17 April – 17 May 2020)

AUTHOR'S NOTE

These poems were written between the 17th of April and the 16th of May 2020. The sequence began with a few tentative lines written in a sick bed, after I'd already been ill for a month with a virus that matched Covid-19 symptoms.

Writing them became a daily mental exercise, an attempt to regain sharpness, corollary to the physical exercise I began to take from that first poem on, up and down the river walk that leads from my home to the sea at Cramond, when I'd meditate on my mood, perhaps some news story, or something I saw as I walked – or rather trudged like a very old and vulnerable person. The poems were written quickly on returning home, directly into Facebook status updates, and not really revisited afterwards.

The process of recovery was slow and at the time of writing, I am still a little unwell, though much improved. In the spirit of instant response which marked the writing, this collection is rapidly produced through the most immediate channel, and dedicated to all my friends near and far, whose responses to the poems as I posted them became a vital communication with the world during lockdown. It was a part of what I came to think of as, not livestreams, but a "love-stream" between us all, those sharing their thoughts and ideas, their art and craft, and those responding.

17.5.2020

I reach the garden at last

17.4.20

A month of pestilence indoors
and the vegetable plot ignored is
full of tiny blue flowers, all waving and smiling,

Signing sarcastically

> Forget-me-not
> forget-me-not
>
> forget-me-not

I am losing the habit of speech

21.4.2020

Language itself grows strange.
I forget the names of all I knew.
Colour, shape and texture blend.

Those things there, what are they called?
Those people, what is it that they do?

How do those little words go
sense to make situations of?

Soon, I will only meow
or bark
or quack.

My tweets will all be bird-like.

I sense the sadness

22.4.2020

New-leaf trees can almost mask
loss that lingers, a mist among them.

They do not care a twig
what humans carry round within
those stupid little heads —

news of illness, death, the ache
of separation, all irrelevant.

Birds fly in, and birds fly out.
The higher skies are silent.

Below, the humans wander,
avoiding touch as if it were
forbidden in this slow dance.

They smile and nod, turn their faces
to the trees that sway, regardless.

But I sense their sadness.

I have no poetry

25.4.2020

I have porridge.

All too grey,
too confused,
this morning.

The horizon
between sense
and information gone,

lost in mist,
last night's dream escape
itself forgotten.

Yesterday's sarcasm
was never truly funny,
just wild defence, against folly.

I pour on a little milk,
watch as it pools.

Can I eat this simple prose?
Can I thole this tasteless morsel?

I don't care too much for money

26.4.2020

Must be six weeks since it jangled in my pocket,
since coins were important – or indeed notes.

That community cafe where they didn't take cards,
I think, when I drove home from the festival of poets.

It can't buy me breath, nor health, nor touch now.
Not even my supplies from the local Tesco –

a dead commodity nobody wants, if it can't
pay the cashier for a bottle of Prosecco.

I dandle none, dander to the shore, no where
to go and nothing there to buy when I arrive.

Other matters matter more now — new-born
values that are somehow very old and wise,

precious as those four tiny ducklings that
repay my real expense of energy in walking

by two trembling minutes of splash-play —
instinctive, feathery balls, together frolicking.

Live, little ones. Avoid the crows.

Flourish.

I want to feel the weather

27.4.2020

Indoor surfaces reflect the same dull scene repeated.
Even the not-so-polished, or decontaminated.

Screens. Dusty Glass. Streaky Windows. Cracked
Mirror. Dull Lamp. Varnished Picture.

Ceramic Glaze. Gloss covers. Tin Foil.
Laminate. Porcelain.

Wood and paint.
Plaster.
And plastic, always plastic.

All pass the dwindling
Light between them till it fades.

But no hint of weather touches me.
The sun doesn't reach, even at sunset.

Just the numb, seeping inwards slowly through
the skin, the eyes, the disengaging brain,

as I press my nose against the flat cold pane
and cough. Inside here, breath is haar — rain, a tear.

I consider going feral

28.4.2020

The garden had seemed a place of shame,
overgrown with a sick spring idleness.

The sign I made last year, old already,
stonework, pocked with isles of moss.

The pond, a pool of rotting leaves and twigs,
the fancy shop-bought windbreak, broken.

The lawn, a sunny dandelion thick-pile,
the cloche, an ocean of forget-me-not.

Yet the cherry tree still drops white blossom,
the lilac bloom still casts an aromatic spell.

I check the chaos, find beauty firmly rooted,
smiling as the bees fulfil their careful duties.

Two tabbies prowl through long grass, catching
nothing but the wind from a butterfly's wing.

All kinds of creatures, most tinier than human
eyes can spot, creep in this miniature universe.

The soil is seething, a healthy mass of friable life.
Seeds sprout, unsown. I feel somewhat unsettled

to be so little missed. This summer, maybe I should
just observe, let all unfold, this constant wilding?

Our straight lines, close-crop hedges, all that mowing,
the wish for outside to be neat like inside, seem wrong.

Let me roam around the long grass, as the cats are,
roll about in sunshine. I know I'll heal much faster.

I don't know where the ejector seat button is

  29.4.2020

Not that I'm anybody's martini
but this has shaken me.

I realise the truisms, how tenuous our
grip on life is, the dangers we face daily —

and I'm no special agent, with or without
those fancy gadgets at the ready.

I realise, too, how fast we're ageing,
in living through epochal change,

as if while time has halted socially,
it had privately accelerated.

This before-and-after marks
another phase, another stage,

for sure, but we're not there yet —
the after bit. Right now, I'm lost

at home without a mission
or a map. No sports or car.

I can't see anywhere to go. Like
somebody slammed the brakes

and now it's all slo-mo, a free-fall
arcing by in milli-milliseconds

towards the foggy windshield.
The airbag hasn't inflated.

This ain't no movie.

In the silence, I hear many things

5.5.2020

In the absence,
I discovered the forgotten,
and in the timelessness,
I found a little soul.

I'd thought it a myth,
or mystery without solution,
but there it was, all this time,
something transcendental,
beyond consciousness.

It had no meaning.
It had no message.
It had no question.

I would have brought it home
to care for it, had it not
seemed quite content right there,
out in the timeless wilderness.

It wants no feeding.
It wants no rest.
It wants no comfort.

It simply is.
It must be.

I blame the weather gods

6.5.2020

It's done its best to make our sanctioned walks
more tolerable, providing ample opportunity
to get a little sunshine in.

I've read that April was the sunniest here,
the driest, since 1929, with ninety extra hours
of precious vitamin D.

At least, I'd like to think it intentionally kind.
If not, if it was taunting us, with unenjoyable joys,
old TSE was right,

    and the lilac bloom is dying
    for the want of water.

I hear "Take Peace"

6.5.2020

That's what the old folk used to say,
such a familiar idiom, I had to check
to be sure it wasn't English.

Said if somebody was agitated, anxious
or fidgety, maybe pacing about —
someone like me, maybe.

I hear their voices in my head now,
saying, "Boy, tak paes, sit still".
It was a wisdom

I didn't appreciate then.
Now I get it

    I do.

I await renovation

  7.5.2020

I'm feeling strange in strange ways I've never felt before.
Sick, locked in, repressed at a social level, obviously —
but somehow other than those words convey.

Today I saw another of the many signs, where the walk
to Cramond Isle begins, and realised, while reading it,
a substantial part of who I am is currently

    Closed Until Further Notice

I remember the dead on the anniversary of victory

  8.5.2020

Those who died on all sides.
Those who have died to date.

Those who have no one to mourn them.
Those who have gravestones and flowers.

I do not project a number that is acceptable,
that number is total — in time, the sum of all of us.

But I mourn all those who died for lack of care,
whose lives were considered collateral.

I mourn all those who died from want of food
or water, across the fence from plenty.

Weep for those we loved, for those we knew,
who were our people, and were strange to others,

yes — but aren't there tears enough for all,
our strangers too, and human folly?

I look upon a distant coastline

  8.5.2020

Not so long ago, or was it long (how
do we measure these things now?)

I stood across there, on that shore,
and looked at where I'm standing, here.

It was so close, then, an hour away at most.
Now it's months from here at least,

and I'm like a child, gazing, fascinated
by the thought of all the people gazing back —

how do they spend their days?
Do they walk the beach as I do,

feeling child-like themselves,
imagining the city with its spires

and galleries, its shops, and try to guess
when they'll wander through it next?

What wonder this suspense stores up
for us – for some day soon, some future

yet unknown or undefined, a time
when we, like children, can explore

a world we'll rediscover – is immense.
A foreign kingdom calls to me,

an hour or months away – Fife.

I call it now what it is, a culling

10.5.2020

A culling of the old.
A culling of the sick.
A culling of the poor,

a culling of the weak.

I saw no change of heart,
just camouflage and bluster
over insincerity, personal
drama to distract.

Aim stated: immunity.

You heard it too.

I see an old man breaking quarantine and smile

14.5.2020

Ex-Isle, his boat's called.
A bonnie wee Westerly
but seen better days.

She'd been out of the water
since autumn and longs to
be lying at anchor again,

tired of waiting for the old grey
man from the island to come,
to take her out to sea again.

He never says much,
lets the wee radio play
music from far off.

She knows him, though —
his movement, his care.
She trusts his touch.

He misses her greatly as well,
has dreams of sneaking down,
polishing brightwork, caulking.

From the top of the house,
he can just see her mast below —
horizontal, still, so distant, yet

signalling come, where are you?
Tomorrow he'd risk it, he'd visit.

I learn of the Lives of Others

14.5.2020

So glad we've got the chance
to talk alone. Chin-chin.

It was all rather decadent, wasn't it?
Those air miles, the restaurants,
shopping malls, the bars and clubs?

All those theatres and brothels.
The spas and tanning suites,
and those endless, endless cafes.

It couldn't go on. Except, of course
for those in the Party.

Who did those people think they were,
squeezing onto budget jets for two weeks of sun?
The Kardashians? Trumps? Ridiculous. You'd laugh
if it didn't make you money.

All that choice, all that fakery.
They loved it, then. The posing,
the selfies, look-at-me,
FOMO teasing. All so very
very vulgar. But, lucrative.

A kind of mad consumption
in the old sense — a rampant disease,
a debilitation of the soul by
over-exposure to a fatal spore,
desire.

Except for those in the Party.
We don't make a fuss.
We don't need masks.
We are tested daily.

Another drink?

We can have whatever we want.

If you hear of anything,
you'll let the Bureau know,
of course.

I video-conference with my selves

16.5.2020

What is there, isn't always, but
avatars.

The online versions selected.
Simulation.

Which has its virtues, no doubt.
In some ways.

No contamination for one thing.
No shared air.

But it isn't actually live life.
Though live-ish.

It's the mirror world, and how it
consumes us.

We see ourselves first, always.
Performing.

Reversed, reflected, inflected.
Some troll self

sitting in the screen's corner
pretending,

who won't leave the room but
interrupts

even the most intelligent of
observations

with some self-reflexive
revelation

that we are not at all
present but

forever in process of transit.
Time-lagged.

A cipher-self emoji-self.
Winking and

saying, you are not there,
we are just

energy, constantly moving
between us.

No wonder I sometimes forget
who I am

in the breath between speech
and silence.

In the flicker of pixels.

I prepare the Pyre

17.5.2020

They become like plague clothes, these poems,
to be destroyed, burned somehow,
cast out of mind and sight.

Symbols of a time I now desperately need to forget.
And even forget-me-nots have their season —
even their blues burn, then fade.

Hope can heal, but once the healing's done
it's necessary to let it go — when that happens,
you put the wish beyond your reach.

These clothes have served me well.

Strike the match.

Born on Shetland in 1958, Robert Alan Jamieson is a poet and novelist based in Edinburgh, recently retired from the University of Edinburgh where he tutored Creative Writing for twenty years. Prior to that, he was co-editor of Edinburgh Review *between 1993 and 1998, William Soutar Fellow 1993-1996, and Writer-in-Residence at the Universities of Glasgow and Strathclyde from 1998 to 2001. His major publications include five novels and four collections of poetry:* Soor Hearts *(Paul Harris, 1984);* Thin Wealth *(Polygon, 1986);* Shoormal *(Polygon, 1986);* A Day At The Office *(Polygon, 1991);* Beyond The Far Haaf *(Vanderbeek & Imrie, 1993);* Nort Atlantik Drift *(Luath, 2007);* Da Happie Laand *(Luath, 2010);* macCloud Falls *(Luath, 2017); and the extraordinary* Plague Clothes *(Taproot, 2020), written as he recovered from Covid-19.*

BIDING

———

Amanda Thomson

Look to the old dictionaries.

I've been thinking a lot about time lately. Perhaps it's been because for the first time in ages I've been in one place for an extended period, in this spring to summer of 2020. I've watched the first buds on the larches and alders, seen the thin film of yellow pollen from the Scots pines cover every surface at the very end of May, and waited for, and watched the swallows and the martins return; the young have fledged now and sit, quivering at first, like novice tightrope walkers, on the electricity wires outside the house. I heard my first willow warbler on April 17th, and my first cuckoo of the year on the 24th, the day my neighbour, who's lived here far longer than I have, predicted they'd return.

In these long summer hours of daylight, my understanding of duration alters and in old Scots Language dictionaries, I find words and phrases for the nuances of light and how a northern thread of it lingers from the end of one day to the beginning of the next, *at the head of the dim*, midsummer twilight between sunset and sunrise.

> *scraigh-o' day*, the first appearance of dawn
> *grey o' the morning*, dawn of the day
> *greking*, peep of day
> *day-sky*, the appearance of the sky at break of day
> *the scaud o' day*, the daybreak
> *lichtening*, dawn
> *neb-o'-the-morning*, the time between dawn and sunrise
> *creek o' day*, daybreak
> *dawing*, dawn of day
> *scaud o' day*, daybreak
> *morning-mun*, increasing daylight
> *between the sun and the sky*, the interval between daybreak and sunrise

sky, the light at the eastern horizon before sun-rise, or at the western after sunset; thus, "was ye up afore the sin the day?" "ay, afore the sky", or "the sky winna set this hour yet"

Each *dayligaun* now, the roe deer hover at the edges of the field, close to the bracken and junipers and the woods behind, and we watch the woodcock rode above the trees in geometric lines, and we wait for the hares to appear. In the time before the flick of a light-switch, there's a gentle easing into the night.

the gray, twilight
sockin-hour, the portion of time between day-light and candle light
neuk-time, the twilight; in reference to its being the season for pastime or gossiping among work-people
gloaming-shot, a twilight interval which workmen within doors take before using lights
undern, the third hour of the artificial day, according to the ancient reckoning, i.e. nine o'clock
nichting-time, the day when out-door labour ceases during the winter season, i.e., when daylight closes
fore-nicht, the early part of night, the interval between twilight and bedtime
heel of the twilight, the termination of twilight

In these old dictionaries time stretches beyond the hours of the day to months of the year and so many of the words and descriptions are rooted in nature and the land:

Craw Sunday, the first Sunday in March, on which crows were sup-posed to begin to build their nests.
Gowk-storm, a storm consisting of several days of tempestuous weather, believed by the peasantry periodically to take place about the beginning of April, at the time that the gowk, or cuckoo, visits the country.
Worm month, a designation given to the month of July, from the hatching of many kinds of reptiles in this month.

And then, at the far end of the summer, *Stooky Sunday*, the Sunday at harvest when the greatest number of stooks are seen in the field. Beyond this, the *breakback moon*, so called by the harvest labourers because of the additional work it entails. *Go-harvest, Go-hairt, -harst*, the latter end of summer; the time from the end of harvest till the beginning of winter. *Lang halter time*, the season of the year when fields being cleared, travellers and others claimed a common rite of passage.

There's an immediacy to the knowledge of forthcoming weather too, usually rooted in experience and what is visible, and usually in the soon to be, or the near present: *heavy-heartit*, (used of the atmosphere) lowering, threatening rain; *gow*, a halo, circle round the sun or moon, a "brough", portending bad weather. Even other phrases that are longer in term refer to near predictable Scottish weather events: *May-gobs*, cold weather about the second week of May, *Lammas-flood, -rain, -spate*, heavy rain and floods about "Lammas".

We've always reached to nature and the earth, and some of us still do, for alignment, solace, comparison. In these old dictionaries I come across phases like, *neb-o'-the-mire-snipe*, the utmost extremity, and *cheepart*, a meadow pipit or a small person with a shrill voice. *Drizzen*, to low as a cow or ox, sometimes applied to a sluggard groaning over his work. *Weather-gaw*, part of one side of a rainbow; any change in the atmosphere, known from experience to presage bad weather; any day too good for the season, indicating that it will be succeeded by bad weather; anything so uncommonly favourable, as to seem an indication of a reverse. *Ferny-buss*, a clump of ferns; a bush or fern; as in "it's either a tod or a ferny-buss", it's something or other, no matter what. *Peak*, to chirp; to squeak ; to speak in a whisper or thin, weak voice; to complain of poverty, n. the chirp of a bird; the squeak of a mouse; an insignificant voice; a small person with a thin, weak voice.

I've loved the phrase *to spurrie-how*, to run as fast as a sparrowhawk flies, since I found it. It speaks again of that first reach of metaphor to what is known and what is seen and imagined. I listened to a podcast recently where they described how weather forecasting as we know it today came about at the time of the invention of the telegraph, when news and the sharing of information could move faster than clouds, and we could become one step ahead. I have an App on my phone which tells me the rain here will start in three minutes and end 35 minutes later.

Now, nature is not necessarily our first port of call when we think of speed and we can think in terms of light years and, perhaps, long nows. We measure upload speeds and download speeds in terms of milliseconds, and we can travel around the world or be connected and alerted to actions and atrocities and movements and thinking in ways which were unimaginable mere decades ago. Daily we're asked to think in abstracts and what ifs in speeds and times beyond the human-scale.

From the eighteenth century, we've had an awareness of deep time and have looked beyond our present existence to a geological scale that measures time and change in millions of years. Just over a couple of hours drive northwest from where I stay lies Sutherland and the Knockan Crag. It sits within and overlooks Norman MacCaig's favoured landscape, and he writes of this area,

Glaciers, grinding West, gouged out
these valleys, rasping the brown sandstone,
and left, on the hard rock below –
the ruffled foreland –
this frieze of mountains, filed
on the blue air

Knockan Crag is said to be one of the first important sites of modern geology, and it's a place where it's easy to see the Moine Thrust, where two continents crashed together and older rock pushed and crushed and folded and rested on top of younger rocks, disrupting layers of time. "At Knockan Crag" the Tourist Board tells us, "you can bridge 500 million years of history with your bare hands."

But now we're told we're living in the Anthropocene, and we're still thinking of it in terms of decades and centuries, and not in the millions of geological years such 'cenes are usually measured in. It's a strange thing to have to think about our own responsibilities within an ongoing timespan of earth that's hitherto been rooted in the slow formation of rocks and changes in climate that have had nothing to do with humanity. We're adding plastic and carbon and radioactive isotopes to layers of time that have been seen and shown in rock strata. Now there are interconnections to rock and minerals and how we've used this earth, and they're present in histories and projections of future times near and far that are written and being re-written as I write.

We're in a strange time of looking out and over, peeking over lockdown walls with trepidation, and wondering how and when the things of the world might connect, and might impact on and implicate us, and our behaviour. So much since March 2020 has felt day-to-day and so immediate, so local; within a pandemic that has swept, is sweeping still, across the world. But at the same

time we do look out, we have to, and we look out across the world in ways
that our forebearers would never have thought possible, and see change, and
possibilities for change that, perhaps, at the beginning of 2020 we would
never have thought possible. We read about carbon emissions falling because
of the reductions in travel by air, land and sea. We see with horror the murder of George Floyd and watch or participate in or comment on subsequent
protests against racism and police brutality, and monuments to racists are
pulled down. We follow #climatestrike and #blacklivesmatter and #meto,
and hope we get through this pandemic, though we wonder whether anything
on a structural level will shift or remain shifted. Some of us watch a doomsday clock – an ongoing commentary on nuclear proliferation and now, the
climate emergency – which was moving ever closer to midnight even before
Covid-19 ("Doomsday clock lurches to 100 seconds to midnight – closest to
catastrophe yet", *The Guardian*, 2020).

Years and decades and centuries. How we understand the past will
impact on our sense of the present, and thereafter, our possible futures. Even
discussions about when the Anthropocene starts complicate and implicate in
different ways (Simon Lewis and Mark Maslin, "Defining the Anthropocene",
Nature, 2015). Should we pinpoint its start from the time of Columbus and
into the sixteenth century with the beginnings of the exchange of species
between the "Old" and "New" worlds? Some might argue that it started at
the advent of the Industrial Revolution. The historian T.C. Smout, writing the
social history of Scotland noted, "to the economic historian the success of the
first phase of the industrial revolution is succeeded by the success of iron and
coal in the second, then after 1860 by the triumph of steel, ships, jute, tweed
and high farming ... to the social historian – or at least to me – things seem
rather different." He writes – and these early years are when the Jamieson
dictionary (1846) was compiled – "The age of great industrial triumphs was
an age of appalling social deprivation" (T. C. Smout, *A Century of the Scottish
People 1830–1950*, 2010). Now, with hindsight, success is re-written in the
context of carbon emissions and pollution, and some have argued the Anthropocene really began at a time much closer to now, with the detonation of the
first atomic bombs and the radioactivity cast up into the atmosphere from
the 1950s ("The Anthropocene epoch: scientists declare dawn of human-in-
fluenced age, *The Guardian*, 2016).

Smout draws attention to the humanity impacted on by the industrial,
but Kathryn Yusoff adds more, revealing the seam of colour running through
the Anthropocene (Katheryn Yusoff, *A Billion Black Anthropocenes or None*,

2018). She's interested in changing what she calls the "grammar" and "language" of geology, adding another corporeality and responsibility to it. If the Anthropocene started with Columbus, or thereabouts, and the beginning of the trade and the movement of species between the Europe and the Americas then, "the collision of the old and new" covers over the friction of a less smooth, more corporeal set of racialized violences. These are exchanges which are "the directed colonial violence of forced eviction from land, enslavement on plantations, in rubber factories and mines, and the indirect violence of pathogens through forced contact and rape …" (Katheryn Yusoff, *A Billion Black Anthropocenes or None*, 2018). Of the Industrial Revolution, Yusoff writes, "In 1833, Parliament finally abolished slavery in the British Caribbean, and the taxpayer payout of £20 million in 'compensation' [to slave owners!] built the material, geophysical (railways, mines, factories), and imperial infrastructure of Britain and its colonial enterprises and empire" (Katheryn Yusoff, *A Billion Black Anthropocenes or None*, 2018). If it started with atomic testing, then, "Nuclear testing marks the displacement and exposure of indigenous peoples in the Pacific Islands and the radiation of Native American and Aboriginal peoples in North America and Australia" (Katheryn Yusoff, *A Billion Black Anthropocenes or None*, 2018).

She writes of this Anthropocene, "the end of this world has already happened for some subjects, and it is the prerequisite for the possibilities of imagining 'living and breathing again' for others" (Katheryn Yusoff, *A Billion Black Anthropocenes or None*, 2018). This pandemic, and the time of it has further exposed inequities. Those of us who are lucky can sit in our local bubbles and wonder, worry how much of what has happened has changed minds or made those who think in a particular way anyway just a little bit more resolved, one way or the other, to try and act and behave more proactively – for good or bad. And how many of us still feel that quiver of powerlessness and limitation that we've always felt in the world; overwhelmed by considerable failures to value human life, in that same way that we can't quite comprehend the vastness of deep time or the complications of what needs to be done to make things better, on the existential scale that the call to arms that correction to this Anthropocene trajectory as it stands, needs.

In these old dictionaries, *eard-din* means thunder; thunder in the earth; an earthquake; and I can only think that it's a composite meaning earth noise, and how interesting there's that conflation of air and land, air and rock. And we'll bide here, on some days walking up to the moor in the hope of hearing *wheeples* or *wherries*, and watching and listening to the *sirdouns*, *pews* and *chirls*.

How easy it's been, in some ways to quiet the noise, or drown out that which we don't want to hear, or it can take all our strength to listen to, and understand and find a way to act on what we are listening to. And I find myself returning to this old dictionary, these old words and phrases, wondering whether this is or will be *a hearkenin' win'*, a comparative lull in a storm, followed by a destructive blast.

To *sirdoun*, v. to emit a plaintive cry, as some birds do

To *wheeple*, v. to whistle like a whaup (curlew), to whistle a shrill, melancholy note, as plovers do

To *whirry awa'*, v. to fly off with such noise as a partridge or moorcock makes when it springs from the ground

To pew, n, v the plaintive cry of birds; the least breath of wind or smoke; the least ripple on the sea; (applied to birds) to emit a mournful sound

To chirl, v. to chirp, warble merrily; to whistle shrilly; to emit a low, melancholy sound, as birds do in winter or before a storm; to laugh immoderately, n. a low, melancholy sound; chirping.

Amanda Thomson is a visual artist and writer who lives and works in in Glasgow and Strathspey. Much of her work — in art and writing — is about the Highlands of Scotland, its landscape and nature, and how we are located (and locate ourselves) in the world. Her first book, A Scots Dictionary of Nature, *was published by Saraband Books in 2018.*

POEM

——

Don Paterson

EASTER 2020

In the ICUs and care homes they are drowning in their beds
drowning in themselves, like christ, their airways down to threads

while a blue glove opens FaceTime on an iPad to discover
another new contender for Worst Family Photo Ever

We love you. Goodbye Dad. And even if they understand
there's no breath left for their last word. *Into their hands.*

Meanwhile in the post of hell we call the cabinet
the rats have figured out the means and gnaw the ends to fit

the headless chickens count themselves but miss the standing duck
and the goats survey the goatscape for just where to pass the buck

the pig has hidden in the toilet since he came down sick
when it turned out happy *birthday to me* didn't do the trick

and he almost looks into his soul, but bounced back to steer
his usual course through what he thinks his buddies want to hear

*So if we tell them "stay alert" and then they all get ill
well that's on them, it's not our fault the bug's invisible*

and they still don't know essential's *Latin for gets paid jack shit
and hero's Greek for you go first and take the fucking hit*

*and no one knows the body count if we don't show the chart —
Now let's all get the taps back on before the riots start*

So one rat texts a laptop jockey at The Daily Scare
who wants his Polish cleaner back and his kids out of his hair

who raises up one winedark hand to throw the dog a cork
and types out with the other 'Let Our Angels Back to Work'

Meanwhile stuck in lockdown we all stare at the TV
where a nurse from County Monaghan in home-made PPE

ignores the hack and turns around to face the lens alone
with a stare as hard as nails and a promise cast in stone

if we see your family out we will love them as our own

*Originally from Dundee, Scotland, Don Paterson left school at 16 and moved to London to
pursue music and join a band. He found success with the jazz-folk ensemble* Lammas, *but was
captivated by poetry upon encountering poet Tony Harrison, among others. He is the author of
nine collections of poems, most recently* 40 Sonnets *(Faber, 2015) and* Zonal *(Faber, 2020),
as well as several poetry anthologies and collections of aphorisms. He continues to perform as
a jazz guitarist and lives in Dundee, Scotland.*

ON NOT WALKING

—

Alec Finlay

On the colours of pain.

if you can walk
a half mile
places connect

if you can walk
100 yards
then that's it

28.V.20

I do irony well. Selected for a residency with Paths for All that would explore walking, creativity, and disability, I end up spending three months unable to walk. I promised myself I'd be able to by the end of this essay.

That's not quite true. I can walk down the stairs to the back garden and lay among the lockdown daisies. I can make a minor walk to the recycling bins over the road. In extremis, I think I can still make the corner shop for coconut milk and bacon.

But then comes the desire to go around the block, past the fuchsia, and back by the sculpture workshop. Call it a 250m loop, seven-minute dauner. I've done it six times since March and had as many relapses, each lasting three or four days, waking at 4 or 5 am, panting, aching with lactic muscles, exhausted. A dump bin of wasted days. That's what coronavirus does to a vulnerable immune system. There are thousands of people sharing this experience many for the first time. Their world feels strange.

the odd walker
on the path

with an aura
of danger

24.III.20

How I miss walking. My desk looks over an arterial footpath which was once a busy rail-line to the docks. While I've hardly seen anyone during lockdown, I do see people all the time, and their dogs, prams, and bikes. They pass behind the glass, or, on a good day, with the windows held open by a pile of books, I can hear their chatter and the dogs barking.

There are starlings nesting in the wall and gulls on the roof. In the faraway is the torso of the Pentlands.

fresh snow picks out
old paths on the hills

Poverty is seeing other people enjoy what you can't. Still, everyone can take some pleasure in other's pleasures. But a delight that's permanently denied rankles. Never, you say, but that's not fair.

From the kitchen window I can see patches of the Firth and a harbour lighthouse. This marks my trad. walk — more a stroll — my everyday luxury, my Jaffa cake. These past months it's been my dream to go back down Whale Brae and see the little boats.

I can see the sea
but it's so long

since I could walk
to the harbour

14.VI.20

The measure of our pace changes our world.

The rhythm of our walk sets our clock.

We begin as toddlers, who toddle, and then, after a long, long walk along the *via active* of our lives, we gradually decline into doddlers, who doddle. In a walking lifetime the allotted span is supposed to follow the slow patterns of ageing. Our ability to walk should diminish as slowly as tree rings grow. Periods of illness have the appearance of a poor Summer, closing the gaps between the rings.

I became a dodderer at 21. That isn't quite true. I could walk a-ways if I had to, but the outcome – the *lag*, as I called it – would result in days of agony that made life unbearable. Relapses don't follow the standard pattern of muscular tiredness. The lag in the legs isn't a hiker's stiffness following a day on the hill. For someone with ME or long-term coronavirus, or any number of chronic illnesses, the onset of exhaustion from a short walk, sometimes of a hundred yards or less, may be delayed and the duration of their relapse may extend for days, even weeks. Lactic acid sits on the muscles like beads of mustard. Face it out, another bout of pain the body won't flush.

Disabilities vary. Some impairments force themselves on the body permanently. Some illnesses impose fatigue, without fail, in the days *after* an activity.

Fatigue isn't tiredness. Pain isn't an ache. It's the inability to have any thoughts or joys beyond a jagged bodily sensation. Sometimes it feels as if weights and irons have been attached to your legs. This isn't just a physical problem, it's existential. It can feel like dying, or it can make you feel that you need to die. It can also make the possible so tender and magical.

> *we know where*
> *energy comes from*
> *but where does it go?*

I remember an evening 20 years ago when, after three tough days in bed, I made myself go outside for some air. It was one of those episodes of illness that slip giddyingly beyond familiar symptoms, when function isn't so much impaired as disfigured. My flat was on one of the roads that lead off The Meadows. The park was within reach. Walking slowly around the imaginary touchline of a jackets-for-goals footie game, the sensation came over me that I may not make it home. I'd come 200 metres.

The disparity between the jouissance of the game, with its fluid triangles, and my shuffle was intense and invisible. My legs felt excruciating, shins aching, but there were no bones broken. What was happening? It didn't feel like an episode of routine exhaustion. I was determined not to fall down in front of the footballers. In the belly of my thigh muscles the tissue had turned to junket laced with coal dust. I made it home.

Swimming might feel great – so floaty, what could go wrong – but watch out for kryptonite later in the week. Pain reactions may bear no relation to how you felt when you were doing a thing. It's one of the most perplexing things about a chronic illness: how the exhaustion bears no relation to what caused it. It's fundamentally unjust, like being on the receiving end of an irrational outburst of anger. The exchange rate is always loaded in favour of the disease.

Expect nothing good, only losses. Adapt to limits willingly. Keep trying. Don't allow yourself to feel in exile from those parts of the world that are out of bounds. Smile wryly at all the times you walked too far because you were shy to say to a companion, *well, actually, I need to stop here*, even though they think we've barely begun the walk.

Hoc est corpus. This is my body. I have no other.

Fear comes on whenever you re-enter the mechanism of illness. That's what a disease is like: it isn't an emotionally incapable jellyfish that stings, it's a machine; honed, relentless, impersonal. This virus especially, SARS-CoV-2, sets its cryptic workings walking in a chain of 30,000 "A", "T", "G" or "C" letters, delivering havoc throughout the immune system. The mechanism leaves some unaffected and mangles other's lungs permanently, or it kills them.

———

lexicon of fatigue

I'm *slepi*, weary
fatigat, so wearied
relinxed, fatigued
afoundred numbed
with exhaustion
and *upspent*, oh so
exhausted

(composed *from a Dictionary of Old English*)

A *relapse*. A *boom-and-bust*. A *completely buggered*. These are some of the terms used by the "professionally" ill to refer to an episode.

All over Britain there are people who have recently come off ventilators and walked, very slowly, back into this world. Many will need months of rehabilitation. They will be learning these terms and inventing their own.

> *the wabbit week*
>
> *rested*
> *tired*
> *exhausted*
> *fatigued*
> *very fatigued*
> *totally fatigued*
> *fatigued as f**k*

The repetition of pain becomes unbearable – though it must be borne – because each time the machine switches into gear one recognises that it will endure for a tightly knotted parcel of time. When the door opens and you're pushed through, you don't get out until you've been shunted into every room. Even if you only cross the line a little you may receive the same punishment as if you'd fallen far out of bounds.

My old pain cycle lasted five days, with the third being the worst. I used to count back and try to guess which event had been responsible. Remembrance of walks past. It took two decades to sand my recovery down to two days, if the weather was fine. Coronavirus has pushed it back up to four. And that's for a walk of 100m.

We speak of fright in terms of *fight* or *flight*. But those who can't walk have no option but to face tigers and trolls. To find yourself in a landscape and not be able to walk is to experience beauty in the eye and, at the same time, feel the body exposed. The routes that paths follow matter much more.

Mental calculations become a habit – to *that stile*, *this hazel*, or as far as *the fank*? Is that a shortcut? Perhaps, around that bend in the path, there's the most beautiful birchwood, or some beehives, a dun fragrant with bog myrtle, or an ice cream in the perfect cone? Should I? Can I?

Gradients matter as much as distances. Do the sums. Calculate the likely pain. Consider what's planned for the next days and whether you can afford to pay the debt.

Cycles of relapse and recovery heap up and become eyesores. That mechanism of symptoms and their cycle becomes the thing you most wish to avoid. This places the subject body in direct opposition to the joyful walk.

>*if the walk is the joy*
>*then where is joy*
>*without walking?*

Nothing blunts human responsiveness like pain. Nothing makes kindness more desirable. Blessings on the lover who rubs your legs gently and wards away pain. Blessings on the oil burner and tea tree. Blessings on the bucket of hot water. Sort-of-blessings on the cold bath. Blessings on pillows between the knees. Blessings on sunshine to lie in. Blessings on a cup of tea.

Rest, real rest, is a thing which happens when pain is absent. Sometimes you have to rest before you can rest. Anyone with critical levels of fatigue will tell you that lying down, waiting for toxins to dissolve and flush out of the body, is *not* resting. It's hard work and takes endurance. There's nothing passive about pain except your posture.

How the land strikes the legs differs when illness and age bear down upon us. For some illness is learning how to live in a body that has lost its rhythm. Others have fences drawn around them by pain. While, for others, constraints are permanent, physical, and multiplied by natural and man-made obstacles.

For the constrained walker limits aren't precise, however carefully they calculate. The effect of a walk will depend on how a person is on the day it meets a bit of land. Each person with chronic illness carries their own pocketful of harsh experiences with which they gauge the next walk and its limits. Over time, as experience is gained, a rough-and-ready regimen is improvised in which common-sense is a path. The mind begins to form imaginary lines marked *far enough*, *too far*, and *far too far*.

>*you always try to*
>*carry a line*
>*ahead of you*
>
>*so as to not cross*
>*into all the pain*
>*that follows*

Still, it isn't easy to account for how slopes use different muscles, or the effects of heat, cold, and damp.

If doctoring is a matter of reading the form and calculating the odds, then managing a chronic illness is playing Patience. It takes years to learn one's own specifics in different contexts. From the onset, characterised by a rush of symptoms and collapse of life as it once existed, over months, or years, one has to figure out how the mechanism of symptoms works, what triggers it, what oils it, what placates the pain?

Terrain is an allergy test. Walking up a brief incline has different aerobic consequences to daunering along a lane, but how much of a difference in terms of pain? How do you react to steps? Heather's a bugger, isn't it?

Like old John Anderson in his snowy years, I've explored the foot of many a mountain. Once I clambered over a bog for a couple of hours to reach the very bottom of Sgurr nan Gillean. I've spent a day reading, sat among the ruined shielings by Allt a' Garbh-choire, while friends got smaller climbing up Càrn an Tuirc. I've failed to reach Loch a' Mhadaidh Mor. I'd been on Berneray seven times before someone gave me a run over to the West Beach and I could walk back to the hostel.

As a boy I walked down and back up a stony track of three-quarters of a mile length for the school bus. On my good days, before coronavirus, that distance was a symbolic marker for the hem of my walks. Step beyond that and I will (nearly) always relapse.

Now, after corona. I couldn't make it to the first gate of the track.

Just as the coastline of Tahiti appears enormous in the maps of the Surrealists so, to people with constrained walking, a hill looks thick with contours. All these wavy lines are fine to look at and hopeless to walk over.

My friend Alison Lloyd is an artist skilled in guiding people. She has no physical illness, but walking helps her feel less anxious. Trained in micro-navigation techniques which climbers use to navigate at altitude, Alison translated these to the flat to make walking art. She invites walkers to visualise a contouring mountain walk at pavement level and has used visualisation to help people re-enact the traverse across a cornice in the Cuillins, while making on a slow walk around a Leicester roundabout.

Contouring is a technical skill used in the mountains when visibility is poor. It enables the walker to define a safe route, remaining at a constant height and following a contour as if it were an imagined path through the landscape. It's applied map logic. Alison describes contouring as *"a way of walking slowly that concentrates on my immediate surroundings."* Capable of topping any Munro that she wishes, this slow steady line became her signature walk. The applicability of this skill for those who cannot walk far is clear, for it enriches any walk.

In terms of my original disease, ME, confronted by sceptical and stumped doctors and specialists I've fantasised leading a special expedition of the ill. I think of this as my *I'm at the end of my endurance walk*. The medics wear white coats and hiking boots. I'm carrying a tartan blanket. They walk either side of me, warily, rather bored, but politely encouraging, enjoying the scenery. We continue together, or me among them, across hills and mountains, through pinewoods, fording a shingly river, until the crucial moment comes. Is it on the first day? Do I walk on into the night? Do I take us even further, impossibly far? Well now I can go no farther. They nod approvingly. They can't deny that I tried. In their minds the purpose of the experiment is to prove I can walk this great distance without collapsing, and therefore I am essentially fine. In reply I speak up: *hold on, stay a while*. Now I will force them to observe the symptoms as they take hold. This is the real experiment.

Day one of the relapse and they're already becoming impatient. *Well, of course you're stiff, it was a long walk.* On day two I have to say *steady lads, you're not leaving yet*. The pain reaches a peak on days three and four. My spindleshanks are full of pins, I've dark shadows under my eyes, and a solid ridge of muscle across my waist where my breathing has turned to gravel.

I can't describe the end of this fantasy because, of course, they lost interest on the second morning and left before anything was proven on my side of the argument. But I understand that cycle is the crux of my disease. I can feel when the mitochondrial generator goes into over-drive and cells sputter and dim into lassitude. Just don't call it *feeling tired*.

A few years ago, a friend and I were staying at Loch Maree hotel. We were the only visitors. There was an atmosphere of tweed and Victorian fishing expeditions. I was exhausted from a minor walk we'd done the day before, or the day before that, so I let the pain have its way and rested with the maps. My friend headed off for a day climbing Slioch, *The Spear*. That evening he'd tell me how, despite its wonderful profile, the mountain was a slog, and how magical the little islands appeared from the wide-angle summit.

By the afternoon I'm still exhausted and in pain, but the hotel's dark, and I wanted to at least see the woods. I headed down the road looking for a way in. When batteries are that low there's nothing more frustrating than the delay in finding the path, for that's where the walk really begins, beyond the asphalt. Distances matter.

Just off the road I found a grove of old oaks with moss stumps and a damp holiday hut. What I remember most is the strange buzz in my body as the respiratory capability of each cell scrabbled for energy. Recent research suggests there is a crisis upstream of the cell mitochondria, perhaps in the carrying stream of oxygen. Breath makes a walk as much as steps. This may be why the mangled lungs of post-coronavirus produces such similar symptoms to ME. My lungs have felt traumatised for weeks, as if the bronchial veins had had been clumsily soldered and some of the lobes filled in. Each inhalation is a wee project.

———

ME is *The Crash*, a phrase which describes the inability of the compromised body to recover. *You look so well*, people say.

Someone with ME will have a picture of their disease, but it looks like pages of automatic writing scribbled down in the middle of the night. Meaning can be made out, if you want it to and look carefully, sometimes upside down. You don't get to sit in front of X-rays and have complex symptoms patiently explained. The medical science is like an account of scattered dust in a far galaxy.

You have to work these kinds of illness out yourself, over years, by reading, feeling how your body works, finding what helps, what makes things worse, and learning how to rest, and how to adapt your walking. It is the walk and sleep that are, for the chronically ill, two of the essential measures of how they are.

With the arrival of coronavirus my walking shrunk to the odd day, 100m, maybe 200m, at most 250m when I had a better spell, in April. After each short walk – walklet? – my diaphragm would strain and boom, forming a hypertonic muscle, and my legs would ache as if I'd run a marathon. Now that I'm over 90 days into my Coronavirus term, without remission, I've been trying a very, very, very short walk each day. The constrained walking that comes with any chronic illness increases the scale of a walk map. One comes to measure the distance of a walk by The Lamppost or an individual tree. I've made it as far as the birch, and then, next day, one tree on, to the pine, which is 100m, and 103m. And now I'm paying for it. The need to find a balance been maintaining some pliability in my leg muscles and avoiding such a dose of pain and fatigue that days are lost isn't easy.

The lobby who imagine ME – or any neurological disease – as a shyness from activity couldn't be more wrong. I want to walk every day. I want to go further. I want to reach the bus stop. I want to get back to the harbour. But, since I did those two walklets, my body has felt like an assemblage of test tubes filled with various colours of pain.

———

In this time of limit I keep remembering a minor walk I used to take with a friend in Glen Feardar. We'd park where the road became a track and walk a couple of hundred yards to a wooden bridge over the Felagie. The name is a compound of two Gaelic words, *féith*, a bog stream or slow burn, and *léig*, the marshy pool that the water winds out of. By the point where we met the Felagie it has become the perfect miniature river, happy-go-lucky between rocks, birches, and Bog Myrtle, whose scent made this micro-landscape as complete. It's one of the few places I could still imagine doing one of my corona-lag walks that would amount to what can be called a *walk*. This is one reason that ecologies, gardens, and paths matter. They offer a greater richness in exchange for fewer steps. They are energy-efficient landscapes.

A poet friend once sent me her latest book of poems, inscribed, in unsteady letters, "from before". She'd had a stroke: these were the last poems she'd written in that other life.

I'd become used to my condition as it was, from before. A minor walk wasn't an issue, which means that enough of the world is possible. Ah, to be as we were. The problem isn't walking, for me, but that coronavirus made my body mislay the ability to recover. It's still fond of old habits and wants to go back to them, to be me walking a wee way along the path, but my mangled lungs say no.

Everyone with ME tries to push through the barrier of the possible time and again, to see if they can walk, or run, or bicycle. They are trying to get back to before. In the moment it's sometimes possible to feel one can. For a few steps, or a walk that goes further, and too far. There are moments of elation when the body feels like its old self and you imagine that, thanks to the magical character of a place, or the right kind of sunshine, or love, you can go further.

I remember a walk like that above Dunkeld, when a pinewood path opened out on a stepped slope of wildflowers and birches that didn't exist on the map. I felt I could walk that ridge forever. And so I did, for two miles. And then I remember the pain that I endured, in a narrow bed in the Taybank for the next two days, which I carried home.

There are moments one slips into the complex thought processes: *this disease is making me a better person*, or, *I've changed, I've healed, now I can walk*, or *I've freed the breath within me*. Illness is a bag of questions, so people are bound to pull out answers, especially if they are in short supply from medical science. Kindness heals pain, it doesn't cure it.

More than anything, someone with ME, fibromyalgia, lupus, or any such disease, wants to get beyond the strangeness of what their body has become.

Many find that the first months, or years, of their new illness are taken up with quixotic attempts to elude the mechanism. Bittersweet memories of what our bodies could do, before the catastrophe, keep us trying to walk old paths, but the results rarely vary. Harsh lessons. A weakness is a weakness is a weakness.

Over time, a wariness comes in the wake of all that weariness. Episodes of pain mount up until there are too many. They block out too much of the light.

There are too many holidays in which the too-long walk to the beach made on the day you arrive leads to days in a strange bed with only a window of fresh sky to look at.

My friend Chris Dooks is a bonnie fighter. *"In the first ten years of M.E. I wasted a lot of time waiting to get better. That's the natural impulse isn't it? Curl up, head down, let the storm pass. But what if it is like one of those two hundred-year storms on Jupiter? In the second half of my M.E. career — and it is a career, I decided to be ill in other places. I've passed out in Amsterdam and, more recently, cycled twenty-two miles on my electric bike to Rosslyn. That was my Kilimanjaro!"*

My philosophy is that doing too much is inevitable, but I find that being careful, learning to draw the line, is a way to avoid repetitive disasters which hurt the spirit. The persistence of pain will lead some people, including me at times, to contemplate an end. This isn't to feel suicidal: it's to feel one can no longer bide in a body dominated by pain. Seeking the mean, I try to avoid relapses. But whether you are doing too much or too little depends upon what energy you have. The impact of coronavirus has changed the treaty I'd insisted my disease made with the world. Now they are at war again.

For many people with long-term coronavirus symptoms, or *corona-lag*, this line drawing is the new lesson for this week, and the next, and probably a few more after that. It takes a long time to adjust between wishes and abilities, to test what you can do and what it will cost.

> there are the things to walk away from —
> ah, but what when you can't walk?

In cities you can count street blocks and sometimes there are buses. What a help a bus pass would be for everyone with invisible or chronic illness – don't imagine they can all get one now. Officialdom has no time for: *sometimes I can walk X, but sometimes only Y and sometimes not a Z*. For stick users and wheelies there's a chance of passing the tests, but a condition like ME prompts the query: *can you walk X distance? Yes, but*. No chance to explain what happens to you *after* the walk. No pass. Think of all the avoidable pain. And think of all those recuperating from corona-lag, who won't be able to walk, or not as far. They will need transport.

Doctors know almost nothing about ME and, since the illness became dominated by psychiatry in the late 1990s, what they hear doesn't always help. Medical scientists I speak to are confident there will be a spike in cases as a result of coronavirus. A substantial new community will become ill because of the virus and this may change attitudes.

You still come across horror stories, like the dismissive GP who sent a new case outside to run laps around the medical centre and prove to themselves there's nothing wrong. Or a child who has been lying in a darkened room being made to get up and jump into a swimming pools to sink or swim. It doesn't bear thinking about. Our outrage at past medical scandals is always big enough to obscure those of the present.

———

It was a walk that got me removed from disability benefits back into the day. I was the country fool who admitted walking the five blocks to his interview for a disability assessment. That starter question, *how did you get here?*, got me kicked off and the rest of the interview was over in a jiffy. Like there was a bus I could have got? I never had the opportunity to explain that I got out of my sick bed to walk in and I'd be in bed that afternoon and the next day resting the ache of the walk back. The face of that DSS GP has never left me, he had jowls like Scooby Doo.

———

Many years ago, at a birthday party, someone had the idea of gathering a group of my friends together as a bearer party to gift me a mountain ascent. On the following morning they planned to meet at breakfast time, place me in an old rush chair and, using broomsticks as handles, carry me to the top of Arthur's

Seat. I shrank with embarrassment at this kindness. The idea of being raised on a throne, being seen to be helped, was so kind that I wanted to curl up in a ball. It was a relief that everyone who solemnly promised to turn-up in the wee hours was predictably too hungover the next day.

———

the snow fetches back
her walk for candles

to pen imagined flowers
through the dark hours

10.II.20

I have *not* walked in some beautiful places. Sometimes I have also been walked for. How does that work?

If a walk has an aim, to see particular tree, collect water from a hill burn, or photograph a distant spring, that can be fulfilled for someone. It isn't walking, but in my work as an artist and poet mapping landscapes I've often shared projects with poets and artists who can go wherever I'm unable to, in what could be termed, *walking for.*

To the everyday walker this may make little sense. What use is a walk without walking? But to a poet, for whom the imagination is a mobile instrument of witness, it's the best second-best thing there is.

of course, I recall
episodes of rage
and the rain of wee fists,

but there were also
hours lolling in
an orchard, a candle

lit for Finnish
Christmas, the time
she tipped into Allt

Slapin to fish out
a chittering lamb
and, best of all, a long

walk she made out
of kindness across an
expanse of moor

that I couldn't reach
muffled up in her
green parka she loved

to tell how she'd forded
her wee legs through
the river to spite

the spate which proves
that in time some
divides cease to exist

During my time with corona, because I can no longer walk or bus to the shops, I've been dependent on food deliveries. The knock on the door opened to find parcels and bags left on the mat remind me of a similar (inter-)dependence that marked my childhood. I grew up in a shepherd's cottage on a country hillside and my family was weird enough not to own a car. We depended on three delivery vans which would each arrive on a day of the week, delivering groceries, fish, bread, rhubarb tarts and sweeties. This country economy had a reciprocal aspect, as I could sell the grocer's van punnets of gooseberries and red and black currants for pocket money, which I'd use to order wargames that would, in turn, arrive in the post van. When it snowed provisions were left in a wooden box at the foot of the track and, Little House on the Prairie style, we would drag a sled down to fetch them.

This is the kind of slow network which we will need to recover in order to reduce climate breakdown. To a needs-must extent, coronavirus renewed community distribution, adding a more urgent task of helping the vulnerable, to the veg boxes, wine and beer boxes, and the panoply of deliveries that help life mosey along. Lockdown has at least meant we're always in. I've appreciated everyone who does the fetching for me.

———

I am sacred I may never walk again, or never recover the half-mile range I had. It's easier for the disabled when constraints are shared in the way lockdown demands. I've half dreaded the day when everyone else returns to their everyday workplaces and my disability shows up, like Ph paper turned violet.

Even though I'm determined to heal, perhaps I will have to rely on those who *walk for* and those who deliver?

Is the end of walking the end of life, or just of a life? Thousands of people are asking themselves the same questions, having been through the hoped-for recoveries and rebuffs that mark post-corona.

A couple of years ago I came up with a *walking for* art project: the *proxy walk*. I haven't realised one yet and, thanks to coronavirus, my role seems to have changed from *walker* to *recipient*.

For any proxy walk, on the same day, for one hour, the receiver remembers a walk in a place they have nominated, and the proxy walker goes there, walks for them, and describes the place as they passed through it. The resulting text is a proxy walk made of two very different memories.

I've since been told of another artist who gifts such walks, for women, and a nurse in a care home who does the same thing for elderly residents. A proxy walk can happen anywhere. Before this spell of not walking I liked to consider the social implications of people placing their walking at another person's disposal, redistributing energy between people in an act of altruistic Romanticism. Now I have to consider it.

All limits create new possibilities. Not every promise can be fulfilled.

———

an optimism
that can allow

that continues
that continues

and can allow
the possibility

of a reason
for pessimism

(after Joan Retallack and John Cage)

VI.2020

Alec Finlay is an artist and poet whose work crosses over a range of media forms. He has published over forty books and won seven Scottish Design Awards, including two Grand Prix Awards. Recent publications include a far-off land *(morning star, 2018),* gathering *(Hauser & Wirth, 2018),* minnmouth *(morning star, 2017) and* A Variety of Cultures *(Jupiter Artland, 2016). He lives in Edinburgh.*

THE CORNICHE CARRIAGE CLOCK:
A SEQUENCE
(for Cyril O'Regan)

John F. Deane

About time.

The grove is long lost, though extant in memory —
prime, majestic

> *breathfilled in breeze and storm*
> > *flushed in off the Atlantic*

I have climbed back up the knobbled bark and branches
to sit high and solitary

> *content, watchful*

like a sated harrier, in a crotch of bark and bole
one with the time, and times, the root and canopy

one with the ragged mat of ochre-dull pine-needles
and the soft moistening of persistent rains

where I am isolate, one with the winds
hidden under the everyday, a barren air-scape

> *sky-wide*

in the delighting scent and stickiness
of dark-gold resin on the hands

> *animal, mineral*

THE SCOTS PINE GROVE

Time past, passed in the Scots Pine grove,
was a listening, child-heart, to the trees, their soft-sift
mysterious whispering

                    with the snow falling
and thickening the air, till you could imagine a measured
hosting of phantoms through the murk, the layers

               of pine-needles on the earth
stiffening in the chill.

                 Where I sat, nested high
and sheltered among the branches, I knew a muddled
melancholy and delight, sensing something of the loneliness

of the soul:
           being already that old man who would be
           holding memory of the child I was,

                 time a mere deception —

as the soft hooting of the owl that will shade the killing
of a lightsome creature, vole or shrew or fieldmouse,

foraging alone among the ravellings below.

IN RETROSPECT

The way round the field of wonder was to creep-crawl

on your knees, splendid in the rhododendron hedge,

through otherworlds of shadowy importance and satisfying

risks; to be amongst the secret creatures, the creepers,

the eye-bright, the burrowers; no mercy sought, you ventured

bravely, everything against you, you – hero, and victor. Pause:

and know the heart thumping, the attar of furze-petals opening,

the squeaky-clean hubbub of the world turning. For one discreet

animating hour, you were not who you had to be, there was only

faithfulness to the project, flesh pricked by thorns, your *geansaí*

an unravelling of threads. Now age has leached the animality

from the field but cleaves still to those days that hold a light

and chequered importance, the dreams that come ahead

of cares, and history from the brightly-coloured storybooks.

TURF

The bank we laboured on was deep, from heather-scraw
down to the blackest waters; it held the histories

of winds and rains, of bog-oak roots, and the slow, slow
passing of the centuries; in its original darkness the peat

guarded a hoard of knowledge, but we worked and pillaged,
moulding turves to warm for a while our western bones,

cherishing the flicker of flames that eased the evenings,
the murmurings of shifting sods and ash that told

of the falling away of time. We found no golden torcs
but have always valued the contorted forms of turf,

like stored memories, like dreams of Ireland. Dusk
we, restful around the hearth, counted our beads, rehearsed

the sacred mysteries, and the great wrongs done to us.

ABOUT TIME

It's a question of time, the irritating ticking of the carriage

clock while you try to focus on "I am" … Still, when you do

shimmy into God's presence, God shimmies into yours;

when you touch on quiet, your name written, you may hear

God's murmuring – although you have not yet quite learned

the language; when you watch a summer sunset turn from

rose to damson, you will know a pianissimo air is being played

on the strings of a cosmic violin, though your ears are not yet

quite attuned to it; you remember those who have flown over

into that music and have learned the Maestro's handling,

you sense their gossiping and gaiety, how they cavort around

you, your heart ringing. For you it's a question of time, the was

of being, the now of presence, the coming-to-be of absence.

AH, BRIGHT WINGS

Today the sky
                    turned a sea-glass green, the sea
was the thrush-egg blue of the sky;

nearby the mountain river played
            a boulder music over the steepest falls;

in a stiff wind
                    the bog-brown water in the lake
flung small storms of butterfly-white froth;

I was wondering if the eels –
            the way pennants flutter in a breeze –
were wiggling their stringy clean-gold bodies

to hold their place in the disturbed disturbing
waters, when an insect, size of a full stop

landed on my page, paused, touched on the word
            "intent", then
(mind of its own, bones, heart, lungs) lifted away

into the air: pilgrim, too, Odysseus
over this bewildering and phenomenal creation.

OF LIGHT AND DARKNESS

I hear now, through the window, the breaking waves
of a high tide; the moon drops a long
shivering track across the sea and all of the bay
lies calm and peaceful;
                                    I cannot sleep, I am gripped
by a time long past, of darkness and light, world,
closed and static, faithful, and *doloroso*;

beyond the city's lights, the spaciousness of cosmos,
beyond and beyond, unfathomable;
there is a gloom encompasses me, root and stalk,
a fear the Christ might well
                                    not be so, not at the core
of this awful process, and that, our fire out,
we will melt like sods of ash back into earth.

———

They were frightening, the sean-bheans, ancient
as Slieve More, and as hacked,
with words of affection only for the animals
as the buckets clattered; once
                                    they gathered in the front room,
grandfather coffined down in the cold parlour;
the sean-fhears too, stubbled dark and watchful,

chewing on the stems of white-clay pipes, swallowing
porter from the bottle and gulping down fists
of whiskey; men on one side, women
on the other, and I, scarce ten years old
                                    tending them. *Lacrimosa*,
the infolded room, bleak light from
high candles and smoky, hesitant oil-lamps.

———

Those days the women called like cries of the hooded crow
from the high reaches; twig-fashioned broom
to sweep boy and goose out of the hen-shitted yard;
and one road-wanderer
                              hoisted her fardel of skirts
and let her Shannon flow freely on the cart road;
those days the men, with talk of weathers and stiffening

bones, with odour of shed and stable, grey stains
on the Sunday suit, were deft with the old brown
kitchen knife to cleave the head
off a cocky hen;
                        old men, old women,
in laceless black boots and grey woollen stockings,
faithful to the Mother of a recalcitrant son Jesus.

—

I cannot sleep; I am penned in; there is darkness
even where there is light; I fear unfaith, its
stone certainties. Time hurries on; it harries us.
There is a cruise-ship, a city en fête,
                           easing itself smoothly out
on the Irish Sea; we have come far, but a life
strains towards light and spaciousness, rest for the soul.

THE ENTANGLED BANK

It soothes me, the high, uneven stone ditch,
greened over with lichens and moss, where a concrete

pillar holds the hinges of the garden gate: beyond —
the garden, potatoes in regimented drills, offering

their wistful blooms. He gathers stones, almost
boulders, and in gaps and cavities, the soil

accumulates, dead leaves and seeds until the wall
is a wildflower wonderment, vetch and bindweed,

shy violet, pimpernel, and curious robins singing
in the trees, vole and fieldmouse secretive in the cracks.

I see myself clambering over, relishing this
Darwin's delighting entangled bank and, within me,

sense of the mystery, its everyday miracle and hallows.
I see him, in soiled vest, braces stretched over muscle

and back, stoop, lift, placing the heavy stones, one by one,
and building. Grandmother calls, they are lovers, the century

turning; it is spring forever, the golden hyacinth is blooming
on the compost heap. The ditch is flawed, letting energy flow,

letting wildness find its lovely way through. Grandfather sees
that it is good. It will do, he says, and I smile, knowing.

THE CARRIAGE CLOCK

Tread softly here; he lies ill; ill-tempered, too;
pray for him, urgently, soft-whispering.
Saturdays, 8 o'clock, the old man lifted the carriage clock
from its place of honour, mantelpiece, centre,

opened the glass door at the back, fitted the brass key,
wound, anti-clockwise, counting aloud,
nine turns; hung the key back, replaced the clock:
all regular, slow march, about turn, stand at east. That

was long ago; time is unforgiving, the mighty fortresses
come tumbling down. Tiny dewdrops
on his yellowing moustache, he lived a little apart, old-style,
Constabulary. Royalist, out of favour. We are not lost,

she will say, the old woman who took her loneliness
to heart; we, she will say, are small people, ordinary
with our small fields and hedgerows, our lives
hidden with Christ in God. And yes, I loved him,

she will say, with his brass buttons, his bicycle clips,
his gruff tenderness. We are forgiven, and we
forgive. At times, she will say, out of her grief,
even Father, Son and Holy Ghost may require forgiveness.

THE BARRACKS

The village, a scatter of poorer houses. "Tóin
an tSean-Bhaile", back-side of the old home-place;

the R.I.C., "royal" though no
king or queen, prince or princess had ever hiked this way;

it was files, blue ink out of an ink-pot, blots on the page;
nothing shattering: cattle loose, lamps on bicycles –

the ocean surf hummed a soothing song on the rare
sunshine days,

               but there was the sweat of damp
on the dark-green walls, turf half-smoking in the grate.

The lighthouse across the bay was comfort in the long
lonesome evenings; stars were whelming in their abundance

and the terrible longevity at their core;
                     to be part of this

however minuscule, was, in itself, magnificence;
to love, be loved, he knew, is worth beyond all, but he

did not have the words, the telling gestures. Irishman –
resented and resenting, he went into exile:

                 London, Birmingham,

came home when the noise died down. History, we know,
corrodes, the way the ocean gnaws at the roots of rock.

GRANDMOTHER

There is a time for war, the Book says and she

was intimate with war, each with its seasons

serving the interests of the small, whimpering gods;

intimate, too, with death, her missal swollen

with cards, sons, daughter, husband, the dead with their

smiling faces, with their dispatches from beyond

where love and violets thrive. When grandfather died

she let the carriage-clock, with her expectations, wind

down, and stop. This, too, is love; oh sleeping Lord,

do you not see, hear, how we hurt? Now, where I write

a winter storm is complaining in the chimney;

I have been gifted the corniche carriage clock, have

wound it up again, inheriting its ticking, its ritual

remembering, the sorrow, the righteousness, the love.

I sit at peace, near the irregular
breathe-in breathe-out of the Irish Sea,
focusing on the difficult task
                                    of prayer;

decades back, I came climbing down
from my green nesting high in the pines,
child-heart unknowing that I was present
                                    with grandfather God

and that Christ-child had been seated by me.
In these my earthbound years I hurt
for the cut daffodils that open their hearts
                                    in a glass jar

on the pantry shelf; hurt for the lambs,
spring in their step, purified
for the Easter seasoning; world, tree
                                    and carriage clock,

all of this, the full heart hopes, is Eucharist;
with all of time and memory,
flesh-bread and blood-wine, matter —
                                    dusk filling

the felled pines, the lingering scent of resin and decay,
animal, mineral, convergent pattern
and impetus of this sanctuary cosmos.

John F. Deane was born in 1943 on Achill Island, Co Mayo. He is the author of two novels and ten collections of poems, most recently Snow Falling on Chestnut Hill: New and Selected Poems *(2012),* Semibreve *(2015) and* Dear Pilgrims, *all from Carcanet Press. He is also the author of a memoir,* Give Dust a Tongue *(Columba, 2015). In 1979, he founded Poetry Ireland, the national poetry organization, and* Poetry Ireland Review. *He divides his time between Dublin and Leitrim.*

DÁNTA

—

Simon Ó Faoláin

DÉITHE SLÉIBHE

(I) Síonáí

Ceal Shíonáí ceart d'ár gcuid féin
Dheineamar scrios ar na cnoic,
— Ag bagairt scaotha caorach romhainn
Ar nós lócaistí —
Chun go mbeadh fásach againn
Oiriúnach d'ár gcomhrá le dia.

Mar, in ainneoin a sciatháin,
Ní idirghabhálaí ár ndiongbhála
Í an chearc fhraoigh
Ná colm na síochána.

Ní sin atá uainn,
Ach dhá intinn — duine agus a dhia —
I lár dísirt mharbh ghlas:
Sin is foirfeacht naofa ann.

(II) Na Beanna

Is ní thugtaí riamh orthu ach sin,
a gcruthanna amuigh ar imeall na spéire
ag guailleáil a chéile
geall is go rabhadar
ag cúntairt tabhairne lá aonaigh.

Na Beanna,
is níor thug aon bhailitheoir
ainm aonair aon bheann acu
leis riamh ón gceantar.

Na Beanna,
mar ní hionainn agus rudaí ollmhóra eile,
ní thógadar riamh aon chéim níos giorra.

(III) Fiach

A bhráthair,
A bhráthair bíobhanta,
Ag beannú dom le glothar
Ar an gcnoc

A bhráthair,
A bhráthair bíobalta,
Réidh chun m'ionathar
A stracadh amach

(IV) Míréir Chognaíoch

Ní haon chabhair
Fianaise na cuimhne
Do ghníomh an chreidimh

An barr,
– Féach air –
Bhíos in airde ansan
san éitear
Ní dhá uair ó shin

Fastaím!
Nó an deamhan aeir
nó gabhar sléibhe
atá ionam?

(V) Oilimpeas

I ndiaidh trombháistí ar ardchlár Bhréanainn,
Agus barr na mbeann fós i gcuibhreann néalta
Foilsítear easa nárbh ann dóibh inné,
Gach líne ingearach eangach ghabhlach
Chomh geal bán beo, leictreach le cumhacht
I gcoinne chúlra na carraige gruama
Le splanc thintrí ón mbinn anuas
Reoite in am, níos fíre ná fírinne:

Tá uamhan im' shící, preab im' chroí,
Agus codladh grifín i ngach géag go barraicín.

LASNAIRDE

Iontas liom fós
gach crann de chrannaibh:

Is mó den spéir
i measc a méaranta
agus is mó ithir
idir a mbarraicíní
ná atá ann de chrann.

Táid chomh daingean
dlúth iontu féin
gur ar éigin go mothaíonn
siad duine

(agus mothaíonn,
trína gcéadfaí
sainiúla crannda féin)

Ach mar a bheadh searradh
a ritheann tríot
nuair a shiúltar
ar fhód do bháis,

Is gur chosúil dóibh
go bhfuilimidne
chomh teibí céanna
le coincheap sleamhan fealsaimh,

Is chomh neamhbhuan
le bearradh an deimhis
ar bharr locha,

Is chomh deacair a shamhlú

Simon Ó Faoláin was born in Dublin and raised in the Corca Dhuibhne Gaeltacht in Co Kerry. He trained as an archaeologist and for many years worked in the academic and commercial spheres, authoring and co-authoring several academic books. Now a full-time Irish-language writer and translator, he has published three books of poetry: Anam Mhadra *(Dog's Soul, 2008),* As Gaineamh *(Out of Sand, 2011), and* Fé Sholas Luaineach *(By Unsteady Light, 2014), all from Coiscéim, as well as an illustrated chapbook,* Baile do Bhí *(A Home that Was, 2014, Púca Press). Amongst the awards for his work are the Glen Dimplex Prize, The Strong Prize, The Walter Macken Prize, The Colm Cille Prize (twice) and The Foras na Gaeilge Prize (four times). His latest two books are translations:* An Corrmhíol *(The Midge, Coiscéim), an Irish translation of the Scottish Gaelic long poem* A' Mheanbhchuileag *by Fearghas Mac Fionnlaigh; and* An Fheadóg Fia *(The Deer Whistle, Southword Imprints), translations from the Chinese poet Jidi Majia. He is Director of An Fhéile Bheag Filíochta, an annual bilingual poetry and arts festival in Baile an Fheirtéaraigh, and Editor of the Irish language literary journal* Aneas. *He is also a noted sean-nós singer with a particular interest in the songs of the great West Kerry singer Seán de hÓra.*

NA CLOCHA IS NA CARRAIGEACHA

Cathal Ó Searcaigh

Do Paddy Bushe.

1

Amanta labhrann siad
go neamhbhalbh
i dTost.

Tigeann siad astu féin
i gcnead
a scoilteann iad.

2

Ná síl go bhfuil siad
ina gcnap chodlata
leis na cianta.

Tá céad spréach na cruinne
á gcoinneáil go síor
ina ndúiseacht.

3

Na clocha greanta seo —
iarmhar na glóire,
fuílleach na caithréime!

Tá buaine iontu
nach raibh riamh sa duine
a dheasaigh iad.

4

Leagaim mo lámha orthu,
á gcuimilt go ceanúil;
a gcuislí ársa,

Is screamh chnámhach
a gcraicinn
ag téamh faoi mo mhéara,

Ag brú dáimhe orthu
I ndúil is go ligfidís
a n-aithne liom

Agus a gcuid Rún.
Ach na clocha stuama seo
fanann siad ciúin,

Cuachta i dtost chianach
nach ngéilleann d'fhocla
ná a gcuid faisnéise.

5

D'fhoinsigh siadsan fosta
as an Bhriathar Spreagtha
a thíolaic is a thiomáineann

Dán glórmhar na Cruinne;
Iadsan na consain chruaidhe
i measc bhog-ghutaí an uisce.

6

Corroíche is an spéir
ag drithliú ina caor thine
os a gcionn.

Tig cumhaidh orthu
ag cuimhneamh ar Ré
phléascach a n-óige.

Is mar a d'fhuaraigh
an mianach iontu
le haois.

7

Ní gá duit gáire
a dhéanamh ná gol.

Níl aon ghleo ionat
le tú a choinneáil

Ó do shuí chlochrighin
ar do mharana bhuan.

Tá tú istigh leat féin
gan súil is gan fuinneog.

Ní gá duit síneadh
as do dhlús féin

Le sásamh a fháil
mar a dhéanann crann,

Mar a dhéanann duine.
Maireann tú go teann

I do mhianach féin.
Ní thiocfaidh sé riamh

De mhian ort athrú
is a mhalairt a shantú.

8

Anseo tá bhur ndúlsáith
agaibh de chiúnas

Le sibh a choinneáil
cothaithe san uaigneas.

9

An domhan teann
ina mbuanaíonn sibh

Níl boige ann ná sní,
níl crith ann ná cuimhní

Ach tá seasmhacht ann
thar acmhainn an duine.

10

Le d'aoibh mharánta
atá chomh snoite le cnámh,

Is fada tú ag feitheamh
leis an bhéic thíoránta

A d'ardódh a bhfuil ionat
ó thalamh is ó thámh.

11

Fuadaíodh tú ón tSliabh
i ré mhórshní
an oighearshrutha

Is caitheadh tú i leataobh
i log na hAbhna
i dtalamh deoranta

Is mhair tú ann i d'aonar
'do chlúdach féin
le crotal is le caonach.

Ach féachann tú go cumhúil
san aird ó thuaidh
ar do chríocha bunaidh

Is crothnaíonn tú go buan
an Mháthaircharraig
as ar foinsíodh thú.

12
Ní bhainfear asat go deo
an cruas seo
atá ionat ó dhúchas

Is ní chuirfear thú
as do dhóchas
go bhfuil tú bithbheo.

Is cé go meilfear go mion
a bhfuil ionat
i muileann na haimsire

Ní chuirfear riamh ar ceal
do chruacht docht —
Sin d'anam geal —

Go fiú agus tú spíonta
i ngraibhéal,
i ngaineamh, i ngráinníní dusta

Beidh an chruacht seo leat
trí shaol na saol
is isteach sa tsíoraíocht.

From his recently published collection, Laoithe Cumainn agus Dánta Eile *(Arlen House, 2020).*

Cathal Ó Searcaigh was born and grew up on a hill farm in Mín a' Leá, Gort an Choirce, an Irish-speaking glen and Gaeltacht community in the northwest of County Donegal. The author of 18 volumes of poetry, three plays and four works of prose, he is a leading figure in the remarkable renaissance of Irish-language writing in our time. A major selection of his poetry from all of his previous collections, Crann na Teanga / The Language Tree, *was published by The Irish Pages Press in 2018. Colm Tóibín has written of his poetry: "There is a section of landscape in Donegal in the North of Ireland near Falcarragh, overlooking Tory Island, which has been utterly transformed over the past decades by the poems written in Irish by Cathal Ó Searcaigh." He is a member of Aosdána, and continues to live on the home ground of his parents.*

MEABHRÚ

—

Eithne Ní Ghallchobhair

Mhúscail sé i mbroinn an dorchadais lár-oíche. Ba theolaigh a leabaidh luí. Chorraigh sé a chorp. Shínigh a cholpacha ar a bhfaid is ar a leithid an uile threo sa leabaidh – na géaga a bhronn neamhspléachas air, na géaga a bhain fómhar. Géaga saothraithe: oibrithe saoil. Mhothaigh sé fuacht feanntach na mbrailíní ag cuimilt a chraicinn de réir mar a shínigh sé cosa agus bosa, de réir mar a bhog sé méara agus ladhra gearrghiota ar shiúl ón áit inar chaith siad an oíche. Tharraing sé anáil úrdhomhain. Isteach fríd a ghaosán, amach fríd a bhéal. Isteach agus Amach. B'shin an cleas a d'fhoghlaim sé chun a bheith istigh ann féin go hiomlán. B'shin an gnás a bhí le cleachtadh aige ag tús agus ag deireadh lae. Isteach agus Amach. Go rithimeach agus go réidh. Cha raibh foscailt súl go fóill ann. Go díreach, cha raibh gá.

Cha raibh gá dó a shúile a fhoscailt óir bhí a fhios aige go beacht cad é bhí ina thimpeall. Thoisigh sé ag éirí go spadánta – a cheann, a mhuineál ag ardú ón cheannadhairt. D'airigh sé a fheadán droma ag beathú agus ag beochan leis an bhogadh, leis an tsíneadh, alt i ndiaidh ailt, siúnta i ndiaidh siúnta, go dtí go raibh sé ina shuí in airde. Chnag speabhraídí an chodlata go trom é ach chaithfeadh sé éirí agus imeacht agus tabhairt faoin bhóthar ar an toirt. D'fhoscail sé a shúile go mall. Cha raibh dadaí fad a radhairc sa dorchadas. Ba chuma leis agus ba róchuma. Óir, cha raibh sé le coimheád amach roimhe a thuilleadh, cha raibh sé le cuimhneamh siar. Scaoilfeadh sé na geasa agus bheadh sé saor. Bheadh sé beo sa bhomaite beatha ar analú, ar aer. Isteach agus Amach. Go rithimeach agus go réidh.

Chíor sé barrmhéara a chliotóige isteach fríd a fholt fhada fhionn agus bhain searradh amach as a cheann. Chuimil bos dá shúile, dá mhalaí. Analú úrdhomhain. D'fhan sé. D'fhan sé ansin go socair. D'fhan sé sa tsocracht go ciúin – gan corr ná carr as, gan gíog ná míog as … go dtí go raibh sé réidh. Agus nuair a bhí … an uair sin amháin … d'éirigh de bhocléim amach as an leabaidh chlúimh, chaith a dhá chois faoi ar an talamh fhuar, chaith air a cheirteach gan cás, gan cúram, chaith air a chulaith chatha, chaith air a chuid airm, chaith mála canbhais ar a leath-ghualainn. Thóg sé a sheoltaí beaga bucóideacha bacóideacha agus thug sé aghaidh le ceo. Tharraing sé doras donn, meirgeach an veain ina dhiaidh go garbh agus ar shiúl leis de shiúl, de phreab, de léim. Ar shiúl leis go bríoch, ar shiúl leis go briosc. Ar shiúl leis go costarnocht, go ceanntarnocht. Ar shiúl leis amach ar na cuibhrinn fhéarmhara i modar-dhoircheacht na moch-mhaidine. Bhí gríosach glan, beo faoi bhonnaí a chos, gan barr cleite isteach ná bun cleite amach. Thóg sé an drúcht dubh, draíochta le achan choiscéim choirpúil a ghlac sé. Thug míle is fiche de thuras aigne agus intinne i gceiliúradh gaoithe is gealaí. Agus mhothaigh sé an drúcht — an drúcht dubh, draíochta, an drúcht fionnfhuar, fliuch — ag smeadráil suas síos ar bhonnaí agus ar shála fuadracha a chos. Bhí eanglach ar a ladhra. Eanglach. Ach mhothaigh sé iad, d'airigh sé iad. Na crúba a tugadh dó chun siúil, na spága a bronnadh air chun turais. Lean sé leis den tsiúl. A chorróga ag luascadh, a ghlúine ag lúbadh, a mhurnáin ag bogadh, a ladhra ag cromadh. Gan rith, gan rás, gan róscaoil shiúil sé leis ag baint an drúchta — an drúcht dubh, draíochta — faoi chiúnas chalma sa cheo. Bhí an talamh faoi chosa s'aige cnapánach, bhí sé clochach, cortha, cam ach bhuail sé an bóthar go dícheallach, bhuail sé an bóthar le dúthracht.

Bhog sé leis, d'éist sé, d'amharc sé agus rinne boladh an aeir. Ar thóir tuigbheála feirmeora ar thalamh a bhí sé, ar lorg tuigbheála iascaire ar abhainn. Thiocfadh a leas agus a láidriú ón talamh. Thiocfadh a neart agus a athnuachan ón domhan. Thóg sé an drúcht dubh, draíochta agus é ar a shála thar mhullaí maola, thar dhíoga doimhne, thar bhóithre briste, thar aibhneacha aimpléiseacha. Thug pocléim thar an tsraith loinge a shlogfadh go hioscaid go héasca é. Chrúbaigh faoi gheata iarainn a bhí ró-mheirgeach le dul in airde air. Bheannaigh sé don tobar. D'umhlaigh sé don bhallóg. Bhí fuinneamh agus fuadar faoi. Isteach agus Amach. Faoi ghaisteacht agus faoi gheasa a bhí sé, faoi theas agus trí thine. Ón chréafóg, ó na haibhneacha a fáisceadh é. Óch, thóg sé an drúcht dubh, draíochta agus shiúil sé, shiúil sé, shiúil.

Stracháil sé fríd an raithneach, tharraing sé fríd an fhraoch. Cos luath, cos tapaidh. Ní dhearna sé stad ná mórchónaí gur fhág sé an breac-fhiántas scáfar ina dhiaidh, gur tháinig boladh lusa agus luibhe chuige ar eiteog aoibhinn gaoithe. Isteach. Amach. Stad sé ansin. Isteach fríd an ghaosán. Amach fríd an bhéal. Stad sé agus smaoitigh sé. Agus, nuair a bhí sé réidh … an uair sin amháin … thug rúid reatha chun coille craobhaigh. Isteach leis sa choill crann critheach. Isteach leis, isteach, isteach … istigh.

Shiúil sé leis fríd an choill fá choiscéim stráiciúil, shollúnta. Aiteann is eidhneán fite fuaite fríd a chéile, cuileann is coll taobh le taobh ina gclann. Géaga agus gasanna, cipíní agus cifleogaí ina gcnapanna, ina gcarnáin ag criongán leo go beo. Duilleoga móra, duilleoga beaga ina luí ar an talamh ag feo, iad fliuch, iad fuar, iad fuinniúil ar chraiceann chréachtach cos. Agus mhothaigh sé na duilleoga. D'aithin sé an fliuchadh agus an fuacht mar fhilíocht. Bhí an bealach a ghlac sé go n-uige seo go mí-chothrom, corrach. Isteach fríd an ghaosán. Amach fríd an bhéal. Isteach agus Amach.

Stad sé den tsiúl in athuair agus chuir sé cluas le héisteacht. Mhothaigh sé éanacha ag múscailt sna crainn os a chionn. D'airigh sé péisteanna ar seachrán go híseal ag bun. Chuala sé dordán fonnmhar, fórsach na mbeach agus iad ag crónán go glóir-réimeach, go glan-ghuthach, glinn le tréan urrúntachta agus misnigh. Sheol siad leo go sócúlach ó bhláth go bláth. Sheol siad leo go mánla deiseal agus treiseal. Sheol siad i mbun ceoil, i mbun cainte, i mbun cuideachta. Callán íseal, obair uasal i mbolg-láthair an imshaothair. Chuala sé na sciatháin leathair agus iad ar scaoil de rúid dheireanach a n-oíche, iad ag scoilteadh, ag scaipeadh, ag stróiceadh an aeir go haigeanta, aerach, suairc. Sciurd siad leo go dúdheifreach fríd na bunghéaga brioscarnacha, iad ag cogarnaigh leofa go fann, iad go fiafraitheach ar eiteog.

Bhog damhán alla leis go croíúil ar chraobh lena thaobh. Bhí sé caol agus cúng, ligthe agus lúfar. Lucharán dubh na n-ocht gcos ag iomramh leis ar a sheandícheall. Ar crochadh ar chraobh a bhí sé, ar an uaigneas dá leoínte féin. Ba bheag a shuimse a bheith i lúb na cuideachta. Stiúrfadh sé a churach féin gan treibh, gan teach, gan taoide. Bhí a aird dírithe ar an tsníomhadh, ar an chíoradh, ar an chriathrú. Muna raibh méid ná meáchan ann bhí luascadh coirp agus líofacht ann. Choinnigh sé leis go cothrom, go cúramach, go comair, go ciúin. Thiocfadh sé ar chuileog roimh am a choda – b'shin a chúis, a rún. Bheadh a leor-dhóthain bídh faoin am sin aige. Foighde an fhíodóra. Cogadh coganta na ndúl.

Chuala sé siosarnach lán-bhríoch na gcrann le achan fheothan agus le achan leath-leoithne gaoithe a bhuail iad. Chuala sé síor-chreathadach na nduilleog. Barr na gcrann ag lúbadh agus ag cúbadh leis an ghaoth, bun na gcrann ag bog-chorraí faoi fhoscadh, faoi dhídean na sinsear. Chuala sé a anáil féin agus a chosa i dtaca abair agus duilleog. Isteach agus Amach. Go rithimeach. Go réidh. Bhog sé a ladhra aniar agus siar, anonn agus anall. Mhothaigh sé an fás, an flosc, an fuinneamh sa talamh. Shúigh sé isteach é. Bhí sé ina bheatha, ina mhórshláinte. Bhrúigh sé amach é. Bhí sé faoi fhaoiseamh, faoi shó. D'airigh sé drúcht na maidine … Óch! an drúcht dubh, draíochta. Biseach agus borradh, áilleacht agus aoibhneas. Bhí ceann agus colainn ag cneasú i mbreacsholas thús lae. Agus, nuair a bhí sé réidh … an uair sin amháin …

Shiúil sé go costarnocht, go ceanntarnocht, ceann s'aige crom go talamh. Bhí croí na coille ag éirí ní ba challánaí agus bhog sé go héasca faoi scáth.

Mhothaigh sé na héanacha ag ceol go híseal ar ghéag, cuid acu ag foluain, cuid acu ag bíogarnach – na mochóirí meidhreacha, meanmnacha. Cheol siad leo gan stad, gan snagaireacht agus iad i lúb an chruinnithe. Cheol siad leo go maorga, go maisiúil agus iad i gcrúb an chomhluadair. Bhí scréach na coirre glaise ann, bhí grágaíl na bpréachán; an spideog, an riabhóg, an ghlasóg, an bhuíóg, an rí rua. Bhí lonradh ag teacht ar shaol na coille le grágarnach agus gocarsach éan. Brille breaille breacadh lae. Éanacha Earraigh ag úrthús a ré. Mhothaigh sé feothan éadrom gaoithe ag séideadh ina araicis, ag feadaíl ina chluasa, ag cuimilt a chraicinn. Tháinig blaiseadh d'aer thais an Earraigh ar a bheola. Sháigh sé amach a theanga thirim agus ligh sé iad go fonnmhar. Thóg sé a cheann. Bhí gathanna ioldathacha ar a ndícheall ag iarraidh síneadh, briseadh, pléascadh isteach fríd bharr na gcrann agus a ngéaganna bairr. Stad sé faoi thom agus smaointigh sé. Isteach agus Amach. Agus nuair a bhí sé réidh ... an uair sin amháin ... lean sé leis ag bóithreoireacht agus shiúil sé, shiúil sé, shiúil.

Chuir sé cluas le héisteacht. Chuala sé ceolaire casarnaí ag cantaireacht go glinn. Ba mhaith an t-ainm aige é mar éan – é i bhfolach san fhothair agus sa fhraoch. Ag ceol leis de réir mar a bhog sé. Ag cantaireacht leis de réir mar a shocraigh sé. Bhí áiméar aige a bheith i bhfolach i dtiúchan agus i ndoimhneas coille. Ba mhór leis an dorchadas agus faoi cheilt a chaithfeadh sé a shaol. Cúthail gan a bheith ar bhealach ar bith ciúin -boc beag, bríomhar, breabhsánta. Duanaire donn a bhí ann, a bhí i ndiaidh a theacht ar eiteog ón Afraic. Chnag tallann é tabhairt chun turais. Líon fonn é tabhairt faoin spéir. Stad sé agus smaointigh sé. Isteach agus Amach. Go rithimeach. Go réidh. Char thug an ceolaire casarnaí seo aitheantas do thír ná do theorainn. Thóg sé a chuid seoltaí gan chosaint, gan chosnamh. Cha raibh ábhar rí ná ábhar banríona a chuirfeadh bac ná buairt airsean a bheith dílís dá phór, dá fhuil. Bí ag caint ar chrógacht, ar ghaisciúlacht. Scuir a cheol fríd an cheo mar cheiliúradh ard, ealaíonta. Isteach agus Amach. Agus nuair a bhí sé réidh ... an uair sin amháin ...

Chuir sé cluas le héisteacht. Chuala sé ceol an tuirne lín ag ardú agus ag ísliú le brí. Las an port mall, tomhaiste anam an tsiúlóire, óch! las sé a chroí. Óir, shíl sé nach gcluinfeadh sé go deo é – an t-éinín seo a bhí ag meath agus ag gannú, an t-éinín seo a bhí ag imeacht ó chlár-imeall an domhain. An t-éinín mear-shiúlach a raibh an t-an-iontas agus an t-an-áilleacht ina cheithre cnámha go smior. Bheannaigh an siúltóir don éan. Bheannaigh sé dá chlann. Mhol sé é. Cheol sé é. Binn-cheol, barr-cheol, caoin-cheol, sár-cheol. Ceol an ómóis. Feadaíl na fáilte.

D'eitil na leamhain, na féileacáin oíche go síoraí seasta thart timpeall air. Bhí gile agus gleoiteacht iontu an tráth sin de mhaidin. Ba bheag a bhfaitíos agus ba ghairid a bhfeitheamh. Ach, bhí fad a théide ag an tsiúltóir – ní raibh tráth suí ná seasaimh ann. Agus, nuair a bhí sé réidh … an uair sin amháin …

D'fhág sé an choill ina dhiaidh. Bhog sé leis gan foscadh toir ná toim, sheol sé leis gan dídean sean-chrainn ná crainn úir. Chonaic sé sruthán cúrach ag caismirneach agus ag lúbadh go lonrach le fána leitreach, an t-uisce glioscarnach á stealladh féin in aghaidh na gcarraigeacha ar achan bhruach. Stad síos ar imeall uisce sruthlaithe. Stad suas faoi mhoch-theas éirí gréine.

Rith cat fiáin breac-liath trasna a chosáin, a ghnúis dhorcha go dú-dhorránach, dú-néaltach. Cat feargach, fíochmhar, fad-fhiaclach. Cat chomh giobach le fraoch, dreach na hainise agus an tsíor-ocrais ar a aghaidh fhada, fhiata.

"*Cé tusa atá ag tógáil callóide ag an am mhí-oiriúnach seo?*
Cé tusa atá ag tógáil achrainn le fainne geal an lae?"

Créatúr cnámhach, creatlach ag cuartú cuireadh chun catha. Chonaic an siúltóir na súile srámacha ag stánadh ar ais air gan niachas, gan náire. Ba iomaí scéal beatha agus báis a luigh faoi cheilt ar chúl an dá shúil sin. Bhreathnaigh an créatúr roimhe, ar a dheis agus ar a chlí. Bhí sé ar caor thine, ar buille, ar mire, ar mire ar fad. Cat coille colgach, cat caithréimeach, cam, claon. Níor fhan sé ach an géar-bhomaite féin. Níor fhan, ach d'imigh de rúid go dearg-dheifreach, go te, tógtha ag déanamh talaimh mhéith de na túrtógaí. *Is maith le achan chat iasc ach ní maith leis a chrúb a fhliuchadh.*

Agus nuair a bhí seisean réidh … an uair sin amháin … dálta an chait, ar shiúl leis sna bonnaí rí-rua reatha, aghaidh le grian, cúl le gaoth.

Chuir solas na gréine fad lena radharc agus d'amharc sé i bhfad uaidh amach i dtreo na sléibhte. Na sléibhte a bheathaigh caoirigh agus carria, a chothaigh éanacha na gcnoc. Na sléibhte a thug foscadh agus dídean d'achan neach bheo. Na sléibhte a thug cead a gcinn do shiúltóirí dul in airde ar dhroimeanna agus ar ghuaillí s'acu. Na sléibhte a lig don chaonach fás orthu. Na sléibhte a leasaigh luibheanna. Sléibhte arbh iad a tharraing lucht lorg faoisimh agus fiántais. Sléibhte arbh iad a tharraing lucht lorg mianraí agus óir.

Is óch, is óch, a shléibhte mo chroí, go dtabhartar slán sibh in éadan na sainte.
Is óch, is óch, a shléibhte mo chroí, go bhfágtar sibh i mbarr bhur sláinte.

Chonaic sé i bhfad uaidh cosáin chúnga na gcaorach ag síneadh aniar agus siar. Chonaic sé i bhfad uaidh ciorcail agus cearnógaí de choillte scaipthe thall is abhus, gan a bheith ard, gan a bheith íseal, ach iad ina seasamh ansin, préamhaithe go mórtasach ar achan chearn den tír. Chonaic sé na ballaí buana cloiche deartha agus tógtha ag fir agus ag mná na nglúnta siar ag leagan teorainneacha dochta, beachta amach dá dteaghlaigh – deartháir le taobh dearthár ar thalamh aon bhó. Lean sé mullach na gcnoc lena shúile chomh fada agus a thiocfadh leis. Sléibhte Iarthar Éireann. Portaigh agus boglaigh. Isteach agus Amach. Go rithimeach. Go réidh.

Chrom agus chuimil a lámha ar an drúcht dubh, draíochta agus tharraing barr-mhéara a chiotóige fríd a fholt fhada fhionn. Chuimil sé a bhos dá shúile, dá mhalaí. D'airigh sé an mhúscailt ann féin. Mhothaigh sé an beocht. Thug sé faoi deara go raibh an ghrian ag éirí go hard anois, ag taitneamh go soilseach anuas air agus spéartha an lae ag nochtadh. Thug sé fá deara na deora drúchta aonaracha ar an fhéar, na ribí ag lonradh, ag soilsiú leofa go geal, ríméadach. Thrampáil agus bhratráil agus phreab sé a chosa ar an drúcht dubh, draíochta. Na bonnaí, na sála, na ladhra. Bhí sé beo agus beathach ar a thuras lae. Bhí sé sin agus é go hiomlán ar strae. Stad sé. Stad suas síos. Stad den bhogadh agus sheas amuigh ar an uaigneas go tostach. Bhain sé blaiseadh as úr as aer thais an Earraigh. Isteach. Amach. Go rithimeach. Agus nuair a bhí sé réidh … Shiúil sé leis go fuinniúil, go fiosrach, fiafraitheach – eireaball go hiomlán in airde.

Shiúil sé go dtáinig sé fhad le stollaire de charraig dhonn-liath a bhí ag gobadh amach as cuibhreann fhéarmhar. Shuigh sé ar a ghogaidí go buacach. Bhí a sprioc bainte amach aige le scaradh oíche agus lae. Ba léir dó iomlán gealaí na hoíche aréir ar crochadh idir na scamaill. Ba léir na cosa faoin ghréin ag síneadh anuas agus isteach ar gcúl na gcnoc. Óch! Isteach fríd an ghaosán. Óch! Amach fríd an bhéal. Dhírigh sé ar na dathanna a bhí ag briseadh amach os a chomhair. Óch! Isteach fríd an ghaosán agus amach fríd an bhéal. Dathanna spéire nár nochtaigh riamh, in aon am, ach amháin le barr-thús maidine agus le bun-deireadh lae. Scáthanna órbhuí, cróndearga, gealchorcra, glasa, ag fás amach as achan ghéag go míorúilteach, go diaga. Isteach agus Amach. Dhírigh sé ar chuiteoga, ar mhíoltóga agus iad ag eitilt go ró-chóngarach, go ró-lonrach dá shúile. Isteach agus Amach. Saoirse. Saoirse. Saoirse aigne agus alt. Dhruid sé a shúile agus rinne sé a cheiliúradh féin. Isteach fríd an ghaosán. Amach fríd an bhéal. Bhí cóngaracht talúna aige, bhí fad-radharc súl aige, bhí glinn-chluas éisteachta aige, béal le foscailt agus le druidim aige. Isteach agus Amach. Chuala sé glug glag giodamach guagach – fuaim sruthháin le fána. Chuala sé monabar, bonamar agus dordán thart ar a cheann. Chuala gaoth éadrom

Earraigh. Isteach agus Amach. Chuala ciúnas. Go rithimeach, réidh. D'fhoscail sé a shúile agus d'amharc sé in athuair. Na maolchnoic rua amach roimhe, na mór-chnoic fhéarmhara, ghlasa. Na gleannta rite, na beanna bearnacha. Bhí siad sin uilig ann, bhí sin agus tuilleadh.

Scaip na scamaill ag síobadh leofa ar shiúl agus shuigh sé leis go socair ar an uaigneas. D'airigh sé smior ina chuid cnámh, fuinneamh ina chuid feola agus fola. Colainn faoi scíste, intinn faoi shuaimhneas. Shuigh sé i sámhnéal i moch-sholas Earraigh. Shuigh sé go sochma faoi mheadaracht gréine is gealaí. D'éist sé leis na mínte, d'éist sé leis na móinte, d'éist sé leis an mhéid a bhí le ráit acu – agus bhí neart le ráit acu, mar a bhíonn, mar a bhí, mar a bheas go deo. D'éist sé leis an cheo a bhí ag éirí, leis na scamaill a bhí ag bogadaí leofa de dhearg-rúid trasna na spéire. D'éist sé leis na cnoic. D'éist sé leis an charraig faoi. Bhí an ubh agus an t-éan aige, bhí an craiceann agus a luach aige – an toirtín mór agus an bheannacht.

A story-teller – who learnt who her craft from the last living traditional story-tellers in Donegal – Eithne Ní Ghallchobhair works for The Royal Irish Academy *on the* Foclóir Stairiúil na Gaeilge. *She lives in Ardara, Co Donegal.*

DHÁ DÁNTA

Róisín Sheehy

CÚIRT Ó BHEAN DEN LUCHT SIÚIL
Do Nóra Ó Rielly

Nuair a thagann Nóra
Tugann sí leithi mianach tincéire
Tinte cnámh, míle beannacht
Nuair a thagann Nóra
Tugaim di mo shean bhalcaisí
'san seainseáil deireanach i mo phóca
Nuair a thagann Nóra
Tugann sí leithi bainne na ngamhna, uibhe seabhaic
a chneasódh mo chraiceann ataithe
Nuair a thagann Nóra
Bíonn na gardaí ar dalladh í a stopadh
Goideann bean i motor glas a mála
Nuair a thagann Nóra
Tuigim go maith gur tháinig
 mise ón lucht siúil
Nuair a thagann Nóra
Téim ag snámh leis na capaill
i Loch Bhaile Uí Scanláin
's in Abhainn na Siúire
Nuair a thagann
Nuair a thagann
Nuair a thagann Nóra

Tuigim go ró mhaith
gur tháinig mise ó
phréamh an ghrá

A VISIT FROM A TRAVELER WOMAN
For Nóra Ó Rielly

When Nóra calls
she brings with her
a thousand blessings, bonfire nights
When Nóra calls
I give her my old clothes
the last change in my pocket
When Nóra calls
she carries goat's milk, hawk eggs
to heal my swollen skin
When Nóra calls
the guards are mad to stop her
a woman in a green car steals her bag
When Nóra calls
I know that I come
from the travelers
When Nóra calls
I go bathing with the horses
at Ballyscanlan Lake, the River Suir
When Nóra
when Nóra
when Nóra calls …

I know for sure
I was birthed
into love

MURÚCHA AN OIRTHIR

Le hais na haille scriobhas dán
Inar chaith Áine í féin le h-aill,
In ainneoin a h-iarrachta damanta
tháinig Gearóid uirthi
's thug i dtír í
ar Thráig na mBó.

D'fhágas mo dhán faoin gcarraig
's d'imigh liom i gcaitheamh mo shaoil,
Roimh deireadh an tSamhraidh
bhí sé ina scéal mór
gur chaith Áine í féin le h-aill
ach tháinig Gearóid uirthi
's thug i dtír í ar Thráig na mBó.

Chuimhníos láithreach ar mo dhán
's ritheas i dtreo na carriage
an áit inar leagas é.
Cé bheadh rogham ach Áine,
Í caochta ag an ghaoth
a bhí ag séadadh
a gruaig finne catach;
"A Áine bhfuileann tú chomh mór
I bpoll an bhróin
Go gcaithfeá tú féin le h-aill?"

"Táim sochair ar an dtalamh seo
ar feadh tamaill eile
ach nuair a bhíonn sé
ina bharra taoide,
níl aon leigheas agam ar"

Sar a bhí deireadh ráite
tháinig Gearóid an slí
mo dhán ina ghlaic;
"Is tusa atá thíos leis seo",
Shín sé chugam mo dhán;
"Féach m'ainmse 's ainm Áine
Strac suas é, strac suas é".

Dheineas smidiriní de mo dhán
ach thuigeas nach raibh
aon mhaitheas ann,
Nuair a bhí sé ina ré lán
chaith Áine í féin le h-aill,
Léim Gearóid isteach ina diaidh
's thug i dtír í ar Thráig na mBó.

Theanntaigh sé a lámh
timpeal uirthi
's phóg a craiceann ataithe,
Le teas 's meachan na colaíochta
d'iompaigh an lanúin ina mhurúcha
's d'imigh leo leis an taoide
sar a bhíomarna
caochta ag an gceo.

Róisín Sheehy writes poetry and plays. Her work has appeared in Poetry Ireland Review, Comhar, *and* Strokestown Poetry Anthology 2019, *and been broadcast on RTÉ Radio 1 and Raidió na Gaeltachta.* Snámh na Saoirse, *her debut play, was awarded a Stewart Parker Trust Award. She lives in Waterford*

THE FREEDOM OF THE PRESS
(1943?)

———

George Orwell

By the known rules of ancient liberty …
Unless, of course, we speak of "trousers".

GEORGE ORWELL'S PROPOSED PREFACE TO *ANIMAL FARM*

This book was first thought of, so far as the central idea goes, in 1937, but was not written down until about the end of 1943. By the time when it came to be written it was obvious that there would be great difficulty in getting it published (in spite of the present book shortage which ensures that anything describable as a book will "sell"), and in the event it was refused by four publishers. Only one of these had any ideological motive. Two had been publishing anti-Russian books for years, and the other had no noticeable political colour. One publisher actually started by accepting the book, but after making the preliminary arrangements he decided to consult the Ministry of Information, who appear to have warned him, or at any rate strongly advised him, against publishing it. Here is an extract from his letter:

> I mentioned the reaction I had had from an important official in the Ministry of Information with regard to *Animal Farm*. I must confess that this expression of opinion has given me seriously to think … I can see now that it might be regarded as something which it was highly ill-advised to publish at the present time. If the fable were addressed generally to dictators and dictatorships at large then publication would be all right, but the fable does follow, as I see now, so completely the progress of the Russian Soviets and their two dictators, that it can apply only to Russia, to the exclusion of the other dictatorships. Another thing: it would be less offensive if the predominant caste in the fable were not pigs (see *Author's Note* below). I think the choice of pigs as the ruling caste will no doubt give offence to many people, and particularly to anyone who is a bit touchy, as undoubtedly the Russians are.

This kind of thing is not a good symptom. Obviously it is not desirable that a government department should have any power of censorship (except security censorship, which no one objects to in war time) over books which are not officially sponsored. But the chief danger to freedom of thought and speech at this moment is not the direct interference of the MOI or any official body. If publishers and editors exert themselves to keep certain topics out of print, it is not because they are frightened of prosecution but because they are frightened of public opinion. In this country intellectual cowardice is the worst enemy a writer or journalist has to face, and that fact does not seem to me to have had the discussion it deserves.

Any fair-minded person with journalistic experience will admit that during this war official censorship has not been particularly irksome. We have not been subjected to the kind of totalitarian "co-ordination" that it might have been reasonable to expect. The press has some justified grievances, but on the whole the Government has behaved well and has been surprisingly tolerant of minority opinions. The sinister fact about literary censorship in England is that it is largely voluntary.

Unpopular ideas can be silenced, and inconvenient facts kept dark, without the need for any official ban. Anyone who has lived long in a foreign country will know of instances of sensational items of news – things which on their own merits would get the big headlines – being kept right out of the British press, not because the Government intervened but because of a general tacit agreement that "it wouldn't do" to mention that particular fact. So far as the daily newspapers go, this is easy to understand. The British press is extremely centralised, and most of it is owned by wealthy men who have every motive to be dishonest on certain important topics. But the same kind of veiled censorship also operates in books and periodicals, as well as in plays, films and radio. At any given moment there is an orthodoxy, a body of ideas which it is assumed that all right-thinking people will accept without question. It is not exactly forbidden to say this, that or the other, but it is "not done" to say it, just as in mid-Victorian times it was "not done" to mention trousers in the presence of a lady. Anyone who challenges the prevailing orthodoxy finds himself silenced with surprising effectiveness. A genuinely unfashionable opinion is almost never given a fair hearing, either in the popular press or in the highbrow periodicals.

At this moment what is demanded by the prevailing orthodoxy is an uncritical admiration of Soviet Russia. Everyone knows this, nearly everyone acts on it. Any serious criticism of the Soviet régime, any disclosure of facts which the Soviet government would prefer to keep hidden, is next door to unprintable. And this nation-wide conspiracy to flatter our ally takes place, curiously enough, against a background of genuine intellectual tolerance. For though you are not allowed to criticise the Soviet government, at least you are reasonably free to criticise our own. Hardly anyone will print an attack on Stalin, but it is quite safe to attack Churchill, at any rate in books and periodicals. And throughout five years of war, during two or three of which we were fighting for national survival, countless books, pamphlets and articles advocating a compromise peace have been published without interference. More, they have been published without exciting much disapproval. So long as the prestige of the USSR is not involved, the principle of free speech has been reasonably well upheld. There are other forbidden topics, and I shall mention some of them presently, but the prevailing attitude towards the USSR is much the most serious symptom. It is, as it were, spontaneous, and is not due to the action of any pressure group.

The servility with which the greater part of the English intelligentsia have swallowed and repeated Russian propaganda from 1941 onwards would be quite astounding if it were not that they have behaved similarly on several earlier occasions. On one controversial issue after another the Russian viewpoint has been accepted without examination and then publicised with complete disregard to historical truth or intellectual decency. To name only one instance, the BBC celebrated the twenty-fifth anniversary of the Red Army without mentioning Trotsky. This was about as accurate as commemorating the battle of Trafalgar without mentioning Nelson, but it evoked no protest from the English intelligentsia. In the internal struggles in the various occupied countries, the British press has in almost all cases sided with the faction favoured by the Russians and libelled the opposing faction, sometimes suppressing material evidence in order to do so. A particularly glaring case was that of Colonel Mihailovich, the Jugoslav Chetnik leader. The Russians, who had their own Jugoslav protege in Marshal Tito, accused Mihailovich of collaborating with the Germans. This accusation was promptly taken up by the British press: Mihailovich's supporters were given no chance of answering it, and facts contradicting it were simply kept out of print. In July of 1943 the Germans offered a reward of 100,000 gold crowns for the capture of Tito, and a similar reward for the capture of Mihailovich. The British press "splashed" the reward for Tito, but only one paper mentioned (in small print) the reward for Mihailovich: and the charges of collaborating with the Germans continued. Very similar things happened during the Spanish civil war. Then, too, the factions on the Republican side which the Russians were determined to crush were recklessly libelled in the English leftwing press, and any statement in their defence even in letter form, was refused publication. At present, not only is serious criticism of the USSR considered reprehensible, but even the fact of the existence of such criticism is kept secret in some cases. For example, shortly before his death Trotsky had written a biography of Stalin. One may assume that it was not an altogether unbiased book, but obviously it was saleable. An American publisher had arranged to issue it and the book was in print – I believe the review copies had been sent out – when the USSR entered the war. The book was immediately withdrawn. Not a word about this has ever appeared in the British press, though clearly the existence of such a book, and its suppression, was a news item worth a few paragraphs.

It is important to distinguish between the kind of censorship that the English literary intelligentsia voluntarily impose upon themselves, and the censorship that can sometimes be enforced by pressure groups. Notoriously, certain topics cannot be discussed because of "vested interests". The best-known case is the patent medicine racket. Again, the Catholic Church has considerable influence in the press and can silence criticism of itself to some extent. A scandal involving a Catholic priest is almost never given publicity, whereas an Anglican priest who gets into trouble (e.g. the Rector of Stiffkey) is headline news. It is very rare for anything of an anti-Catholic tendency to appear on the stage or in a film. Any actor can tell you that a play or film which attacks or makes fun of the Catholic Church is liable to be boycotted in the press and will probably be a failure. But this kind of thing is harmless, or at least it is understandable. Any large organisation will look after its own interests as best it can, and overt propaganda is not a thing to object to. One would no more expect *The Daily Worker* to publicise unfavourable facts about the USSR than one would expect *The Catholic Herald* to denounce the Pope. But then every thinking person knows *The Daily Worker* and *The Catholic Herald* for what they are. What is disquieting is that where the USSR and its policies are concerned one cannot expect intelligent criticism or even, in many cases, plain honesty from Liberal writers and journalists who are under no direct pressure to falsify their opinions. Stalin is sacrosanct and certain aspects of his policy must not be seriously discussed. This rule has been almost universally observed since 1941, but it had operated, to a greater extent than is sometimes realised, for ten years earlier than that. Throughout that time, criticism of the Soviet régime from the left could only obtain a hearing with difficulty. There was a huge output of anti-Russian literature, but nearly all of it was from the Conservative angle and manifestly dishonest, out of date and actuated by sordid motives. On the other side there was an equally huge and almost equally dishonest stream of pro-Russian propaganda, and what amounted to a boycott on anyone who tried to discuss all-important questions in a grown-up manner. You could, indeed, publish anti-Russian books, but to do so was to make sure of being ignored or misrepresented by nearly the whole of the highbrow press. Both publicly and privately you were warned that it was "not done". What you said might possibly be true, but it was "inopportune" and played into the hands of this or that reactionary interest. This attitude was usually defended on the ground that the international situation, and the urgent need for an Anglo-Russian alliance, demanded it; but it was clear that this was a rationalisation. The English intelligentsia, or a great part of it, had developed a nationalistic loyalty towards me USSR, and in their hearts they felt that to cast any doubt on the wisdom of Stalin was a kind of blasphemy. Events in Russia and events elsewhere were to be judged by different standards. The endless executions in the purges of 1936-8 were applauded by life-long opponents of capital punishment, and it was considered equally proper to publicise famines when they happened in India and to conceal them when they happened in the Ukraine. And if this was true before the war, the intellectual atmosphere is certainly no better now.

But now to come back to this book of mine. The reaction towards it of most English intellectuals will be quite simple: "It oughtn't to have been published". Naturally, those reviewers who understand the art of denigration will not attack it on political grounds but on literary ones. They will say that it is a dull, silly book and a disgraceful waste of paper. This may well be true, but it is obviously not the whole of the story. One does not say that a book "ought not to have been published" merely because it is a bad book. After all, acres of rubbish are printed daily and no one bothers. The English intelligentsia, or most of them, will object to this book because it traduces their Leader and (as they see it) does harm to the cause of progress. If it did the opposite they would have nothing to say against it, even if its literary faults were ten times as glaring as they are. The success of, for instance, the Left Book Club over a period of four or five years shows how willing they are to tolerate both scurrility and slipshod writing, provided that it tells them what they want to hear.

The issue involved here is quite a simple one: Is every opinion, however unpopular – however foolish, even – entitled to a hearing? Put it in that form and nearly any English intellectual will feel that he ought to say "Yes". But give it a concrete shape, and ask, "How about an attack on Stalin? Is that entitled to a hearing?", and the answer more often than not will be "No". In that case the current orthodoxy happens to be challenged, and so the principle of free speech lapses. Now, when one demands liberty of speech and of the press, one is not demanding absolute liberty. There always must be, or at any rate there always will be, some degree of censorship, so long as organised societies endure. But freedom, as Rosa Luxembourg [sic] said, is "freedom for the other fellow". The same principle is contained in the famous words of Voltaire: "I detest what you say; I will defend to the death your right to say it". If the intellectual liberty which without a doubt has been one of the distinguishing marks of western civilisation means anything at all, it means that everyone shall have the right to say and to print what he believes to be the truth, provided only that it does not harm the rest of the community in some quite unmistakable way. Both capitalist democracy and the western versions of Socialism have till recently taken that principle for granted. Our Government, as I have already pointed out, still makes some show of respecting it. The ordinary people in the street – partly, perhaps, because they are not sufficiently interested in ideas to be intolerant about them – still vaguely hold that "I suppose everyone's got a right to their own opinion". It is only, or at any rate it is chiefly, the literary and scientific intelligentsia, the very people who ought to be the guardians of liberty, who are beginning to despise it, in theory as well as in practice.

One of the peculiar phenomena of our time is the renegade Liberal. Over and above the familiar Marxist claim that "bourgeois liberty" is an illusion, there is now a widespread tendency to argue that one can only defend democracy by totalitarian methods. If one loves democracy, the argument runs, one must crush its enemies by no matter what means. And who are its enemies? It always appears that they are not only those who attack it openly and consciously, but those who "objectively" endanger it by spreading mistaken doctrines. In other words, defending democracy involves destroying all independence of thought. This argument was used, for instance, to justify the Russian purges. The most ardent Russophile hardly believed that all of the victims were guilty of all the things they were accused of: but by holding heretical opinions they "objectively" harmed the régime, and therefore it was quite right not only to massacre them but to discredit them by false accusations. The same argument was used to justify the quite conscious lying that went on in the leftwing press about the Trotskyists and other Republican minorities in the Spanish civil war. And it was used again as a reason for yelping against habeas corpus when Mosley was released in 1943.

These people don't see that if you encourage totalitarian methods, the time may come when they will be used against you instead of for you. Make a habit of imprisoning Fascists without trial, and perhaps the process won't stop at Fascists. Soon after the suppressed *Daily Worker* had been reinstated, I was lecturing to a workingmen's college in South London. The audience were working-class and lower-middle class intellectuals — the same sort of audience that one used to meet at Left Book Club branches. The lecture had touched on the freedom of the press, and at the end, to my astonishment, several questioners stood up and asked me: Did I not think that the lifting of the ban on *The Daily Worker* was a great mistake? When asked why, they said that it was a paper of doubtful loyalty and ought not to be tolerated in war time. I found myself defending *The Daily Worker*, which has gone out of its way to libel me more than once. But where had these people learned this essentially totalitarian outlook? Pretty certainly they had learned it from the Communists themselves! Tolerance and decency are deeply rooted in England, but they are not indestructible, and they have to be kept alive partly by conscious effort. The result of preaching totalitarian doctrines is to weaken the instinct by means of which free peoples know what is or is not dangerous. The case of Mosley illustrates this. In 1940 it was perfectly right to intern Mosley, whether or not he had committed any technical crime. We were fighting for our lives and could not allow a possible quisling to go free. To keep him shut up, without trial, in 1943 was an outrage. The general failure to see this was a bad symptom, though it is true that the agitation against Mosley's release was partly factitious and partly a rationalisation of other discontents. But how much of the present slide towards Fascist ways of thought is traceable to the "anti-Fascism" of the past ten years and the unscrupulousness it has entailed?

It is important to realise that the current Russomania is only a symptom of the general weakening of the western liberal tradition. Had the MOI chipped in and definitely vetoed the publication of this book, the bulk of the English intelligentsia would have seen nothing disquieting in this. Uncritical loyalty to the USSR happens to be the current orthodoxy, and where the supposed interests of the USSR are involved they are willing to tolerate not only censorship but the deliberate falsification of history. To name one instance. At the death of John Reed, the author of *Ten Days That Shook the World* — firsthand account of the early days of the Russian Revolution — the copyright of the book passed into the hands of the British Communist Party, to whom I believe Reed had bequeathed it. Some years later the British Communists, having destroyed the original edition of the book as completely as they could, issued a garbled version from which they had eliminated mentions of Trotsky and also omitted the introduction written by Lenin. If a radical intelligentsia had still existed in Britain, this act of forgery would have been exposed and denounced in every literary paper in the country. As it was there was little or no protest. To many English intellectuals it seemed quite a natural thing to do. And this tolerance or plain dishonesty means much more than that admiration for Russia happens to be fashionable at this moment. Quite possibly that particular fashion will not last. For all I know, by the time this book is published my view of the Soviet régime may be the generally-accepted one. But what use would that be in itself? To exchange one orthodoxy for another is not necessarily an advance. The enemy is the gramophone mind, whether or not one agrees with the record that is being played at the moment.

I am well acquainted with all the arguments against freedom of thought and speech – the arguments which claim that it cannot exist, and the arguments which claim that it ought not to. I answer simply that they don't convince me and that our civilisation over a period of four hundred years has been founded on the opposite notice. For quite a decade past I have believed that the existing Russian régime is a mainly evil thing, and I claim the right to say so, in spite of the fact that we are allies with the USSR in a war which I want to see won. If I had to choose a text to justify myself, I should choose the line from Milton:

By the known rules of ancient liberty.

The word *ancient* emphasises the fact that intellectual freedom is a deep-rooted tradition without which our characteristic western culture could only doubtfully exist. From that tradition many of our intellectuals are visibly turning away. They have accepted the principle that a book should be published or suppressed, praised or damned, not on its merits but according to political expediency. And others who do not actually hold this view assent to it from sheer cowardice. An example of this is the failure of the numerous and vocal English pacifists to raise their voices against the prevalent worship of Russian militarism. According to those pacifists, all violence is evil, and they have urged us at every stage of the war to give in or at least to make a compromise peace. But how many of them have ever suggested that war is also evil when it is waged by the Red Army? Apparently the Russians have a right to defend themselves, whereas for us to do [so] is a deadly sin. One can only explain this contradiction in one way: that is, by a cowardly desire to keep in with the bulk of the intelligentsia, whose patriotism is directed towards the USSR rather than towards Britain. I know that the English intelligentsia have plenty of reason for their timidity and dishonesty, indeed I know by heart the arguments by which they justify themselves. But at least let us have no more nonsense about defending liberty against Fascism. If liberty means anything at all it means the right to tell people what they do not want to hear. The common people still vaguely subscribe to that doctrine and act on it. In our country – it is not the same in all countries: it was not so in republican France, and it is not so in the USA today – it is the liberals who fear liberty and the intellectuals who want to do dirt on the intellect: it is to draw attention to that fact that I have written this preface.

Author's Note: "It is not quite clear whether this suggested modification is Mr ...'s own idea, or originated with the Ministry of Information; but it seems to have the official ring about it."

Editor's Note: General Draža Mihailović was the leader of the Četniks (Serbian ultra-nationalist paramilitaries) during the Second World War. It has been extensively documented by historians that the Četniks were responsible for numerous atrocities against Muslim and Catholic civilians during the war, and from 1942 onwards collaborated extensively with the Nazis, Nedić's puppet regime in Serbia, and even with the Utaše (Croatian Fascist) puppet state, despite the latter's genocidal persecution of Serbs. It is unlikely, however, that Orwell had a detailed knowledge of the collaborationist and genocidal character of the Četniks, or that he would have seemingly endorsed them if he had known. Mihailovic was tried and executed by the Yugoslav authorities in 1946.

This was Orwell's proposed Preface to Animal Farm, *rejected by the publisher and so first published in the* Times Literary Supplement *on 15 September 1972 with an introduction by Sir Bernard Crick. Ian Angus found the original manuscript in 1972.*

George Orwell (1903 – 1950) was one of the twentieth century's greatest English-language writers.

GOING FOR A WALK
(1921)

—

Joseph Roth

As if to a costume party.

What I see, what I see. What I see is the day in all its absurdity and triviality. A horse, harnessed to a cab, staring with lowered head into its nose bag, not knowing that horses originally came into the world without cabs; a small boy playing with marbles on the pavement – he watches the purposeful bustle of the grownups all around him, and, himself full of the delights of idleness has no inkling that he already represents the acme of creation, but instead yearns to be grown up; a policeman who fancies himself as the still point at the center of a whirlpool of activity, and the pillar of authority – enemy to the street, and placed there to supervise it and accept its tribute in the form of good order.

I see a girl, framed in an open window, who is a part of the wall and yearns to be freed from its embrace, which is all she knows of the world. A man, pressed into the shadows of a public square, collecting bits of paper and ciga-rette butts. An advertising kiosk placed at the end of a street, like its epigram, with a little weathervane on it to proclaim which way the wind is blowing down that particular street. A fat man in a cream-colored jacket, smoking a cigar, he looks like a grease spot in human form on this summer's day. A café terrace planted with colorful ladies, waiting to be plucked. White-jacketed waiters, navy blue porters, newspaper sellers, a hotel, an elevator boy, a Negro.

What I see is the old man with the tin trumpet on the Kurfürstendamm. And the motion of a waiter on the café terrace, swishing at a fly, has more content in it than the lives of all the customers on the café terrace. The fly gets away, and the waiter is disappointed. Why so much hostility to a fly, O waiter? A war cripple who finds a nail file. Someone, a lady, has lost the nail file in the place where he happens to sit down. Of course the beggar starts filing his nails – what else is he to do? The coincidence that has left the nail file in his possession and the trifling movement of filing his nails are enough to lift him about a thousand social classes, symbolically speaking. A dog running after a ball, then stopping in front of it, static now and inanimate – unable to grasp how some stupid, brainless rubber thing only a moment ago could have been so lively and spirited – is the hero of a momentary drama. It's only the minutiae of life that are important.

Strolling around on a May morning, what do I care about the vast issues of world history as expressed in newspaper editorials? Or even the fate of some individual, a potential tragic hero, someone who has lost his wife or come into an inheritance or cheated on his wife or in one way or another makes some lofty appeal to us? Confronted with the truly microscopic, all loftiness is hopeless, completely meaningless. The diminutive of the parts is more impressive than the monumentality of the whole. I no longer have any use for the sweeping gestures of heroes on the global stage. I'm going for a walk.

Seeing an advertising kiosk on which facts such as, for instance, Manoli cigarettes are blazoned out as if they were an ultimatum or a *memento mori*, I completely lose my patience. An ultimatum is just as inconsequential as a cigarette, because it's expressed in exactly the same way. Whatever is heralded or touted can only be of little weight or consequence. And it seems to me there is nothing these days that is not heralded. Therein lies its greatness. Typography, to us, has become the arbiter of perspective and value. The most important, the less important, and the unimportant only *appear* to be important, less important, unimportant. It's their image that tells us their worth, not their being. The event of the week is whatever – in print, in gesture, in sweeping arm movements – has been declared the event of the week. Nothing is, everything claims to be. But in the face of the sunshine that spreads ruthlessly over walls, streets, railway tracks, beams in at the window, beams out of windows in myriad reflections, anything puffed up and inessential can have no being. In the end (led astray as I am by print, by the presence of typography as an adjudicator of value) I come to believe that everything we take seriously – the ultimatum, the Manoli cigarettes – is unimportant.

Meanwhile, at the edge of the city, where I have been told nature is to be found, it isn't nature at all, but a sort of picture-book nature. It seems to me too much has been printed about nature for it to remain what it used to be. On the outskirts of our cities, in place of nature, we are presented with a sort of idea of nature. A woman standing at the edge of the woods, shielding her eyes with the umbrella she has brought along just in case, scanning the horizon, and seeing a spot that seems familiar from some painting, exclaims: "Isn't this just so picturesque!" It's the degradation of nature to a painter's model. It's not such a rare degradation either, because our relationship to nature has become warped. You see, nature has acquired a purpose where we are concerned. Its task is to amuse us. It no longer exists for its own sake. It exists to satisfy a function. In summer it provides woods where we can picnic and doze, lakes where we can row, meadows where we can bask, sunsets to send us into raptures, mountains for walking tours, and beauty spots as destinations for our excursions and day-trips. We have Baedeker-ized nature.

But what I see hasn't made it into the Baedeker. What I see is the sudden, unexpected, and wholly meaningless rising and falling of a swarm of mosquitoes over a tree trunk. The silhouette of a man laden with firewood on a forest path. The eager profile of a spray of jasmine tumbling over a wall. The vibration of a child's voice, fading away into the air. The inaudible, sleeping melody of a distant, even an unreal life.

I don't understand the people I see putting their best foot forward to enjoy nature. There's a difference between a forest and a sidewalk. "Recreation" is no necessity, if that's the expressed objective of the hiker. "Nature" is no institution.

Western Europeans set out into nature as if to a costume party. They have a sort of waxed jacket relationship with nature. I saw hikers who were accountants in civilian life. What did they need their walking sticks for? The ground is so flat and smooth that a fountain pen would have served them just as well. But the man doesn't see the flat and smooth ground. He sees "nature". If he were going sailing, presumably he would don the white linen suit he inherited from his grandfather, who was also a weekend sailor. He has no ears for the plashing of a wave, and he doesn't know that the bursting of a bubble is a significant thing. The day that nature became a site for recreation was the end.

In consequence of which, my outing was that of a curmudgeonly soul, and I wish I hadn't undertaken it.

Berliner Börsen-Courier, 24 May 1921

Joseph Roth (1894-1939) was an Austrian journalist and novelist writing in German, best known for his family saga Radetsky March *(1932) about the decline and fall of the Austro-Hungarian Empire; his novel of Jewish life* Job *(1930); and his seminal essay "The Wandering Jews" (1927). He was born and grew up in Brody, a small town near Lemberg in East Galicia, part of the easternmost reaches of what was then the Austro-Hungarian Empire and is now in Ukraine. He is widely considered the quintessential chronicler of late Austria-Hungary. Most of his work has been translated into English (as here) by Michael Hoffman.*

AFRICA IS PEOPLE

———

Chinua Achebe

For contingent humanity: simple trouble in seven words.

I believe it was in the first weeks of 1989 that I received an invitation to an anniversary meeting – the twenty-fifth year, or something like that – of the Organisation for Economic Co-operation and Development (OECD), in Paris. I accepted without quite figuring out what I could possibly contribute to such a meeting/celebration. My initial puzzlement continued right into the meeting itself. In fact it grew as the proceedings got underway. Here was I, an African novelist among predominantly Western bankers and economists; a guest, as it were, from the world's poverty-stricken provinces at a gathering of the rich and powerful in the metropolis. As I listened to them – Europeans, Americans, Canadians, Australians – I was left in no doubt, by the assurance they displayed, that these were the masters of our world, savoring the benefits of their success. They read and discussed papers on economic and development matters in different regions of the world. They talked in particular about the magic bullet of the 1980s, structural adjustment, specially designed for those parts of the world where economies had gone completely haywire. The matter was really simple, the experts seemed to be saying: the only reason for failure to develop was indiscipline of all kinds, and the remedy a quick, sharp administration of shock treatment that would yank the sufferer out of the swamp of improvidence back onto the high and firm road of free-market economy. The most recurrent prescriptions for this condition were the removal of subsidies on food and fuel and the devaluation of the national currency. Yes, the experts conceded, some pain would inevitably accompany these measures, but such pain was transitory and, in any case, negligible in comparison to the disaster that would surely take place if nothing was done now.

Then the governor of the Bank of Kenya made his presentation. As I recall the events, he was probably the only other African at that session. He asked the experts to consider the case of Zambia, which according to him had accepted, and had been practising, a structural adjustment regime for many years, and whose economic condition was now worse than it had been when they began their treatment. An American expert who seemed to command great attention and was accorded high deference in the room spoke again. He repeated what had already been said many times before. "Be patient, it will work, in time. Trust me" – or words to that effect.

Suddenly I received something like a stab of insight and it became clear to me why I had been invited, what I was doing there in that strange assembly. I signaled my desire to speak and was given the floor. I told them what I had just recognized. I said that what was going on before me was a *fiction workshop*, no more and no less! Here you are, spinning your fine theories, to be tried out in your imaginary laboratories. You are developing new drugs and feeding them to a bunch of laboratory guinea pigs and hoping for the best. I have news for you. Africa is not fiction. Africa is people, real people. Have you thought of that? You are brilliant people, world experts. You may even have the very best intentions. But have you thought, *really* thought, of Africa as people? I will tell you the experience of my own country, Nigeria, with structural adjustment. After two years of this remedy, we saw the country's minimum wage plummet in value from the equivalent of fifteen British pounds a month to five pounds. This is not a lab report; it is not a mathematical exercise. We are talking about someone whose income, which is already miserable enough, is now cut down to one-third of what it was two years ago. And this flesh-and-blood man has a wife and children. You say he should simply go home and tell them to be patient. Now let me ask you this question. Would you recommend a similar remedy to your own people and your own government? How do you sell such a project to an elected president? You are asking him to commit political suicide, or perhaps to get rid of elections altogether until he has fixed the economy. Do you realize that's what you are doing?

I thought I could read astonishment on some of the faces on the opposite side of the huge circular table of the conference room. Or perhaps it was just my optimistic imagination. But one thing I do know for a fact. The director-general (or whatever he was called) of the OECD, beside whom I was sitting, a Dutchman and quite a giant, had muttered to me, under his breath, at least twice: "Give it to them!"

I came away from that strange conference with enhanced optimism for the human condition. For who could have imagined that in the very heart of the enemy's citadel a friend like that Dutchman might be lurking, happy enough to set my cat among his own pigeons! "Africa is people" may seem too simple and too obvious to some of us. But I have found in the course of my travels through the world that the most simple things can still give us a lot of trouble, even the brightest among us: and this is particularly so in matters concerning Africa. One of the greatest men of the twentieth century, Albert Schweitzer – philosopher, theologian, musician, medical missionary – failed completely to see the most obvious fact about Africa and so went ahead to say: "The African is indeed my brother, but my junior brother." Now, did we or did anyone we know take Dr Schweitzer up on that blasphemy? Oh no. On the contrary, he was admired to the point of adoration, and Lamberene, the very site on African soil where he uttered his outrage, was turned into a place of pilgrimage.

Or let us take another much admired twentieth-century figure, the first writer, as it happens, to grace the cover of the newly-founded *Time* magazine. I am talking, of course, about that extraordinary Polish-born, French-speaking English sea captain and novelist, Joseph Conrad. He recorded in his memoir his first experience of seeing a black man in these remarkable words:

> A certain enormous buck nigger encountered in Haiti fixed my conception of blind, furious, unreasoning rage, as manifested in the human animal to the end of my days. Of the nigger I used to dream for years afterwards.

My attention was first drawn to these observations of Conrad's in a scholarly work, not very widely known, by Jonah Raskin. Its title was *The Mythology of Imperialism*, and it was published in 1971 by Random House. I mention this because Mr Raskin's title defines the cultural source out of which Conrad derived his words and ideas. Conrad's fixation, admitted so openly by him in his memoir, and conspicuously present in his fiction, has gone largely unremarked in literary and scholarly evaluations of his work. Why? Because it is grounded quite firmly in that mythology of imperialism which has so effectively conditioned contemporary civilization and its modes of education. Imperial domination required a new language to describe the world it had created and the people it had subjugated. Not surprisingly, this new language did not celebrate these subject peoples nor toast them as heroes. Rather, it painted them in the most lurid colors. Africa, being European imperialism's prime target, with hardly a square foot escaping the fate of imperial occupation, naturally received the full measure of this adverse definition. Add to that the massive derogatory endeavor of the previous three centuries of the Atlantic slave trade to label black people, and we can begin to get some idea of the magnitude of the problem we may have today with the simple concept: *Africa is people.*

James Baldwin made an analogous point about black people in America, descendants of Africa. In his essay "Fifth Avenue, Uptown", he wrote:

> Negroes want to be treated like men: a perfectly straightforward statement containing seven words. People who have mastered Kant, Hegel, Shakespeare, Marx, Freud and the Bible find this statement impenetrable.

The point of all this is to alert us to the image burden that Africa bears today and makes us recognize how that image has molded contemporary attitudes, including perhaps our own, to that continent.

Do I hear in my mind's ear someone sighing wearily: "There we go again, another session of whining and complaining!"? Let me assure you that I personally abhor and detest whiners. Those who know me will already know this. To those who don't, I recommend a little pamphlet I wrote at a critical point in my country's troubles. I called it *The Trouble with Nigeria*, and it is arguably the harshest statement ever made on that unhappy country. It is so harsh that whenever I see one of the many foreign critics of Nigeria quoting gleefully from it I want to strange him! No, I am not an apologist for Africa's many failings. And I am hardheaded enough to realize that we must not be soft on them, must never go out to justify them. But I am also rational enough to realize that we should strive to understand our failings objectively and not simply swallow the mystifications and mythologies cooked up by those whose goodwill we have every reason to suspect.

Now, I understand and accept the logic that if a country mismanages its resources it should be prepared to face the music of hard times. Long ago I wrote a novel about a young African man, well educated, full of promise and good intentions, who nevertheless got his affairs (fiscal and otherwise) in a big mess. And did he pay dearly for it!

I did not blame the banks for his inability to manage his finances. What I did do, or try to do, was offer leads to my readers for exploring the roots of the hero's predicament by separating those factors for which an individual may justly be held accountable from others that are systemic and beyond the individual's control. That critical, analytical adventure to which the book invites its readers will be medicine after death for my hero, but the reader can at least go away with the satisfaction of having tried to be fair and just to the doomed man, and the reward, hopefully, of a little enlightenment on the human condition for himself.

The countries of Africa (especially sub-Saharan Africa) on whom I am focusing my attention are not the only ones who suffer the plight of poverty in the world today. All the so-called Third World peoples are, more or less, in the same net, as indeed are all the poor everywhere, even in the midst of plenty in the First and Second Worlds.

Like the unfortunate young man in my novel, the poor of the world may be guilty of this and that particular fault or foolishness, but if we are fair we will admit that nothing they have done or left undone quite explains all the odds we see stacked up against them. We are sometimes tempted to look upon the poor as so many ne'er-do-wells we can simply ignore. But they will return to haunt our peace, because they are greater than their badge of suffering, because they are human.

I recall watching news on television about fighting in the Horn of Africa, between Ethiopia and Eritrea. As I had come to expect, the news was very short indeed. The only background material the newscaster gave to flesh out the bald announcement of the fight was that Ethiopia and Eritrea were among the world's poorest nations. And he was off, to other news and other places, leaving me a little space to mull over the bad news from Africa. How much additional enlightenment did that piece of information about poverty give the viewer about the fighting or the fighters? Not much. What about telling the viewer, in the same number of words, that Eritrea was a province of Ethiopia until recently? But no. The poverty synecdoche is more attractive and less trouble; you simply reach for it from the handy storehouse of mythology about Africa. No taxing research required here.

But if poverty springs so readily to our minds when we think about Africa, how much do we really know about it?

In 1960 a bloody civil war broke out in Congo soon after its colonizer, Belgium, beat a hasty retreat from the territory. Within months its young, radical, and idealistic prime minister, Patrice Lumumba, was brutally murdered by his rivals, who replaced him with a corrupt demagogue called Mobutu, whose main attraction was presumably his claim to be an anti-communist. Mobutu set about plundering the wealth of this vast country, as large as the whole of Western Europe, and also fomenting trouble in Congo's neighboring countries, aiding and abetting the destabilization of Angola and openly cooperating with the apartheid white-minority regime in South Africa. Mobutu's legacy was truly horrendous. He stole and stashed away billions in foreign banks. He even stole his country's name and rebaptized it Zaire. Today Congo, strategically positioned in the heart of Africa, vast in size and mineral wealth, has also become one of the poorest nations on earth. Whom are we to hold responsible for this: the Congolese people, Mobutu, or his sponsors, the CIA? Who will pay the penalty of structural adjustment? Of course, that question is already irrelevant. The people are already adjusted to grinding poverty and long-range instability.

Congo is by no means the only country in Africa to have foreign powers choose or sustain its leader. It is merely the most scandalous case, in scale and effrontery.

President Clinton was right on target when he apologized to Africa for the unprincipled conduct of American foreign policy during the Cold War, a policy that scorched the young hopes of Africa's independence struggle like seedlings in a drought. I have gone into all this unpleasant matter not to prompt any new apologies but to make all of us wary of those early, facile comments about Africa's incurable poverty or the endemic incapacity of Africans to get their act together and move ahead like everybody else.

I cannot presume to tell world bankers anything about public finance or economics and the rest. I have told you stories. Now let me make a couple of suggestions.

In the late 1990s an organization in Britain called Jubilee 2000 informed me of their noble campaign to persuade leaders of the world's rich nations (the G8 countries) to forgive the debts owed to them by the world's fifty poorest nations. I was made to understand that the British government was half persuaded that it should be done, and the Canadians were possibly of the same view. But, on the negative side, I learned that Japan and Germany were adamantly opposed to the proposal. About the most important factor, America, my informant had this to say: "When asked about cancellation their tongues speak sweetly, like some of Homer's Greeks, but their hearts are closed. It needs another poet to go to them and lay siege to those hearts … will you be that poet?" Subsequently, my wife, noticing perhaps my anxiety, showed me a passage in a book she happened to be reading. "The fact that a message may not be received is no reason not to send it." I was startled by the message and the mystery of its timely surfacing. I also recognized the affinity between this thought and another I knew, wearing its proverbial Igbo dress: "Let us perform the sacrifice and leave the blame on the doorstep of the spirits." That's what I have now done.

Regarding Japan and Germany, beneficiaries both of postwar recon-struction assistance, I did not appeal to their hearts but instead nudged their memories and their sense of irony. And for good measure I told them the parable of Jesus about the servant who was forgiven a huge debt by his master, on leaving whose audience he chanced upon a fellow servant who owed him a very small sum of money. The first servant seized him by the throat and had him tortured and thrown into prison.

My second request to the World Bank went to the very root of the problem – the looting of the wealth of poor nations by corrupt leaders and their cronies. This crime is compounded by the expatriation of these funds into foreign banks, where they are put into the service of foreign economies. Consequently the victim country is defrauded twice, if my economics is correct: it is defrauded of the wealth which is stolen from its treasury and also of the development potential of that wealth forever.

In asking the World Bank to take a lead in the recovery of the stolen resources of poor countries, I did not suggest that such criminal transactions are made through the World Bank. I am also aware that banks are not set up normally to act as a police force. But we live in terrible times when an individual tyrant or a small clique of looters in power can destroy the lives and the future of whole countries and whole populations by their greed. The consequences of these actions can be of truly genocidal proportions.

Herein lies the root of the horrifying statistic to which the president of the World Bank, James Wolfensohn, drew attention: "You will be staggered to know, as I was, that 37 percent of African private wealth is held outside Africa, whereas for Asia the share is 3 percent and for Latin American is it 17 percent."

It would be a great pity, I remarked, if the world were to sit back in the face of these catastrophic statistics and do nothing, merely to preserve codes of banking etiquette and confidentiality formulated for quite other times. The world woke up too late to the inadequacy of these codes in the matter of the Nazi Holocaust gold. We had thus been warned. The cooperation of the world's bank, led by the World Bank Group, in eliminating this great scourge would have given so many poor countries the first real opportunity to begin afresh and take responsibility for their development and progress, and it would have discouraged future marauders of nations. It would also have cleared the world's banking systems of the charges of receiving stolen property and colluding with genocide.

For too long the world has been content to judge peoples and nations in distress largely on the basis of received stereotypes drawn from mythologies of oppression. In 1910, at the height of British imperial dominion, John Buchan, a popular novelist who was also a distinguished imperial civil servant, published a colonialist classic entitled *Prester John*, in which we find the following pronouncement: "That is the difference between white and black, the gift of responsibility."

I do not believe such a difference exists, except in the mythology of domination. Let's put this to the test by giving these poor, black nations the first sporting chance of their lives. The cost is low and the rewards will blow our minds, white and black alike. Trust me!

Let me round this up with a nice little coda. "Africa is people" has another dimension. Africa believes in people, in cooperation with people. If the philosophical dictum of Descartes "I think, therefore I am" represents a European individualistic ideal, the Bantu declaration "*Umuntu ngumuntu ngabantu*" represents an African communal aspiration: "A human is human because of other humans."

Our humanity is contingent on the human of our fellows. No person or group can be human alone. We rise above the animal together, or not at all. If we learned that lesson even this late in the day, we would have taken a truly millennial step forward.

An Igbo from Biafra born in the "Colony and Protectorate of Nigeria", Chinua Achebe (1930 – 2013) is one of modern Africa's greatest writers. His first novel, Things Fall Apart *(1958), often considered his masterpiece, is the most widely read book in modern African literature.*

THE IRISH PROBLEM

—

Gabriel Rosenstock

You won't believe it!

What is the Irish problem? I'm sure the Irish have many of the same problems as everyone else on earth, maybe more, maybe less. So what exactly is the Irish problem we are addressing here?

There's a clue in the name itself, *Irish*. You see, the Irish don't speak Irish! Not anymore. Less than 10% of the population. A lot less! Why is this? Well, there are lots of reasons.

In his book *The Broken Harp* (2014), Tomás Mac Síomóin outlined a grim scenario when describing the fall and decline of the Gaelic world and the terrible effects of colonialism on the Irish psyche. Ghoulish, nightmarish actually, the stuff of monster movies, zombie movies. (More on that presently).

And there's been a cover up. And the cover up continues. And we have to ask ourselves, why can't we clean out the closet once and for all and breathe freely again. Put all those ghosts to rest, jabbering away in Irish, English, Kiltartanese, Cant and whatever you're having yourself.

Mac Síomóin has followed *The Broken Harp* with another book, more conversational in style, *The Gael Becomes Irish* (2020).

Who is Mac Síomóin? He could be described as an Irish cultural exile who has lived in Catalonia for over 20 years. Writer. Journalist. Marxist. Scientist. Poet. Contrarian, according to his detractors. One could say that the Gaelic form of his name is in itself a statement, as most of the surnames and place names of Ireland are known by their Anglicised form, which often lends an air of idiocy to them, whether intended or not.

There's the nub, already. The Irish have accepted Anglicisation and only a dedicated few wear a badge of resistance; one such badge is using the native form of one's name and address. Using the native form of one's name doesn't necessarily mean you can speak, write or read Irish, however. That's part of the Irish problem too. And vice versa! Some of the best Irish speakers I have heard never used anything but the English form of their name.

Many native speakers of Irish in Gaeltacht areas (Irish-speaking) are known by the English form of their names, or avoid the problem of the surname altogether by becoming known under a string of Irish-sounding and English-sounding Christian names, such as Paddy Mháire Dick, which places one on a recognisable family tree. Others have a name that distinguishes them in some manner or other, such as Máire an Bhéarla, meaning "Mary who can speak English." Maybe we should all have that suffix attached to our names!

Vanquished Ancestral Universe

English legislation regarding Anglicisation of names was not uniformly enforced and, so, you sometimes have the added complication of having people of the same family using different forms of their names: O'Houlihan and Holland, for instance. Houston, we have a problem!

But actually, it's not funny. It's serious. It's symptomatic of a widespread disease, a sickness, a virus . . . the virus of colonialism. As Mac Síomóin says,

> "References that reflect his vanquished ancestral universe are replaced by those of the coloniser's civilisation. The linguistically colonised becomes part of the referential universe of the coloniser."

This is undoubtedly true. I remember reading a Sunday newspaper, in hospital, (which I normally avoid like the plague, i.e. hospitals and that particular rag!). The newspaper alluded to didn't contribute to my rehabilitation, I can tell you that much. *Au contraire.*

What attracted my eye (or what appalled it, I should say) was the crossword. It was oozing with what Mac Síomóin calls, above, "the referential universe of the coloniser". Yes, there I was in a hospital bed, and an "Irish" newspaper was worming its way into my mind with vile crossword clues regarding British royalty, British celebs and other questionable forms of life. Three across, four down . . . some bugger or other who was awarded the Victoria Cross. Help! Nurse!

Complete Cultural Colonisation

How do we allow ourselves to be treated in this insidious manner? The answer is simple. Mac Síomóin has got it right: "Linguistic colonialization is complete cultural colonisation."

The Colonial Effect is not some superficial veneer, a silly hat, or bonnet, that we can wear and take off at will, a sly peep at the Chelsea Flower Show, or even the Graham Norton Show, God forbid. No. Mac Síomóin insists otherwise: we are powerless! We're stuck in the mire.

"Colonialism has sunk such deep roots in our psyche that a need to restore the riches that were taken from us no longer has any relevancy for the majority of our fellow citizens."

This is a hard-hitting analysis of the Irish problem, but a necessary one. Whenever it comes up, it is swept under the carpet, or derided. Being mealy-mouthed about the subject would not serve any purpose at all. And Mac Síomóin is right to be riled about all of this. In a sense, it's a matter of life and death because if the Irish language joins the list of those languages that have been dying at a rate of one per fortnight in recent decades, no one is going to turn up for the funeral – out of unspoken shame.

The crossword maker whose Anglocentric ravings upset me in hospital would probably not last very long with that particular newspaper if his research reflected the mores, insights, proverbs, songs, oral and literary culture of Irish, a language which stretches back over three thousand years. No, he'd be out on his ear. So would the literary editor, if he or she decided tomorrow to devote space every Sunday to reviews of Irish-language books.

You would think that someone who makes crosswords for an Irish newspaper – or a literary editor for that matter – would be interested in Irish words, their history and etymology. But no, it's as though his mind has been washed clean of our Gaelic past and the known universe is now merrily filtered through an Anglophone prism.

Mac Síomóin's book reproduces part of an interview with the wonderful Ngũgĩ wa Thiong'o who describes language as a natural computer, a natural hard drive. "When you lose that hard drive", says the great African writer and intellectual, "you lose all the memories and knowledge and information and thoughts carried by that language . . ."

What a frightening prospect! It has something of the quality of a sci-fi film script, doesn't it? Losing all that referential material, and in exchange for what? Make no mistake about it. There's nothing sci-fi about all of this. It is real. It has happened. It continues to happen and we allow it to continue because we have not woken up to the fact that we are being manipulated left, right and centre. Fucked sideways.

Trauma and Language Loss

The trauma associated with language loss is described in Mac Síomóin's previous title, *The Broken Harp*, and some of that deeply disturbing material is recapitulated here again. Why not? We need to know what happened and why it happened. Our educators and teachers also need to know what happened, and why and how it happened, and we need to unveil to Irish schoolchildren, once and for all, and unfold the bloody tapestry of the history of Ireland's senior language.

How on earth can the rising generation acquire a language at school, even the basics, if they don't know its long and chequered history? What do you suggest, that it be taught in a vacuum?

We seem to be living in an anodyne society in which it is impolite to step on another's toe, whatever shape or colour that particular toe might have, whatever its sexual predilections and so on! So, in that light, your average teacher in Ireland is unlikely to quote as follows from Mac Síomóin's book:

> "The catastrophic Irish military defeat at Kinsale in 1603, and the subsequent emigration to the continent of its civic and military leaders, initiated the gradual incorporation – aided by several genocidal interludes – throughout more than three succeeding centuries, of the Irish nation into English cultural and administrative practise. Such a process, plus its fundamental economic aspect, is referred to as colonisation . . ."

Genocidal interludes? Has the Irish educational system the mind, or the heart, or the guts to talk about such things? If it did, wouldn't there be complaints, letters to the newspapers and so on? Whatever about our teachers, and parents, have our children got an appetite for such things? (Or are their appetites too dulled by violent video games?)

Aren't we all living in an age of appeasement now, a golden age of fraternal relations with our brothers and sisters on our neighbouring island? Why open up all those old sores? Why re-arrange the chieftain's bones, as Patrick Kavanagh asked.

Poets Hunted Down

We're not finished yet. Mac Síomóin continues relentlessly. In this violent game, there's only going to be one winner, and one loser:

"Public use of the Irish language was penalised, except where practical considerations made its complete elimination impossible; it was all but completely eliminated from administrative affairs at a time when the native Irish population knew no other language. Poets and popular entertainers were hunted down and their works and musical instruments, when discovered, were destroyed."

Great stuff! Why don't they make a violent video game out of that? Hey, wouldn't that be fun! What will we call this game? I know, *Broken Harps*! I love it! Let's go hunting down some poets. Come on! Let's smash some harps. First to smash 20 harps wins!

Why stop there! There's loads more to come. You ain't heard nothing yet. It just gets better and better:

"All non-Anglican religious practise was prescribed. [*Recte* proscribed]. Roman Catholics, the vast majority of the population, along with Ulster Presbyterians, were subject to Penal Laws, designed to impoverish them and keep them illiterate. Catholic priests who received their training in continental seminaries, were hunted down; rewards were offered for their head . . ."

The Oak Is Felled

Can you visualise it? Another computer game! Hunting priests. Hang them high! It could go viral! Well priests aren't very popular today so it doesn't matter. As long as those nasty Brits didn't touch our trees. They didn't touch our trees, did they?!

"The oak forests which covered Ireland, in which most of our ancestors lived, and from which their fighters emerged to attack their English occupiers, were systematically felled. The wood both fed the furnaces of early industrial England and was used to construct the ships of England's naval fleets."

Ah yes, Rule Britannia!

So, Tomás Mac Síomóin, I've known you and listened to you for over 40 years: maybe your polemics will bear fruit some day soon and we'll have a slew of new video games to beat the band. Who needs dragons and what not when such genuine, colourful violence lies at our very own doorstep? Rich pickings, I say.

Perhaps it's happening already. We've had the film of the "Great Hunger", *Black 47* and now, more recently, *Arracht*. After all, entertainment is the *lingua franca* of the hour and *arracht* means "monster" so it must be monstrously good.

As may be obvious, I go along with Mac Síomóin thesis in most respects, but I would like to conclude by mentioning three areas where we part company.

Firstly, his view of contemporary Irish-language literature is unnecessarily bleak. I think it was ungracious of him not to mention — even in a footnote — the remarkable energy and diversity of the Irish-language IMRAM literature festival, a festival which honoured his own achievements not so long ago. True, many of its events are poorly attended — even stalwarts of the Irish-language movement fail to turn up! Members of the wider arts community also fail to make an appearance, even out of curiosity (unless they are part of an event).

Aha! Yes, but this is part of a larger malaise, as the ever-percipient John Zerzan notes in the current issue — pre-Covid-19 Lockdown — of *Fifth Estate*:

> "Clubs are closing as people retreat further into their little screens. When people go out, they are so very likely to be at their tables on their phones. We do less socialising, have fewer friends . . . More and more is delivered to one's door . . . Everything is available online, even cars."

Maybe IMRAM needs to do a rethink and bring some of its events to us for a while, rather than having a couple of hundred people venturing out into the real world and attending actual events!

I won't be watching any IMRAM events on a smartphone simply because I don't have one: I have a computer screen, yes, but I don't want to witness the diminution of life, or art, on a small screen. I don't want to "watch" music, or view Turner's *The Slave Ship* on any little gadget. It's the leprechaunisation of everybody and everything.

Secondly, I differ with Mac Síomóin when he recommends simplifying the Irish language as taught in schools. Try simplifying chess. Or hurling. Why would you even think of such a thing!

Finally, Mac Síomóin advertises his book by saying that "international considerations increasingly determine our national cultural parameters." Sure. Nobody can argue with that. But the author is a Marxist and, by implication, a statist. We would have had a different book from him had he been an anarchist, a book which would have identified the state itself (whether the British state, the neo-colonial Irish state, or some possible European super-state of the future) as a major part of the Irish problem.

A poet, hakuist, novelist, short-story writer and translator, Gabriel Rosenstock was born in 1949 in Kilfinane, Co Limerick and is a graduate of University College Cork. One of the "Innti" poets that transformed Irish-language poetry in the 1970s, he writes primarily in Irish and is the author or translator of over 50 major books. His most recent collections of poetry are Bliain an Bhandé *(Year of the Goddess,* The Dedalus Press, 2007*),* Sasquatch *(Arlen House, 2014) and* Glengower: Poems for No One in Irish and English *(The Onslaught Press, 2018). He is a member of Aosdána and lives in Dún Laoghaire, Co Dublin.*

VARIETIES OF ISLAM

———

Jacob Agee

Degrees, schools, styles and tones.

The Muslim world is anything but a monolith, despite the pronouncements of Western popular wisdom, of Huntington, Trump, Netanyahu and Co. Since the earliest decades after Muhammad's death, diverse varieties of Islam have existed, sometimes resembling Christian denominations (though attempts to find the Muslim "equivalent" of everything Christian are ridiculous), but the most pronounced differences in Islam have in fact been between degrees and styles of interpretation shared by believers from different sects. Fundamental to intra-Muslim struggle has been whether Islam is interpreted as a personal way of life or as a political system, and to what extent either answer is carried.

All Muslims share the belief that Muhammad was the "seal of the prophets" of the Abrahamic monotheistic tradition (Judaism, Christianity, Islam), a succession that Muslims recognize. For Muslims, Jesus is second only to Muhammed, though the Trinity is rejected and the doctrine of *tawhid*, the absolute oneness of God, is the base of all Muslim theology. Jesus is dearly exalted, his name often supplemented with *peace be upon him*, but he is wholly human. As is Muhammad, who resembles Mary more, being the human one who gave physicality to God's presence on earth; the Qur'an, God's direct words in a human language, is in Islam the closest equivalent to the Christian Jesus who is God as humanity. Hence the historical term "Mohammedan" represents a naïve Western attempt to find direct equivalence with Christianity, namely with Muhammed substituted for Christ. Kwame Anthony Appiah has argued about how the entire concept of "religion" as generally understood, for that matter, is predicated on the Euro-American assumption that everything can be understood through equivalences of Christianity. All Muslims share the Qur'an, though like in Protestantism questions around particular passages, of literalism versus interpretation, have created varieties and interpretations of Islam within single sects more intense than divisions between sects have been for much of history.

The Hadith, the body of collected stories and sayings of the Prophet Muhammad, are the Muslim's closest equivalent to the Gospel, though much more extensive, constituting thousands of stories and hundreds of compilations. (And one scholar has assembled and commented on some of the body of Hadith about Jesus, which also are revered by Muslims: see Tarif Khalidi, *The Muslim Jesus*.) But it is with this body of texts that different sects part ways, for Sunnis, Shia, and Ibadis have their own collections of Hadith. That said, all share the idea of *Sharia*, law codes based on the Qur'an and the Hadith, and *Sunnah*, a code of behaviour based on Muhammad as depicted in the Hadith. Where direct commandments are given in the Qur'an, direct laws are made; for questions not addressed in the Book, the Hadith are scoured for answers; and where the Hadith prove fruitless or the Qur'an is silent or contradicts itself, *Ijtihad*, the reasoning of religious scholars and the religious community, are acceptable. This is very similar to Judaism, which has the Torah (Revelation) as first point of reference, then the Talmud, and then educated Jewish opinion as based on the two texts. Each sect and sub-sect has its own Sharia code and jurisprudence.

The first sectarianization occurred in the decades following Muhammad's death, and was centred around Southern Iraq. The Kharijite movement were early puritans, using the doctrine of *takfir*, denunciation as infidels of any Muslim with differing views: Daesh today use the self-same doctrine to an equally trigger-happy extent. Responsible for the murder of Uthman and Ali, the third and fourth Caliphs, they were a sect who were distinct from other Muslims. The Kharijites no longer exist, but did foreshadow how *degrees* of interpretation, rather than the *content* of interpretations, would prove much more definitive in the history of Islam.

For in the very same period, and through much of Islamic history, there were a plethora of different groups and sects, some political, some theological, but only three survive today, as the three broad sects into which the overwhelming majority of Muslims are divided: Ibadi, Sunni, and Shia.

The Ibadis are the oldest, and smallest (no more than one percent of Muslims), still-existing sect. Like the Kharijites they rejected the rule of Uthman and Ali, but also were opposed to their murders and rejected *takfir*. Their relation to the Kharijites is unclear and contentious, but it appears they split away from them, and after a complex history with the puritan Ummayad dynasty in Damascus, founded their own elected Imamate in Oman. Oman remains their heartland today, the only Ibadi-majority nation and the home of most Ibadis, in fact the only Muslim-majority country with a majority that is neither Sunni nor Shia. They are also found on Zanzibar, a former Omani colony, and in isolated pockets in Algeria and Libya.

Oman is the quietest and most peaceful country in the Arab world, and the nature of Ibadism as it stands now has much responsibility for this. For Ibadism allows for the election of the Leader of the *Umma* (Muslim Community), unlike both the other major sects. While the level of detailed theological differences between sects is beyond the scope of this piece, suffice it to say that Ibadism is, as a whole, the most moderate of the three major sects. Oman is known to be rather puritanical, with a Sharia Law that is on the strict side, yet Ibadis have proven to be the sect most tolerant of other religions and opinions. For example, the late Sultan Qaboos of Oman, a religious leader as well as a political one, allowed settlement of large numbers of non-Ibadis and non-Muslims, including polytheistic Hindus, and in fact gave concessions during the Arab Spring that appeased resentment against his rule. Compared to Saudi Arabia and Iran, and the difference with Sunni and Shia Sharia lawmakers is clear to see.

It may be clear already, but if not, I should state that the three great sects of Islam did not split over differences of doctrine entirely (although they have all developed their own doctrines), rather over questions of leadership of the Muslim Empire. This is how the Sunni-Shia split emerged. While the bulk of the community accepted Abu Bakr as Caliph (a Caliph is a general leader of the Muslim community: simultaneously a political and military leader, and a devout Muslim who should be an example to others), a small group, the *Shi'at Ali*, or "Party of Ali", insisted that the true leader had to be a blood relative of Muhammad, and so recognized his cousin Ali as the true leader. The latter group became the Shia, and the rest became the Sunnis, deriving their name from the *Sunnah*.

The Sunnis recognize the four "Rightly Guided (*Rashidun*) Caliphs", those who knew Muhammad personally, as the legitimate successors of Muhammad and as the first four rulers of the Muslim Empire: Abu Bakr, Umar, Uthman, and Ali. The latter is recognized by the Shia as the first legitimate ruler. The Shia then recognize a chain of Imams, twelve blood descendants of Ali, as their rulers for the next few centuries. Note that "Imam" in Shi'ism thus refers to one of these spiritual Leaders, whereas in Sunnism it is a generic word for the leader of prayers at a mosque. The Shia Imams are deeply spiritual, steeped in mystery and mysticism. Whereas Sunni Caliphs, of whom Sultans were a later version, were political, public and military leaders who rejected and were rejected by the Shia. Islam's Great Schism, like Christianity's, was thus more about political power.

Within each of the two great monoliths, there are numerous subdivisions.

Within Sunnism, it is about *degrees*. For Sunnis are historically split into four main legal and jurisprudential *schools*, defined by the specific Sharia code to which they subscribe, which differ in their severity and traditions. They are the Hanafi, the Shafi'i, the Maliki, and the Hanbali, each school named after the scholar on whose works it is based. Very, very broadly speaking, the Hanafi, who dominate former Ottoman territories, are the most liberal, as this school has historically sought to adapt Sharia to pre-existing cultural traditions in various areas (though note that the Taliban are Hanafi, their ideology being a combination of selective Islam and Pashtun tribal codes).

The Hanbali are the most conservative school, found mostly in the Arabian Peninsula. The Wahhabis are an offshoot who grew out of the Hanbalis in the eighteenth century, based on the teachings of Muhammad Ibn Abd al Wahhab, an early Paisley-type figure from the Najd. They have now become their own school completely, in fact more of a formal sect, known sometimes as Wahhabis, and sometimes (by themselves) as Salafis, upper case. Though salafis, lower case, is also a generic word for Sunni Islamists (i.e., including but not limited to Salafis): for example the Muslim Brotherhood are salafis in terms of their ideology, but are not Salafis, as they are not part of this Saudi-based official sect. The word "salafi" comes from the Arabic *salaf*, denoting the world and morals of the first three generations of Muslims. Numerous other sub-Sunni schools and sects have existed and vanished through the centuries.

Within the Shia, it is much more complicated, as numerous divisions have emerged over what exact Imams are accepted within the official line of succession. The dominant sect are the "Twelvers", who accept Twelve Imams from Ali to Muhammad al-Mahdi. The latter, they believe, is still alive in the world but invisible, and will reappear at the end of time, before the second coming of Jesus, which all Muslims believe in. They believe that this Twelfth Imam, in the meantime, guides the world through the Ayatollahs (Shia clerics). The Twelvers themselves are divided into three branches: the Usuli, the Shaykhi, and the Akhbari. The Usuli and Akhbari split over the degree to which *ijtihad* is accepted and how Hadith are selected, the Usuli being more modern. The Usuli are much more numerous, the Akhbari reduced to a few small communities mostly around Basra. Usuli Twelvers make up the majority of the populations of Iran (where theirs is the State Ideology), Iraq, Bahrain and Azerbaijan. The Shaykhi are a very small sect who emerged in the early nineteenth century, focused on eschatology.

Furthermore, there are a number of other sects that are offshoots of Twelver Shi'ism. Such as the Albanian Bektashi, who fuse belief in the Twelve

Imams with their unique Sufi rituals; the Alevi of Anatolia, who have mixed it with Kurdish and Turkish peasant traditions; and the deliberately secretive Alawites of Western Syria, who seem to be a fusion of vaguely Twelver beliefs with remnants of ancient Levantine Christianity. Though many see the Alawites as a Shia sect – including the Syrian regime partly due to their closeness to Iran, the Assads and other leadership figures being drawn from the Alawites, the ethnic group most favoured by their clientelist system – others have argued for Alawism to be considered a type of Islam in its own right, independent of Shi'ism.

Throughout the history of Shi'ism, however, a number of sects split off from the main line that the Twelvers accept, over disagreements over succession of the Imamate. The very first were the Kaysani, who no longer exist. The next, though, were the Zaidis, who accept Zaid as the true fourth Imam (the Twelvers accept Zayn al Abedin). They still exist in Yemen, constituting around a third of the population there. The Houthis, currently embroiled in the disastrous civil war, are a Zaidi Islamist group.

Then there are the Ishmaelis, who accept that Ishmael was the true Seventh Imam (Twelvers believe his brother Musa al-Kadhim was the rightful Seventh Imam). They are the most complicated of all the Muslim sects, as they are divided into a dozen sub-sects. The main one is the Seveners, who believe that Ishmael was the final Imam. Then there are at least ten more sects who recognize a chain of Imams descended from Ishmael, different from the chain descended from his brother that the Twelvers recognize. Numerous, impossibly complicated disagreements over succession within this post-Ishmael line led to a plethora of different sects, mostly based in Pakistan and India, including the Nizari (led by the Aga Khan, and forming a majority in the extreme East of Afghanistan and some immediately adjacent areas of China, Pakistan and Tajikistan), Musta'ali, Dawoodi Bohra, and many more.

The Druze of Lebanon and Syria are the best known of the Ishmaeli subgroups, accepting the Imamate, and one of Ishmael's descendants as their final Imam. Though their relationship to Ishmaelism is somewhat contentious, since they have a number of pre-Islamic beliefs not shared with any other Muslims, such as the transmigration of the soul. There is also a smaller population of Seveners found in Syria.

Finally, two further groups emerged partly out of Shia Islam. The first is the Ahmadis, whose Messianic Punjabi founder Mirza Ghulam Ahmad (1835-1908) preached that he was a redeemer of Islam, equating himself with the (Twelfth) Imam al-Mahdi. It would be a mistake to call it an offshoot of Shia though, as its system of beliefs is more like a liberal version of Sunni Islam, and they use the Sunni Hadith. It is something of a syncretism of the two, but now is a Muslim denomination in its own right. Their belief that Prophets can still come after Muhammad (who they accept as "seal of the prophets", but define this phrase as meaning not the final prophet but the most perfect) has caused them to be declared as heretics and horrendously persecuted in Sunni-dominated Pakistan. Even in Scotland, in an infamous 2016 case, a much-loved Glaswegian Ahmadi newsagent, Asad Shah, was stabbed to death outside his shop by an English salafi, who pleaded guilty citing that the victim was an open Ahmadi and denied that Muhammed was the final prophet. Note that although Shia have never believed in *prophecy* after Muhammad, Sunni puritans have accused them of as much and brand them heretics, due to their reverence for the Imams, whom they sometimes depict in paintings of the human form, forbidden in Sunni Islam. Ahmadis also have a number of other peculiar beliefs, including that Jesus died on the cross and was resurrected and thereafter lived in Kashmir (all other Muslims believe he was raised to heaven); and that religion and science are two parts of the same thing, entirely compatible, science being the *how* of God's will and creation. (Echoing the Catholic theologian Teilhard de Chardin.)

The second group is the Baha'is. They are now recognized as a world religion in their own right (their founder was Mirza Husayn-Ali Nuru, 1817-1892, known as the "Baha'u'llah") but grew out of a Persian Twelver environment, and their belief in the unity of God is directly descended from *tawhid*. With their background in ecumenical Shia Islam, they believe in the unity of religions, all of which they believe have something to offer to humanity. They are considered heretics by both Sunni and Shia Islamists, and suffer terrible persecution in Iran. Many Baha'is would agree with me in viewing it as *also* a distinct variety of *Islam*, as well as a world religion in its own right.

Having considered all the schools and sects, or denominations, into which Muslims are formally divided, we should now turn to *types* of Muslims. As I have mentioned, different types of Muslims have historically been more important than actual official sects, whose importance I have certainly over-exaggerated with the strict categorization above (for example, regular Sunnis certainly do not define themselves as "Hanafi" or "Shafi"). And of course, Sunni and Shia, like Catholics and Protestants, mostly do not think of themselves in such categories: even considering the sectarian warfare in Iraq and Syria, the (Shia) Islamic Republic of Iran and Hezbollah still fund and support (Sunni) Hamas — Sunni and Shia Islamists still finding some common ground (though relations between the Saudis and Iranians could derail that). And the common idea of just "Muslim" still holds some traction: for example this is how Bosnian Muslims mostly simply see themselves, many having more knowledge of different Christian sects than of different Muslim sects. While there are also ecumenicals, who consciously describe themselves as just "Muslim" and refuse to pick whether they are Sunni or Shia — common amongst Indian Muslims and liberally-minded converts.

There are of course infinite *types* of Muslims, but the two varieties of believers I will look at are Sufis and Islamists. As in between these two opposite groups lie most everything else: personal believers, inner converts, ecumenicals and their foes, those who believe in modernity and those who reject it, as well as the differing degrees to which practising Muslims are influenced by the cultures of their homelands.

Sufis are not a sect in themselves, though some specific brotherhoods may develop an identity of that sort: but if they do, it is more like a specific Hindu *cult* with its own rituals and emphases, but which still recognizes and is recognized by most other Hindus. Sufism is rather a *style*, more like "mystic" or "spiritual" in Christianity, which can be used to describe Christians of a certain *type* found in all denominations; or like "Kabbalah" in Judaism. For there are Sufis amongst Sunnis, Shia, and Ahmadis (whose origins were in a Punjabi Sufi brotherhood). Shi'ism as a whole is actually more Sufic than Sunnism, as rituals and holy places associated with the veneration of the Imams are central to Shia practice, as are passion cults commemorating the martyrdom of Hussein, the first Imam: however, most Sufi orders are Sunni. But clear-cut distinctions are beside the point when dealing with Sufis, as it is in Sufi orders that we are most likely to find syncretism of both Sunni and Shia practices. Sufism is the emotional practice of Islam, attempting to get closer to God through experience and feeling. It is defined by shrines, veneration of saints (even in Sunni orders, there is likely veneration of Shia Imams as saints), and above all spiritual rituals, sometimes centred on music (as in West African Sufi houses), sometimes on dance (as in the Mevlevi of Istanbul), and so on.

Hard-line Sunni Islamists have a serious problem with Sufis, as they view all these traditions as decadent, contrary to the Sunnah, while the association of some Sufi groups with homosexuality and alcohol has been a trope within the vitriol against Sufis. Above all, the Sufi tradition of shrines and mausoleums has attracted salafist wrath, for example in the barbaric destruction by Malian

Islamists of Sufi mausoleums in Timbuktu, where they also attempted to ban all music (Mali having a musical tradition as great as Ireland's). Desecration of Sufi shrines is also common in Pakistan.

This is the other, opposite, type of Muslim, the final variety of Islam I will discuss: political Islam, or Islamism. The first thing to understand is that there is no "church and state", as there is no "church" *per se*: Islam is not a formal organisation in any way comparable to Christian Churches. Rather, it is a shared way of life, an *orthopraxic* system rather than an *orthodoxy*, though the strength of belief is perhaps generally much stronger than in Judaism and much of Christianity. As there is thus no separation – which in the West is very much perceived in terms of physical space – there is no wall between religion and politics; and Islam often has influence on the latter, as the religion itself is totalizing, commanding that every sphere of life, public and private, be rooted in the Qur'an and Hadith.

Indeed, in the Sunni tradition, the Caliphs were supposed to embody the Five Pillars of Islam and emulate the Sunnah. (The five pillars are profession of faith, daily prayer, almsgiving, fasting for Ramadan, and pilgrimage to Mecca: these pillars are also shared – with some qualifications – by all the main Muslim sects.) The Muslim world therefore has historically, in the modern period, had perhaps less innate understanding of sacred and secular as separate zones: Islam as a whole is thus more like Judaism in being an entire way of life, although Jews have perhaps come to understand better the dichotomy between the sacred and secular as a greater proportion of Jews have lived in secularized Western societies. That said, Turkey for example has been more secular than many Western societies, though Erdogan is changing that rapidly, and the Ba'ath parties who have ruled much of the Arab World into this century did create a Western-style secular state system, though thanks to their authoritarian nature they have failed to bring large sections of their populations into the fold of secularism.

Modern political Islamism emerged as a reaction to such states, which they saw as the erosion of the system by which legitimate Muslims, defined by adherence to the Five Pillars of Islam, ruled over Muslims. It had firstly appeared in Egypt, pioneered by Hassan al-Banna (1906-1949), founder of the Muslim Brotherhood, as a traditionalist form of anti-Imperialism, as Muslims there and elsewhere were being ruled over by Western "infidels" and their native collaborators. Then, under the leadership of Sayyid Qutb (1906-1966), it was reinvigorated as a form of opposition to the Western-style secularized leadership that was prevailing in much of the Muslim world, especially the Ba'ath regime in Egypt. Such post-colonial regimes were attempting to separate Mosque and State and were not directed by the Five Pillars.

Sunni Islamism was an attempt to reincarnate the Sunni Caliphate (which had lost its last nominal existence with the creation of the Turkish Republic which ousted the Sultan) and restore the values and identity of the Muslim world, pre-Napoleon (who began the process of European conquest of the Arab World, as emphasized by Edward Said). This has been the essential aim of Sunni Islamists: to delegitimize secular or non-Sunni Muslim rulers by simply calling them apostates, infidels in disguise, and so on – not real Muslims. This was a new strategy, pioneered by Qutb. Further, it has also aimed to undo the middle-eastern borders created by the European powers post-World War One, which have never satisfied Muslim Arabs. As John McHugo has argued, for example, Mosul and Aleppo were always partner cities, but the Franco-British Sykes-Picot line (the modern border of Iraq and Syria) severed them, destroying the traditional economy of both (John McHugo, *Syria: A Recent History*, 2015).

So both Islamists and the Arab Nationalists they declare *takfir* against have sought to undo these borders and recreate something of the old Ottoman Caliphate/Arab Empire. For European ideas of *nation* – a politically limited community with set borders, even where based on old vilayets (Ottoman provinces) – never entirely translated into Arabic, the Arabs having lived for millennia in massive empires (first their own, then under the Turkish Ottomans). So, there was the United Arab Republic, though its falling apart demonstrates Ba'athists' inability to follow through with their ultimate aim of a greater Arab state. Daesh (i.e., so-called "Islamic State"), however, at its zenith of power consciously did away with the Sykes-Picot line, reuniting Sunni Arab territory on both the Syrian and Iraqi sides. Note also its attempt to relink Mosul and Aleppo; and how consciously Sunni was the choice of name for their leader, *Abu Bakr* Al-Baghdadi, the use of the first Caliph's name in direct opposition to Shia beliefs. Daesh, which attempts to actually physically recreate the world of the Prophet and Rightly Guarded Caliphs, however, represents the most literalist form of Sunni Islamism.

The Muslim Brotherhood offers a more moderate form, believing in the creation of a new society based on Sharia and the Sunnah, which they believe to be compatible with aspects of modernity. Rather than erasing modernity, they seek to reform it, and to move gradually towards political union of Muslims in a Sharia state.

It is in the Shia world, however, that Islamism has had the most proportionally large success, with the successful revolution against the ultra-pro-Western Shah, who was branded as an infidel according to the Sunni Qutb's tactic, installing a Shia theocracy in the state whose population accounts for the majority of the world's Shia population. Shia Islamism since then has had more refined goals — namely, to keep the Iranian theocracy alive, and Hezbollah in power in Lebanon, and in the last decade or so, to consolidate the "Shia Crescent" linking them. The latter stretches from Western Afghanistan to the Mediterranean, and is held together by ensuring that an Iran-friendly Shia government stays in power in Iraq, as well as the vaguely-Shia Assad dynasty in Syria. And also, in the last few years, there has been the attempt to facilitate a Shia (Houthi) victory in the Yemeni Civil War. It has so far been largely successful in the Shia Crescent project, though Iran seems to wish ultimately to spread Twelver Islamism in Assad's Syria, and to further its own and Hezbollah's power in Lebanon.

In terms of the relations between strong Muslim believers and the political sphere, they are (in short) more similar to evangelical Protestants who wish to see their beliefs confirmed by legislation binding on everybody. Islam as a whole is more similar to Protestantism, focusing on debates of interpretation of the text, but with the nature of God rarely a source of debate — Islam having largely been free of the theological dramas of early Christianity, more similar to Judaism in how it sees God.

So the DUP, for example, should see Islamists as kin, and we should view Islamists the same way we would likely view such Protestant parties, whose interpretation of Protestantism and its relation to politics is about on par with elements of the Muslim Brotherhood's interpretation of Islam and politics.

So rhetorically — as with the DUP — would I support them? No. Would I encourage anyone to vote for them? No. But would I support the use of violence — including unlimited civilian casualties — to stop them politically? No — and anybody who suggested this as a solution to Evangelicals would likely be in trouble with the law. Yet it is within mainstream politics in the USA, Russia, the UK, Israel, France, China and other great states to advocate such solutions for Islamists. For anti-Islamism is proving much more dangerous in this century (so far) than Islamism itself (when one compares, for example, the civilian death toll of 9/11 to that of the War on Terror). Hubert Butler reached the same conclusion vis-á-vis *anti-Marxism* in relation to *Marxism* in the middle of the last century.

Like it or not, Islamists are here to stay, as surely as the Evangelical Christian parties are. There are perhaps as many Islamists in the West as, say, Communists. And any use of mass violence to try and stop them inevitably creates *rashids* (martyrs), regardless of how the perpetrators dress it up; and in the long term, all these military and political tactics used to repress Islamists only gives them more ammunition, and indeed (for some) endows genuine legitimacy to their ideas – whilst, of course, Western and Eastern Islamaphobic culture is the greatest recruiter of all.

I think that Islamists, though certainly the least attractive variety of Islam, should – insofar as they are not involved in, or advocating, violent or terrorist activities – be invited into full participation in the democratic system, where they will inevitably screw up, and soon enough repulse and put off most Muslims and non-Muslims. And in any case, what is the great ethical difference between those Islamists who advocate violence, and the respectable generals who execute it? What is ultimately so different about preachers who encourage armed Jihad (for Jihad can also be entirely spiritual), and "public" schools, such as the one I attended (Royal Belfast Academical Institution), which encourage their pupils to join the military in which they may well "legally" kill as many? Indeed, some more moderate Islamist parties present a worldview more moderate than DUP Evangelism.

They should all be countered with ideas, through debate. For the only real way to defeat a bad idea – as Hubert Butler once remarked – is with a better one.

Jacob Eoin Agee was born in 1993 and educated in Belfast. He completed a four-year joint honours BA in Jewish and Islamic Studies, with Classics, at Trinity College, Dublin, before receiving an MA in Holocaust and Genocide Studies at the Hugo Valentin Centre, Uppsala University. He is currently undertaking a PhD at Trinity College Dublin, on the essays of Hubert Butler. His poetry has appeared in Poetry Ireland Review 111 *(edited by the poet John F. Deane), the TCD literary journal* Icarus *(three times), and the "New Generation Poets" issue of* Agenda *(edited by Patricia McCarthy). He has also worked as a freelance translator for Fraktura, Croatia's leading literary press, and recently completed a translation of Slavko Goldstein's study of Holocaust denial,* Jasenovac: tragedija, mitomanija, istina/ Jasenovac: Tragedy, Mythomania, Truth. *He divides his time between Ireland and Croatia.*

SERENDIPITY:
A COLLABORATION BETWEEN
SVEN BIRKERTS & CHRIS BENFEY

Sven Birkerts and Chris Benfey

Auras of arrangement.

My friend the writer Chris Benfey and I have for many years had conversations about serendipity. In the summer of 2018 we decided to correspond about the theme. What started as a casual, private back-and-forth soon enough found momentum and led to 100 exchanges (we agreed to that number as a cap). What follows here are entries relating to Seamus Heaney, whom we both knew, though through separate channels. The reflections mainly take up questions of inspiration and faith — in both cases, the having and the losing ...We pick up these themes mid-exchange, at the time of the Seamus Heaney exhibition in Dublin — which Benfey, travelling with his family in Ireland, was lucky enough to attend. — S.B.

SB: Here's a coincidence, one that felt fairly loaded to me. It happened early this morning, no doubt because I was following from my great distance accounts of the headline moments of the Heaney exhibition (you can find anything at all on Twitter). I was dreaming that I was with great concentration trying to write "Seamus Heaney" in imitation of his hand — he had a very distinctive way with cursive, which is of course now in the museum of bygones along with the rotary phone and the Model T. I remember fretting in that dream over whether to tuck the leg of the final Y under or draw it straight, as I normally would my own Y. I decided that he did tuck, giving me the last stroke of my laborious forgery (I can't imagine what sketchy pretext narrative had me doing this).

 After that I woke, the feeling of the dream still in me. It was dark, but I wanted to know what time it was. Taking up my iPhone, I saw that it was 4:20. I also saw that there was an e-mail there from you, sent at 4:12, which would be, what, 10:20 in Dublin. There was no message, just an attachment. I opened it in the dark, squinting at the little screen. You had sent me a photo of the first page of Heaney's "Blackbird of Glanmore" — written out in his hand! Well, well.

CB: When I was deep into writing my little divination pieces, I had a strange dream about Heaney and Tarot. It was strange, among other reasons, because Yeats was the Tarot poet, not Heaney. And when I woke up, I looked around in *Stepping Stones* to see what Heaney had to say about Yeats's mumbo jumbo. As you know, he deprecates what he calls Yeats's "do-it-yourself religion", ascribing it to the fact that Yeats grew up "deprived of religion in his youth", in contrast to Heaney's Catholicism. Heaney comments: "But I suppose – like many Catholics, lapsed or not – I am of the Stephen Dedalus frame of mind: if you desert this system, you're deserting the best there is, and there's no point in exchanging one great coherence for some other *ad hoc* arrangement." I love the scorn there, the Catholic pride, which took me by surprise, and the identification with Stephen Dedalus. As you know, I've been living with Dedalus lately.

The interviewer in *Stepping Stones* notes that the "Squarings" sequence begins with a poem that seems to reject an afterlife. Heaney counters: "But it's also firmly grounded in a sensation of 'scope', of a human relation to the 'shifting brilliancies' and the roaming 'cloud-life.' It's still susceptible to the numinous."

Doesn't this rejoinder speak to so much of our recent concern with the "serious" – with ultimates? I also can't help but notice how closely Heaney's word choice accords with our ongoing thoughts on photography: how you square a photograph; how you try (you especially) to capture the roaming cloud-life and the shifting brilliancies. And of course the opening section of "Squarings" is titled "Lightenings", which Heaney associates with three meanings: a lightening of burdens, an increase in lighting, and an alleviation in the face of impending death. I mean, isn't that the whole game – and Heaney takes his theme from a game of marbles – right there?

Heaney was, I assume, not a church-goer, though I could be wrong. (He was certainly a haunter of churches, especially ancient Irish churches.) And his sense that having lapsed from an orthodox upbringing doesn't remove you from a certain religious aura, or "arrangement", reminds me of my own lapsed Quakerism, in a comforting way. I recently read a piece about Gershom Scholem, and I was surprised – even a little shocked – to learn that he wasn't a practicing Jew, even after his momentous name change, even after his momentous move to Israel. But of course he spent his life, nevertheless, studying the aura, as his friend Benjamin might say, the arrangement.

SB: Of course your good words got me thinking about Seamus. I count knowing him – and I'm pretty sure you do, too – as one of the charmed singularities of my life. And there aren't finally that many.

Musing again on the man, and flashing back to my first meeting him, I realized that it owed a good deal to happenstance, or what felt like happenstance back then. But that account needs some backdrop.

I had my very first glimpse of the man way back in the 1970s and only from a distance. I was living in Ann Arbor and he had come to give a reading in one of the big auditoriums. The scene takes us back to *before*, because the room was not at all crowded. I took him in from afar only because it was then my preference to sit in the back at readings. I don't remember what poems he read, though I do remember that in one he cast himself as "an inner émigré, grown long-haired and thoughtful." That rang some kind of bell for me. And, indeed, he looked the part. He wore his hair long (for Seamus) and there was that unforgettable chiseled face.

It was at least a decade later – I'm not good with dates and sequences – that I was living in Cambridge and working at the bookstore. I knew he had taken up a one-term-a-year teaching post at Harvard, but had not set eyes on him. One late afternoon, I went to the Yenching Library to hear Derek Walcott read – I think it was Walcott. The room was full, but I managed to find a seat in the middle. Taking my first look around the room, I registered a shock. There was the poet Seamus Heaney in an aisle seat. By now, of course, he was a world-famous poet. I could feel how the attention in the room changed when word got out that he was there.

When the reading ended, I made my way back to the inevitable cheese-and-cracker table. I was in a jostling crowd, determined to extract myself quickly. But then I turned my head and saw that Heaney was standing right beside me. I could not let the opportunity pass. I said some admiring – but surely truthful – thing, and then we had a very short exchange. I'm embarrassed to think what a fan-boy I was. I was so thrilled by that short minute of talk that I hurried away so that I could keep the feeling intact. Deciding that a beer was in order, I made my way to One-Potato, Two-Potato, the restaurant just a few doors down from the Harvard Book Store (where I worked then).

The next bit is tricky, for memory, as we know, is the great fabulator. Looking back, I want to say that I felt a premonition as I sat there. But in truth I'm no longer sure. The rest is accurate, though. I was at a side table. At one point I looked up from my beer and saw the poet himself come through the door – by himself. I learned soon enough that what he called the "One P,

Two P" was a regular port of call for him. But that evening it seemed like the most wonderful coincidence. The good luck kept rolling. For after he came through the door he paused to look around, and saw me sitting there. He recognized me from our interchange; he came up and asked if he might join me. You can imagine how I felt.

Curiously – maybe because I was trying so hard to make an impression – I can't remember what we talked about. Poetry, of course, with me very likely firing the "do you like ___?" question at him over and over. But something definitely clicked as we talked, because not long after that he started coming into the bookstore near the end of my evening shift. He had that wonderful conspiratorial way about him. He would lift one asking eyebrow, and then raise his hand ever so slightly and make a tipping motion with his thumb. I would nod back and then hurry over to the One P, Two P as soon as we had locked up.

That was a fairly lengthy setting of the stage for the short reflection that follows. I don't really want to account for our various interactions here. Instead, I want to think about whatever it was that allowed that to-and-fro between us to take place. Naturally, there's no accounting for what happens between people – how things work or don't – but I know that there were some basic recognitions right away. We had the shared love of literature, and of certain poets, obviously; but we also enjoyed a certain kind of darkish humor. (You'll remember that we had a field day of drollery the time you drove into to Cambridge and the three of us had that one meal together – at the restaurant on Mt. Auburn street called … Daedalus!). Certainly Seamus felt my great admiration, and maybe this allowed him to take a slightly paternal posture toward me.

But I'm after something else here – not so much the emotional aspects of liking someone and being liked back, but more the way that sensibilities do and don't mesh. This angle allows me to bring Seamus more directly into our conversation. For of course we both think of him as one of our tutelary spirits.

So much of what we focus on here is present, often overtly, in his poems and essays. We've each noted certain things in our exchange so far: the Latinist's interest in roots, his way of treating those moments of awakening, the "buffetings"; the wells and springs; and the boggy tangles so evocative of origins, not to mention his attentiveness to harbingers, and his implicit reverence for "the music of what happens". All these things and more are on display – but also secreted – in his lines.

That said, I was slightly puzzled by what you found going back to *Stepping Stones*, his saying: "But I suppose – like many Catholics, lapsed or not – I am of the Stephen Daedalus frame of mind: if you desert this system, you're deserting the best there is, and there's no point in exchanging one great coherence for some other *ad hoc* arrangement."

Is that the Stephan Daedalus frame of mind? My sense from our earlier exchange was that when Stephen deserted the church he did not think it the best there is. Rather, he thought it was confining and in many ways ruinous, and that he vowed to fashion through his art a truer coherence. Also, I can't quite believe that Seamus, who was so admiring of the embattled Miłosz – he called him "Pan Miłosz" – would refer to the art alternative as "some other *ad hoc* arrangement". I know he had the strong Catholic upbringing, but I always thought that he, like young Daedalus, was intent on forging the alternative. I realize that I can't let that notion go – it's such a part of the guidance I take from him.

One more thing, speaking of that guidance: his last gesture. That he would write a text to Marie just before he died saying just *noli timere* – be not afraid. Why the Latin? And what was his import—"don't be afraid for me" or, more generally, "don't be afraid of what's to come"? Is it that death is a natural culmination, to be accepted, or was Seamus writing with one foot already on the other side – announcing that there is another side? Was it the old Catholicism speaking? Was that why the Latin? I don't know.

CB: I was puzzled by Seamus's comment, too, about how "there's no point in exchanging one great coherence for some other *ad hoc* arrangement." Having thought about it for a while, though, I think that what he meant by *ad hoc* arrangements was specifically the kind of jerry-built religion that Yeats fashioned in *A Vision*. I *don't* think that Seamus was referring to art. Like Dedalus, he was okay with deserting Catholicism to forge in the smithy of his soul the uncreated conscience of his race, or whatever the wording is. But he didn't feel called upon to also forge a substitute religion there, in the Yeats manner. Art is art. It's not a substitute religion. Of course, it's a great (or small) coherence, as you say, hence our puzzlement with how Seamus puts the whole matter. I think we're dealing with three things here, though, not two: an inherited religion; a made-up religion; and art. Religion and art may have things in common, like the awareness of the "numinous". They may even overlap in certain ways, and even be in competition in certain ways. But they're not the same thing. I'd want to hear more about Miłosz in this regard. Didn't Seamus have great respect for Miłosz's religious commitments? And for Simone Weil's.

Another puzzle to me is why Wittgenstein, who read and admired *Portrait of the Artist as a Young Man*, singled out the long Catholic retreat section as his favorite part of the book. But then, Wittgenstein was fascinated by religion. He felt that philosophy had not somehow put an end to religion, as logical positivists might believe. He felt that philosophy and religion were different things.

I love what you say about Seamus's final text, his last gesture. So interesting about the message being in Latin. "Was that the old Catholicism speaking?" you ask. In some sense, surely. And maybe Horace, too. But isn't there just the slightest – the very slightest – hint of irony, of the glint in the eye, in that text? And texting! (Was he really texting?) What a strange bridge between the old Latin and the new dispensation.

These things were swirling in my head, especially the question of what Seamus meant in his dismissal of *ad hoc* arrangements, when I was walking Allie this morning. An attractive young woman dressed all in black strode towards me, as in a dream, calling my name. It was Katherine S, an economist at Mount Holyoke, trailing a wake of unspeakable tragedy. She seemed like the woman addressed in Baudelaire's "Á Une Passante", a woman in mourning. A year ago, Katherine gave birth to a daughter named Mabel. Everything seemed fine at first. Then it became clear that Mabel wasn't progressing, wasn't growing. Tests determined a severe brain injury, with no clear cause. She lived on and on for seven months, a beautiful child, but developed in none of the ways a normal child grows. And then she died.

I don't know Katherine well though I've always been extremely fond of her, in committees, meetings, that sort of thing. And suddenly we were talking, this morning, about serious things, ultimate things. Are we supposed to be happy? Is there a plan for us, a destiny? When one tragedy happens to us, are we destined for more tragedy? When will the cancer diagnosis come, following hard on the dead child? I thought of Nadezhda Mandelstam's complaint, "But I'm not happy". Osip replied something like, "Whatever gave you the notion that we're supposed to be happy?" I mentioned this to Katherine. She countered with something her therapist had told her: "I tell my patients that I can't make them happy. I can make them well." Katherine found this puzzling, as do I. It sounds a bit Freudian. Life consists of managing our neuroses, etc.

In groping for what to say to Katherine – what is there to say? – I found myself reaching for literary echoes, consolations. Frost's "Home Burial"? No consolation there. The death of Kipling's daughter at age eight? Katherine had never heard of Kipling. Didion's book about her year of magical thinking? Katherine had never heard of Didion.

PORTFOLIO

—

Tisja Kljaković Braić

The Two of Them
(an extract)

Tisja Kljaković Braić was born in 1979 in Split, Croatia, and was educated at the School of Visual Arts, Split. She took a degree in Painting at the Art Academy, again in Split, studying under Gorki Žuvela, and graduated in 2003.

She has exhibited her work in over thirty joint exhibitions, and in over thirty-five solo shows, both in Croatia and overseas.

Her work is included in many individual, national and international collections, including the Zagreb Modern Gallery and the Sveti Krševan Gallery in Šibenik.

These cartoons are taken from her celebrated book The Two of Them (Oni).

Kljaković Braić is the author of a previous similar volume, The Devil in the Girl. She is a member of the Croatian Society of Independent Artists as well as the Croatian Society of Visual Artists.

She continues to live and work in Split.

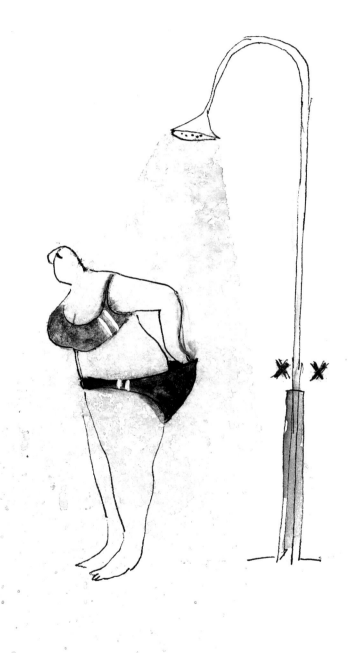

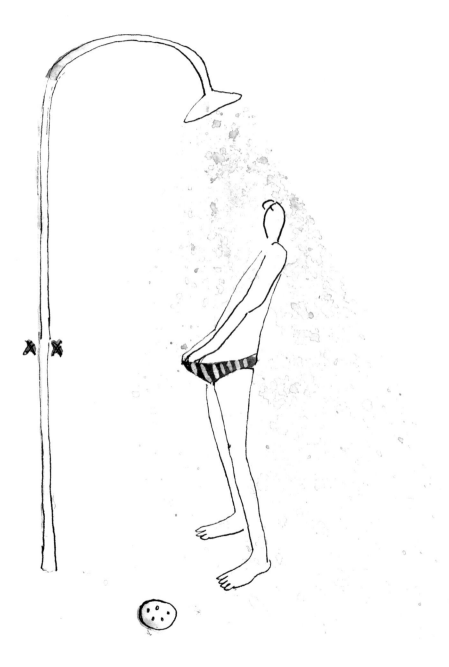

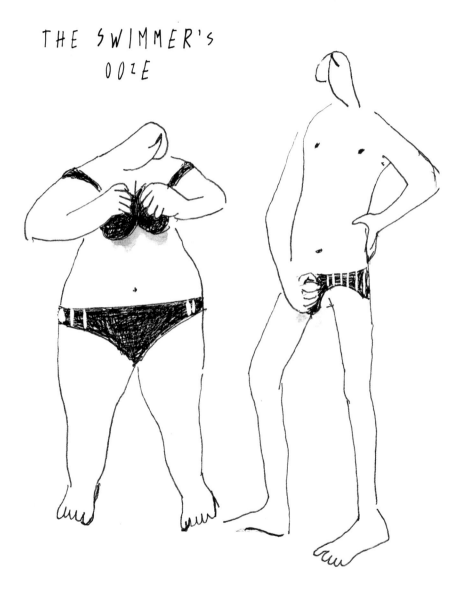

— GIMME
THE LEG

WHAT DID SHE SAY TO YOU
BATHROOM MATS...
THREE PILLOWS
THOSE GLASSES...
THAT'S WHAT LILIA
SAID...
SO I WON'T
GET BACK NOW...
WHICH SHEETS...
ONES WITH THE
FLOWERS...
THEY ONLY
HAVE ELASTICS...

I CAN'T
TAKE IT
ANY
MORE...

A SINGULAR PERSPECTIVE ON DALMATIAN MARRIAGE

—

Jurica Pavičić

There is an ingrained stereotype of the Dalmatian marriage, and the Dalmatian family, as patriarchal. This stereotype is so contagious and common that it is practically pointless to spell it out. The images basically conjure up themselves: of moustachioed, chain-wearing men at the doors, of a patronizing Mišo Kovač; of his tame, loyal wife; of the big mother / mother-in-law for whom the young bride is never good enough, and her son never pampered enough. A scene of noisy households in which cooking and baking go on all day, and the liturgical and calendric years bicker in a regular rhythm of cod, *pašticada*, broad beans, artichokes, Advent dumplings, Istrian Easter brioche, grapes, berries and stuffed sauerkraut. There is also – to be sure – the image of the man, devoted to the public sphere, whose natural habitats are the *kavana* and the *boules* patch, and whose natural interests are politics and ball sports. Finally, there is also another image of the woman, she who switches between the public and private spheres, she who looks after – a major maxim – "three quarters of the house", but also exists in a parallel universe of red wine, cognac and coffee with girlfriends.

This stereotype is so fixed that it is very difficult to challenge, even when the challenge rests on empirical foundations. Many sociologists – from those of the interwar period to Inga Tomić Koludrović, with her sociological study *The Shift to Modernity* – have empirically demonstrated how the myth of Dalmatian patriarchy is *myth* even at its basis. How, in the spheres of work, money and decision-making, the Dalmatian woman is – statistically speaking – more emancipated than, for example, women from continental northern Croatia. Instead of the simple but arresting images of the submissive Mediterranean woman and of southern patriarchy, sociology as well as daily observation offer us an immeasurably more complex dynamic of male-female relations in which traditional culture and modernity are, in a strange way, mixed – an economy dependent on both female employment and traditional domestic functions. It is a world in which economic emancipation and the need for a pretence of the traditional – for the rituals of the permeated household – often go hand in hand.

Milan Begović, Marko Uvodić and Miljenko Smoje have immortalised, in prose narrative, this dynamic of the ostensibly "traditional" Dalmatian family, in different ways and at different phases of development. Two brilliant Dalmatian short story writers, Olja Savičević Ivančević and Tanja Mravak, have created prose worlds inhabited by such families. Most of these depict this dynamic of the Mediterranean family by making use of an alluring mix of wistfulness and humour, delicacy and mockery.

So here we have another book speaking to Mediterranean marriage, with this same entwined sense of delicacy, humour and light mockery. The book, simply called *The Two of Them*, by Split painter and cartoonist Tisja Kljaković Braić, consists of ninety (mostly black-and-white) cartoons in which there exist, in principle, but two figures. Namely, "The Two of Them": A Wife, a woman of unspecified middle age who is at war with surplus kilograms and the metamorphosis of her own body; and A Man, a guy who is, for much of the book, on the couch in his nether garments (or underpants) watching football. Kljaković Braić develops these two figures over ninety situational sketches drawn over a year, and mostly released in phases, in irregular weekly schedules. In terms of genre, the art of Kljaković Braić diverges from the classically accosting cartoon, with its gags and/or lines, being instead lyrical sketches rooted in emotion and neat visuals. Visually, all the sketches are similar. They lie against the backdrop of large white planes, on which the authoress sketches in a simple way, with paunchy contours and abstract situations. Colours – red, yellow, blue – appear only rarely, and always as a kind of gag.

Kljaković Braić's visual minimalism goes hand-in-hand with a thematic minimalism. Hers are little themes, small everyday situations. Like Raymond Carver or Joyce, Kljaković Braić searches for moments of "epiphany", short fragments of reality, sentences or gestures which reveal characters and intrapersonal dynamics. The world of *The Two of Them* is one of the bathroom, kitchen, bed – and only sometimes the beach or car. The "settings" are – literally – the couch, chair, wardrobe and toilet bowl. First and most often, there is the discontent of the chubby Wife with her own looks. Second, there is the cliché of the Wife's dissatisfaction with her wardrobe. Third is the capricious, irrational, football supporter passion of the Husband. A fourth sphere typical of Kljaković Braic's book is that of food: food that is warmed up, or debated and quarrelled over. The caricature of the spouses overwhelmed by a debate on whether they will cook the cod grilled or stewed is only one of many in which Kljaković Braić evokes the centrality of food in the chemistry of the

Mediterranean marriage. Simultaneously, food is also a sphere of saving and economizing, and of instrumentalizing one another, for example in the sketch in which She places before Him a reheated dinner "so it doesn't go to waste".

To be sure, there also appear in Kljaković Braić's sketches, typical battlegrounds in the prolific war between patriarchy and matriarchy (that is, household affairs . . .). Here, the relation between man and woman, curiously, ceases to be a relation between the overburdened servant girl and the male sponger. In place of this, Kljaković Braić offers an unusual glimpse into a Dalmatian marriage in which the Female assumes the role of the competent patron, and the Male is depicted as the immature, incompetent child who puts a pot in the dishwasher, and cannot do any job without ensuring it gets screwed up. "It's easier for me to do it than explain it to you" exclaims She in one of the classic sketches; in another, she simply says to the man "Where did you get these". There is something in front of them on the table, not clear to us if it is dough, vegetables or piles of washed things; less explicit is whether the "emancipated" man has again screwed up an attempt to be useful. Here She needs (her "needs") to assume a role that at least gives her a grain of pleasure – the impression we have the whole time. This role is that of the matriarchal ruler who, as it is said, looks after "three quarters of the house", and is for her spouse (evidently sub-adult in the serious sphere of the household) not only a wife, but also a guardian and a protector.

With the gift of the subtle humourist and the eye of the astute observer, Tisja Kljaković Braić recreates, over ninety sketches, situations that are so typical that they are part of every marriage: though here these sketches are also ones of southern brightness: extrovert, operatic and shameless. Our culture has seen a long line of such southern pairs. We remember, too, Roko and Cicibela, Luigi and Bepina. *The Two of Them* is a beautiful continuation of this tradition.

Translated, from the Croatian, by Jacob Agee.

As I think back to this morning-mourning walk, I realize — it's hardly news, of course — how much you and I experience the world in relation to the writers we love. We depend on this chorus of voices. How could we get through a single day without Seamus, Emerson, Frost, Didion, Milosz, and the rest? The visionary company, as Hart Crane called them.

SB: Yes, yes — I like what you said, differentiating "system" (Yeats) from art itself. I like it in part because Seamus was one of those people I looked to for instruction and inspiration, and if he really had believed that art was somehow a lesser alternative, then I would have to take a contemplative pause and go back to *considering* the constellations in my little firmament.

What you wrote at the close of your last — how much we take our guidance from writers — started me thinking, and eventually led me around to the "last things" discussion you had this morning on your walk. Everything comes down to last things. How not? They are last.

I found myself pondering what you said about our deep attachment to the writers we love, to what you called a "chorus of voices". Of course that's true — we've confirmed as much in these very pages. But then I thought that it's not just the writers and their particular works that we attend to, but also to the kind of "presence" that the works lead us to create. I mean, when you think of Sebald, say, do you think of some particular work or works, or do you think of the person, the life, that those works originate from and that they illuminate? Speaking for myself, I can't but create some semblance of what I imagine to be their writerly identity, and then refer to (address) that identity in my thoughts.

Does this sound strange? You know that I don't mean every writer, just the ones that I have annexed for myself.

CB: I think that I *only* read books now for that felt authorial presence hovering behind the words. I *only* read for wisdom, for help with the serious things, the ultimate things.

It seems hardly credible that we three should have met for our only dinner alone together — you, Seamus, and I — at a restaurant called Dedalus. Can it be possible? And what might it mean? "What is the significance of these similarities, overlaps, and coincidences?" Sebald asks in his chapter on Robert Walser. "Are they rebuses of memory, delusions of the self and of the senses, or rather the schemes and symptoms of an order underlying the chaos of human relationships, and applying equally to the living and the dead, which lies beyond our comprehension?"

Sebald's question is also, it seems to me, at the heart of the ambiguous title of Seamus's *Seeing Things*. I now think that the title works on at least three different levels. First, it means seeing things in the ordinary sense, accurately and realistically, seeing what's *there*. Second, it means seeing things in a mistaken way, as in Sebald's "delusions of the self and of the senses", as when we say, "You're seeing things." And third, it means seeing things in a visionary way, seeing things as poets and other artists see them. This third meaning is the most important one for the book, isn't it? It's what Seamus alludes to, in the sonnet "Fosterling", when he writes, ruefully, "Me waiting until I was nearly fifty / To credit marvels."

Just here I want to make a painful confession. I reviewed (a weird word, "re-saw") *Seeing Things* for Rosanna Warren at *Partisan Review*. I think it was in one of the final issues, maybe the last one. There were other books thrown in, by Howard Nemerov, I think, and maybe Seamus's Philoctetes translation. I couldn't bear to look up my review. I'm pretty sure that *Seeing Things* was pretty much completely lost on me. To my shame, I took to heart in those days Seamus's own downbeat self-assessment, circa 1985, that he was finished as a poet. His anxiety seemed to hit around the publication of *Field Work*. He'd say at readings, "I wrote this when I was still a good poet," before reading something like "Anahorish". For me, the callow and pitiless reviewer, *Seeing Things* felt somehow posthumous, the dying embers of a once great career. I'm sure that I said nice, dutiful things about it, but it has only been very recently that these later – I mean after Seamus turned forty – volumes of his have struck me hard.

At the Dublin exhibition, there was a handwritten page from his private journal on display. I think the date was around 1982. In it, Seamus wrote of how miserable he was, how he said yes to too many things, how he was drinking too much, how he was losing his way. A young Irish poet, Martin Dyar, pointed out the page to me, expressing surprise that Marie had let it be made public. It points to that moment when Seamus felt he had to remake himself as a poet or die as a poet. My sense is that he remade himself in at least two ways. He became a politically engaged poet, in the republic of the conscience poems, or whatever that side of his work should be named, though always in a deeply private way, not just taking sides. But the other way that he remade himself was in the key of *Seeing Things*, as a spiritual poet who "credited marvels".

I feel you've been wary, even resistant, of my pushing this side of Seamus's work already. You're a hedgehog about (or against) religion, I fear (*noli
timere*), while I'm a fox. But again – and I'm sure my repetition of these things
is becoming tiresome – there's a certain openness to religion in *Seeing Things*,
it seems to me. I don't mean the old man is thinking it's time to start going to
church again. I mean instead that Catholicism, and specifically those ancient
stone churches like Clonmacnoise, has been a place where the numinous had
a place, had a voice. What exactly is the status of the miracles mentioned or
retold in the eighth poem in "Squarings", when a ship appears in the oratory
of the Clonmacnoise church? Or the miracle of St. Kevin and the blackbird
in that wonderful poem you sent me a few months back? I absolutely don't
think that miracles like these are what Seamus is referring to when he says
that at age fifty he finds himself able – gives himself permission – to credit
miracles. So what *is* he referring to?

He takes up related questions in another poem from "Squarings", composed entirely of questions. "Where does spirit live?" the poem begins. "Inside
or outside / Things remembered, made things, things unmade?" After many
other questions, he adds a parenthesis: "(Set questions for the ghost of W.B.)"
Surely W.B. is Yeats, and this is another of Seamus's jibes in the direction of
Yeats's mumbo jumbo. But it doesn't mean that Seamus doesn't regard these
questions as urgent, especially with regard to "made things", as in poems.

Again, I reach for a parallel with photography. There was a craze for
"spirit photography" around the time of the Civil War and its aftermath, when
photographers claimed to have fixed Lincoln's ghost, or the ghosts of dead
soldiers, in their negatives. World War I brought another spate of spirit photographs. Conan Doyle was a believer, and of course Yeats was, too. There's a
spirit photograph taken of Yeats in a séance in Paris in 1914. It was thought
that photography could register not only the seen world but the unseen:
seeing things. Sally Mann's Cy Twombly book veers into this world of spirit
photography, I think, as did Jerry Liebling's photographs of the Dickinson
houses, where I specifically claimed – to his mild annoyance – that he was
taking spirit photographs (of shadows, flickerings of light, and other traces
of lives lived).

I think Seamus would reject any such twaddle, any belief in such magic,
except in the most imaginative sense. He'd kick it down to W.B., as we might
kick it down to that other W.B. of the aura, Walter Benjamin. And yet, photography does register another kind of spirit, doesn't it? I'm thinking of what
Seamus calls the "cloud-life".

I think Seamus's world of the numinous was much more like Emerson's. Emerson was always saying that the miraculous did not lie in the waterfalls or the Rocky Mountains or the rainbows, but rather in the ordinary: "the milk in the firkin", etc. Similarly, Seamus, again in an anti-Yeats mode, in *Stepping Stones*: "My starlight came in over the half-door of a house with a clay floor, not over the dome of a Byzantine palace; and, in a hollowed-out part of the floor, there was a cat licking up the starlit milk."

Starlit.

SB: Not to belabor the question of Seamus' investment in Catholicism, but I want to add – lest I sounded too either/or – that of course it's not a simple business. How many of us fully and absolutely believe, or disbelieve? *I believe, help Thou mine unbelief,* etc.

What I really wanted to pick up on was that period you recalled when Seamus thought the gift had deserted him – his apologetic stance in public about poems written after *Field Work*, and then the whole question of artistic inspiration. As we (the all-inclusive "we") tend to simplify the nature of belief, so too do we tend to think of inspiration as a thing that comes and goes, a Muse that makes house calls. But in fact it comes, when it does, in so many forms and intensities. There can be, yes, visitations like what Rilke experienced at Duino, but we might consider also the turned-down-flame sort that might present the writer with a few thrilling sentences or lines, and then dim out ...

Seamus did live with the fear of that waning, if not the complete loss of the power. It was for him, like for many or most of us, intimately bound up with his sense of self-worth. The wonderful run he had early in his career put him on the stage; it was the source of so much adulation. And that adulation is not to be underestimated. It is a mighty validation. So how not feel private diminution when the words no longer come the way they used to? The writer sees him- or herself through the imagined eyes of others. The most hated question – for me, anyway – is "What are you working on now?" If I am not, as I'm mostly not, in full spate, I feel a perceptible inner deflation. We've talked about this. At some level we conflate inspiration with self-worth.

But that deflation has as its counterpart the *in*flation we experience when things the ideas are coming and the words, the right words, seem to arrive at just the slightest beck. Jarrell's pump pumping of its own accord. You put me onto that poem, and I took the title of an essay on writer's block from it. I just now looked back at that essay and I can't resist throwing in a short paragraph, something the Other Birkerts (whoever he is) wrote:

"The memory of the best of the best writing moments haunts, most grievously when the desire is there but the impulse is absent, or when the impulse flickers and sputters but doesn't catch, when the words – which I believe are right there, as if on the other side of the sheerest membrane – will not come. The good runs are not a fortifying memory but a reproach. My younger self – it is always, necessarily, the younger self – mocks me. It's not just writing at stake, but everything. The worth I felt when I worked, *when I was young* – even if that was only yesterday – is gone. This is now and henceforth the way of things; this is the new reality."

Chris Benfey (born 1954, in Pennsylvania) is a distinguished literary critic and scholar of American literature. He is the author of five volumes, most recently Red Brick, Black Mountain, White Clay *(The Penguin Press, 2012), and teaches English at Mount Holyoke College, in Massachusetts.*

One of America's foremost prose writers and literary critics, Sven Birkerts is the author of nine books, including The Gutenberg Elegies: The Fate of Reading in an Electronic Age *(Faber, 1994),* Readings *(Graywolf, 1999),* My Sky Blue Trades: Growing Up Counter in a Contrary Time *(Viking, 2002) and* Changing the Subject: Art and Attention in the Internet Age *(Graywolf, 2015). He is the Director of the Bennington College Writing Seminars, Vermont, and the Editor of the literary journal* AGNI *in Boston.*

CINNABAR SKY

Philip Davison

Thank you, stranger.

She could see a berm to the track bed. Alma pushed through the coarse brambles and made her way down the embankment. She bolstered her resolve by talking aloud to herself. After all, this elderly woman had come to bear witness.

It was a busy stretch of track, but she had timed her descent between trains. She could hear the singsong voices of children playing in one of the gardens that backed onto the cutting. She could hear blackbirds, chaffinches and crows. When she stood still she caught the breeze that lifted the branches of the trees.

It didn't last, of course. The rush of a fast moving suburban train on the near track set her rocking on her brittle ankles. The beast was gone down the track in an instant. In the interval between this and the next train she studied the immediate terrain and judged her position. She braced the tremor in her voice. Had there been anyone listening they might have thought she was praying. Whatever the character of her words, there could be no doubt they were an offering directed into another world.

"You came round by the railings when nobody was looking, yes. Careful not to trip. You didn't want to fall and hurt yourself. Dangerous for children here, but they know, don't they?

"You chose this place, not any other. I see, yes. A long stretch of straight track. Bushes at the side. You stood in here, your heart set. Every reason to succeed. No chance for the driver. None. Say you're sorry."

The rush and clatter of another train, this one on the far track. It was no less unsettling than the first, but Alma stood fast.

"Delays, they said at first. Then, a temporary closure. A medical emergency. An incident on the line. You took what was yours. Faithful to the end. Better off, eah, you dirty little tyke doing that to the driver and his family. You've nothing to say, I know, and for that I'm heartbroken. Nothing wrong with brokenness.

"The world didn't mean it. We're unacquainted, but I'd love you as you are. Now you're too late. Yes. Never mind. Never mind now, I say."

Another train, right to left. This one seemed to hit harder with its air displacement, but Alma took it barefaced.

"The gathering up is done without your father to lift you up, without your mother's hands on your cheeks. Was it peaceful when you did your reconnoitre, when you said to yourself: this is the place, this is how to get knocked out of the world? Did you speak kindly?

"I'll stand in here a minute. I can do nothing for you, precious darling, but let the trains on."

She could hear birdsong again. The notes seemed sharper, more tuneful.

"Look at that evening sky. Knocked through the doors of death and into that fiery red sky. Gone forever and a day. That extra day is to give us hope. You have me going now ... "

A train passing left to right obliterated even the raucous calls of the crows. Another, travelling in the opposite direction, buffeted Alma and made her step back a pace. This one sounded its horn.

But the birdsong came back to her and she listened again to the voices of the children. It was some time before Alma continued.

"You hear the birds ... they'll soon go quiet." She looked again to the evening light. "I speak your name out in my head. Can you hear me?"

She heard footsteps on the adjacent path. A young man stopped by the railings and called to her.

"Are you all right there?"

"I am. I'm all right", Alma called back.

"It's not safe where you are."

"No. It is not."

"Can I help you back onto the path?"

"No."

"You'd be a lot safer up here. Give me your hand. I'll help you up."

"No", said Alma.

"My name is John", said the young man softening his voice a little. "John Lipton ... "

"I know who you are", replied Alma. "You're a stranger. Thank you, stranger."

"I'm sorry – it's just occurred to me", said Lipton, "are you related to the poor man who ... ?" He didn't finish, but made a gesture towards the tracks.

"I am now ... " said Alma. "Lovely evening, isn't it, John Lipton?"

"Yes ... yes, it is." Lipton replied, then added meekly: "I have to get on ... "

"I know you do", said Alma. She hesitated. "Wait ... " she called. She began to make her way to the gap in the brambles on the embankment. "I'm coming up now. Give me your hand."

A novelist, playwright and screenwriter, Philip Davison was born in Dublin in 1957. He is the author of 10 radio plays and eight novels, most recently Eureka Dunes *(Liberties Press, 2017). He is a member of Aosdána, and lives in Dublin.*

SUMMER POEM

—

Chris Preddle

Loss so great — in the causeless why.

THE METAPHYSICS OF SUMMER

1

High trees are higher minds,
forbear
high winds, let go
what the winds bear off,
let go
boughs they were furnished with,
ideas examined,
let fall and finished with.

Under the trees by Mag Brook we converse
in high anxiety. We argue values
outlive who would live by them. We would serve
what's certain, or once was God, or will not fail us.

Christian England's over, and our little age
feels like an ending. We are late, un-Roman,
unredeemed, and irksome at the edge
of Europe. Our inhumanities remain.

Aude walked out with Roland, to a wood
springeth in May. She said, leaves inhere
in the may like love in us. Even here
it's all mortality we move toward.

The magpies of Mag
Brook, makers
of sorrow,
so many gathered and rose
in a bird arch,
a magpie bridge

Weaving Girl
and Cowherd, unequal
lovers
separated by the Silver River,
crossed over,
certainty recovered.

2
I am a girl on a swing
sweating, I reason and sing
in Kaifeng under the Northern Song,
long before Prettified Thing
in petticoats and flounces will be painted by Fragonard.
Go high, low,
sky, below,
go far, near,
far.

High bamboos discuss the cause of the wind,
how cause is course, recourse
and discourse of the wind. Intellectuals and scholars
came up in a clump around us. We suffered the injustice
of policy and politicians, and the Emperor's ambivalence.
He rules All Under Heaven
so I have all the things there are and you have none.
Oppose without action, act
without opposition, says the Tao. But values compel us.
The highest bamboo is merely a grass stem.

Snow has come.
The winter plum
lets go
petals that wish to go.
It is their way
to be carried away.

We fell like a leaf
from favour, to a life
elsewhere.
We dined off celadon ware
in a house of art,
but were often apart.

He died, I lived.
I hardly believed
loss
so great could be set loose.
What we own
we shall disown.

The plum has cast
her blossom. The past
leans
nearer me and I lean
near it. In the snow
leaf buds grow.

3

Human is, for whom
groweth seed and bloweth mead, in whom
the self asks what kind of thing it is,
and even the self itself is a sign
of some unself. A thing
is what we start with, but we suffer
the insufficiency of things, and suffer
the fall of others, and such otherness.
Even time, which falls too soon, is a sign
of the selfmoved other.

Rachel goes in the fair grass walking
out of reach. The seeded grass
followed as she moved across the field, where Jacob sheep
were folded. Absolute
beauty pressed on her like a high atmosphere.
The meadow she had made
arched its earthly back to bear her up.

4

We fail
like apple trees uprooted, or fair Patroclus
undone. (How death interpolates
the continuity of us.) We fall
in love and offer praise like apples,
prayers like opals to
mine onlie fair.
(Undo
my high anxieties.) We feel
we should live forever, it's only fair,
for the absolute
is what we're anxious for. (Fulfil
all that I have at heart, artful
goddess.) We fail,
as the fair Patroclus
fell out of life in the overbearing spearfall.

5

I have sat by the sea
on my heels, to paint a woman painting
her acceptance by the sea. I make the Mediterranean
blue, the shaded grass blue, the sand
blueish, and she wears blue and
blue, and sits on her heels. I put seven of her
sitting on the grass; eleven of her
stand on the beach. Each is made in turn
by painting
acceptable to reason, by the sea.

I am in Europe an erroneous kind
of European. You do not care for me,
errant and aberrant. I am assigned
death, inland. Human, reasoned, let me be.

Trees
that shade us blue and lean to one another,
although I am the other,
have minde on me that was sumtime in ease.

6

We in high discourse, the cicada old,
under a plane in summer by water
cold as a naiad, thought we had compelled

the absolute. We'd know for certain what
certainty there is, how the mere human
could be unpassioned and eternal. Wait,

the seeker cicadas say. No gods remain.
Let go sungod, undergod, Osiris
our self under the sands, those minor

nymphs in sensual meadows. Let go the Rose
of Jericho, the Maid milde we sing of,
her saints and Son-god. Let go Eros,

argue values. No more time for sunning
on the rocks with Jacqueline. In the heat
thin-singing (and the birds picking us off)

we take to dialectic. High art
connects us, we say, to an abstract goodness
eludes us also, like a white hart

of the otherworld. We give no white gardenias
to an abstraction, though it may exist
self-perfect, and the little good in us

would make return to it. O tettix, tettix,
we in the shade, Mark, Graham, Robin, Ken,
Jacqueline and I, see time on its axis

turn away, its purposes unspoken.
We are sick for belief, as one in the hills
for the sea, the sea. So many gods mistaken,

we need redemption still. Mourn also
England, who denies she is of ur-
Europa – her cult and culture nothing else

but Europe's, and no areté of hers
but everyone's. It was the Greeks knew
what reason and its high desires were for,

it is we lorded it to the Pyrenees
with Roland, declared in a humane arcade
no being in dignity is near us,

lived la douceur de vivre (and no iniquity
beyond us), saw the green and turning Somme
loop like mole-ways. So we quite and not quite

kept a civilisation (some or not some
irony of this Iron Age), to a last
western age, our own of the consumer

consumed. We in the body-mind leased
from matter, which fails us, feel the not-I
not-self, the "is" that avails, the lucid

humane demand. Nations say "Not I",
their grand refusal. They do not grant us peace,
the amplitude of peace, but harrow and tine

the poorest, make unkindness into pious
social plans. We choose this quarter-circle
of ground, a quadrant where the timeless pass

as if they lived, conversing in our sickle-
time with us. The river carries away
the metaphysics of summer. We in this School

of Athens Elsewhere, of the causeless why,
grasshopper minds, grouse-heapers, graze happier
here. Here, under branches of apple. Why,

so. Lady of the apples, of the hoops
and hips of rivers, figure of may, Koré
of our discourse drier than gorse in a heap here,

lady of the wood springeth, of crocus-
time, term of this argument and passion
recurs outwith our history that recurs,

love is the absolute in a person,
person in an absolute. Tithonus-old
we shall come, Leaf Queen, to the high dispassion

and final clearness that such love compelled.

Chris Preddle was born in London in 1943, educated at Stonyhurst and Oxford, and has retired from library work to a valley below the Pennines in West Yorkshire, under Mag Hill. His third poetry collection will be The May Figures *(Eyewear, 2021); his second was* Cattle Console Him *(Waywiser, 2010). His work has previously appeared in* Irish Pages, *as well as many Irish and English magazines. He is currently translating the songs and fragments of Sappho.*

AT ALGECIRAS

Gerard McCarthy

At home in the darkness.

When the plane landed in Malaga I headed out through the concourse to the familiar place where there was a bus waiting. The way in was dark; it was late on an October Sunday night and it was raining. When the bus came in to the centre I disembarked on the Alameda Principal. The streets were almost deserted. I found the Hotel Carlos V, in a side-street between the Alcazaba and the cathedral. The reception was empty until a man came along and checked me in to a room on the third floor. He told me I could get water in the lower lounge. The machine produced two bottles for my euro, instead of one. When the man told me I may as well have the two, I decided to take it as a small piece of good fortune as I made my way up to my small single room. I turned off the light, giving way to the darkness. In the morning the darkness lingered, and I realised that it was a room into which only the faintest of daylight ever enters; outside, the window was half way down a deep well formed by four walls, the sunlight far above. I took the lift back down to the lower lounge and purchased a few plastic cups of coffee from a machine there, to assuage the pangs until I had breakfast in the café directly across the road. Afterwards, I had passed the cathedral when I turned back and paid a visit inside, just to breathe in its echoing presences. Outside again my feet took me inexorably in the direction of the sea. Familiarity re-surfaced as I walked along Paseo del Parque, and on to the beach. The morning sunlight was glinting across the water. I followed the example of a few others and went down, taking off my shoes and socks and standing in the shallows of the Mediterranean. My steps brought me back to the harbour. The Pompidou Centre was close by it and, as I approached it, I was startled by the sight of an outdoor exhibition of large photographs of refugees fleeing into Europe, in the immediate aftermath of the voyage of their lives. It is a human flow that has continued across the Mediterranean, from its eastern shores to its western boundary at the strait of Gibraltar. Inside the Pompidou Centre, coincidentally, there was a temporary exhibition with some further representations of refugee journeys: one was in three walls of a room, in which the visitor was surrounded by the sea, to the sound of rowing and glimpses of oars. There was no land visible, and to my eyes it could have been in the waters of Clew Bay. Outside again, with my phone I took some photographs of photographs of refugees.

I walked out the harbour to a café bar I had visited a few years before. It was unchanged. I had two glasses of beer and a plate of patatas bravas. There was a couple outside at a front table who suddenly seemed to get romantic, and then equally suddenly, the man first, the woman next, each resorted to their mobile phone. The intense look on the young man's face and the urgency of his texting were as unreadable as that of an alien species. I left them to it, and walked leisurely out the quay where I loitered awhile as the day darkened before returning to the city streets. My attention was caught by a sign outside a bakery that there was a café upstairs. It was volubly crowded. I had a dish of spicy vegetables there, admiring the speed and diligence and togetherness of the young couple who were running it. Afterwards I sat outside awhile, as the crowds strolled by in the balmy evening, until I made my way back to the hotel reflecting on the harmony that imbued the place, that imbued me too.

The next morning, I left the hotel before dawn. There were few people about as I walked to the beginning of the beach. I sat on a bench above it and could hear faintly the sound of the sea as the sounds of traffic began to build up behind me. I went down to the water's edge in the first glimmer of light. It was only when the sky reddened with sunrise, and the sun itself put in a brief appearance, that I noticed a couple of figures who had been sleeping on the beach, secluded by umbrellas and a pile of deck chairs. I imagined them to be migrants.

I walked up the Alameda Principal, turning off in the confidence that, despite the fact that the streets had not surfaced in my mind in the previous few years, I would find the way. The bus station was immediately familiar. Its café had been extended and refurbished. I thought I recognised one of the men serving. Caught up in his quotidian busyness, he showed no sign of recognition as he served me. I boarded the eleven o'clock bus for Algeciras. There was an Arabic ambience to some of my fellow passengers. I spent the journey looking out at the passing landscape with glimpses of the sea, until the sudden apparition of Gibraltar. Shortly afterwards, the sight of chimneys, cranes and containers announced the onset of the port of Algeciras. I passed out of the bus station through a raggle-taggle crowd around the door. I passed a tourist office with a sign that said it was closed for technical reasons. In contrast to Malaga, the streets looked down at heel. I was coming near the square when a young woman sitting in an alleyway called out "amore amore". I wondered how many years since I received such an importunate solicitation. I passed on. The streets soon gave way to the busy port that is one of the main gateways between Europe and Africa. I walked along across the road from the port, following a sign for the Hotel Reina Cristina.

Yeats and his wife, George, landed in Gibraltar in November 1927, and made the short journey across the bay to the Hotel Reina Cristina. He was suffering a severe bout of ill-health, an inaugural challenge of his old age. From the hotel he wrote the following in a letter to his lost muse, Maud Gonne: "My dear Maud, A multitude of white herons are beginning to roost among the dark branches of the trees outside my windows. They fish in the Mediterranean on the other side of Gibraltar which is some ten miles off, and then fly home to the gardens here for a night's sleep."

It seems that Yeats was in a state of great anxiety while they were staying in the hotel. His wife George wrote a letter home to an associate, Lennox Robinson, in which she said: "WB of course is making his last will and testament at all hours of day and night, hurrying to finish a poem but has not been able to begin yet. 'Of course I shall never be able to go on with the autobio now...' etc etc. All poppycock. However, in the same breath he talks of writing a poem on the herons at Algeciras 'in a few years' time.' What a pillaloo."

George's ironic attitude is corroborated by six photographs of the poet, looking relaxed, and perhaps inebriated, in the gardens of the hotel, along with George, and a friend, Jean Hall; unguarded images of a man, most of whose photographs seem to strike a solemn pose. Despite his anxieties, they are photographs of a man who had more than a decade left, of flourishing and productivity. One of the early fruits of this was a short poem, in the first verse of which the herons of Algeciras were transmuted by Yeats into what he called, "heron-billed birds", that he imagined flying across each evening from their feeding grounds in Morocco to settle in the rich midnight of the garden trees of the hotel. The second verse is set in the Rosses Point of the poet's childhood. He remembers a day he spent gathering shells from Rosses' level shore, and bringing them back in the hope that he might receive the commendation of an older friend. The third and final verse is set at close of day in either place, in which he imagines being questioned by "the Great Questioner": how he might with a fitting confidence reply.

He called the poem: "At Algeciras – A Meditation on Death".

There was an insalubrious aura to the steps I climbed up to the grounds of the hotel, but the entrance was grand. At reception, I was dealt with by a young man. Neither he nor the woman in the background could speak much more English than the dearth of my Spanish. Beside the reception, I looked at a plaque with autographs of celebrities and luminaries, looking to see the name of W. B. Yeats. When I asked, they hadn't heard of him, but the young man pointed out to me a framed photograph behind us of two men: one of them looked out of the frame with the haunted face of Gabriel Garcia Lorca.

I was given a room much more salubrious than my usual hotel accommodation. In the hotel booklet there was a page that mentioned that the hotel was almost entirely burned down in 1928, presumably obliterating the record of the Yeats's stay there the year before. The room had a view as I had requested overlooking the gardens. I took the opportunity to explore them, and I sat for a long interval around five in the afternoon in a secluded place among the trees, in which there were many song birds singing, but I caught no sight of a white heron. Later, in the dusk light I went out to the gate and crossed the road for the view of the port. A sign there spoke of the heyday of the hotel, when there was a beach below it, down to which the guests would descend on the steps that I had climbed as I arrived; steps that now end in a sudden hiatus at the side of a main road. I loitered on awhile. Above the industrial noise of the port, there were occasional cries of what sounded like gulls, but I caught no sighting of any heron in the trees of the garden. I guessed that the many lights and moving traffic had deflected the birds from their traditional flight paths. One possible heron-like bird appeared briefly before disappearing behind a chimney. Before I went to my room, I wandered the corridors, looking at old photographs of the hotel and its environs, particularly a few of the beach that is no more, and the bay between there and Gibraltar that was open sea then, but for the small island called Verde, that had on it what was called a fort, indistinct in the old photograph. However, the prospect that Yeats and his fellow guests would have had was clear, before the green island was enveloped and engulfed by the port that rendered the hotel an old-world island, marooned, surrounded by the industrial new. I was glad to spend the evening in the hotel, feeling an empathy with its maroonedness in the wider world.

In the morning I took a local bus to La Línea, and walked across the road to the border, where my passport was checked on both sides, cursorily, as I stepped onto Gibraltar. The name has a quintessentially British ring to it, but hidden in it is the name of the first Muslim conqueror to come across the straits: Jebel Tariq, meaning Tariq's mountain. I passed through the streets with their Union Jacks, their shops selling fish and chips and souvenirs of England. The mountain that used to be Tariq's loomed above them. When I reached the square, I boarded the number two bus to the most southerly tip of the peninsula, that is called Europa Point. Most of the passengers on the bus were elderly, and most seemed acquainted with one another, talking in rapid fluent Spanish. The woman beside me was engaged with a man in front, from which I could gather they were talking about the planned exit of Britain from the EU. Suddenly the man switched to English as he said in a seemingly native upper-class English voice about the British government, that they should stop negotiating, that they should get up from the table and just say goodbye, we're leaving. The journey was along narrow twisting roads. Most of my fellow passengers had got out before we reached the terminus. The most prominent building in my sight was a mosque, but I went first to the lighthouse, and the memorial to the Polish General Sikorski, whose aircraft crashed there in 1943. The day was murky and windy. I looked down into the turbulent water. The area around the mosque was a building site with many buildings under construction, one that looked like an office block, or a block of apartments, right next to the mosque. The gate was closed, but it opened when I tried it. I tried one door that was locked, but I found an open one around the back and I went inside. A man appeared and asked me did I wish to visit the mosque itself. He showed me the door, and said I should take off my shoes. Then he turned on the lights and disappeared, and I was alone in the large, spartan spiritual space, standing in my stockinged feet, imbibing the silence. The man reappeared as I was leaving. When I thanked him, he said you're welcome, and made a gesture with his palm pressed briefly against his chest.

Back in Algeciras, I sat awhile in the gardens of the hotel, close to a fountain, whose flowing water masked the noise of the port below. I thought of Yeats, wondering where he had been when the photographs of him had been taken. I brought up on my phone his poem, "At Algeciras", wondering was there still the faint ghost of his presence there. The day was darkening early. I saw no herons, but some big gulls were circling and swooping, some seemingly settling in the trees close by. I thought that no heron would now risk the flight across the bay from Gibraltar, above the industrial lights and noise below.

Next morning I walked down the quay to the terminal building where tickets were sold for ferries to Tangier and Ceuta. I responded to the call of a man in one of the cubicles, who very quickly had sold me a return ticket for Ceuta. Soon, I was heading out on the ferry, past the rock of Gibraltar on the port side, across the narrow strait on water that might have been Mediterranean or Atlantic, or the two of them mingled, until we reached the shore of

Africa about an hour later. I marvelled at the ease of it. In Ceuta I marvelled at the ease of wandering up past the surprise of a Lidl supermarket to the centre of the city where I wandered and loitered in the busy streets. To the eye of this brief and distant observer it seemed a harmonious intermingling of southern Europeans and northern Africans, all about their sociable business on a sunny morning. I went in to an Arab market and managed with some gesticulation to purchase three bags of spices to bring home. At the end of our transaction the man seemed a bit bemused by me as he proffered his hand. We shook warmly.

Back out on the street I sat amidst the comings and goings, including a very large cheerful man who was selling lottery tickets, and a woman with presumably her Arab parents, who were meeting for what seemed a special occasion, of which many photographs were being taken. I ambled along the street with frequent breaks for sitting and gawking. I reached a square with a church to Saint Francis: the Plaza de los Reyes. There was a gathering there of about 20 youths who I assumed were migrants, listlessly lounging with pieces of cardboard that they used as mats both for lying on, and for praying. There were many local comings and goings. Some were feeding a large flock of pigeons that seemed to be a habitual presence. A young couple came along with an elaborate camera, and started to film the migrants whose demean-our seemed one of passive acceptance. I left the square, and soon came to a view of the sea. I climbed down through a path of small houses. The sun was entering a late quarter as I sat a long while on a concrete bench, looking at the sea, and across the bay, particularly at a line that I wondered was it the border fence between the Spanish enclave and Morocco. Suddenly, two young men came from behind me. They each had black beards, and their garb was unmistakeably Muslim. One of them deftly leaped over the rail onto a narrow ledge directly above the sea, as if it was a common thing for him to do. It seemed as if they were slightly disconcerted to see me and they moved away momentarily, but they eventually settled on a spot close by me, and they both began praying, prostrating silently. When they were finished they stood a while leaning on the rail above the sea. When I asked them could they speak English, they said they could a little. They confirmed that the line I pointed out to them was indeed the border. One of them said he travelled through it daily on his way to study in Ceuta. He pointed out a hill across the bay, towards which they had been praying, and said that it was his home-place. We chatted for a little while, both of them speaking respectfully to their elder, and we shook hands as they were leaving. The encounter seemed a gift, out of the blue, like life, and it seemed to exonerate the decision to cross to Ceuta, and the day.

Back at the terminal, as I waited for the boat for the return journey, three men came along, two of them comforting the other, older one. It seemed they had all been drinking. The older man was close to crying. I saw him again on the ferry, his eyes closed as if sleeping. Out again on the choppy water of the strait, we passed two small boats seemingly battling, and I couldn't help but wonder: their vulnerability in the immensity put me in mind of a quote I had read, from one of the migrants who had successfully made the journey across the strait to Europe: "Death happens but once; we prefer to risk our lives than to stay there."

I watched from the deck as Africa quickly receded behind us, and the sun slowly descended into the Atlantic beyond the strait. The rock of Gibraltar gradually reared ahead of us, and it was looming to the starboard as we turned back in to the harbour of Algeciras. On my way back to the hotel, I came across a path that was somewhat secluded from the noise and sights of global capitalism around the port below, and I was able to look down at the business of the port, and see it as separate, and at a remove from the world in which I was walking, with the grounds of the hotel beside me. A few sea birds on a roof had me wondering did they have beaks like herons, and, on the edge of the roof of the hotel, the bird I had seen the previous evening was seemingly nesting beside the chimney. I didn't leave the grounds of the hotel for the rest of the day, feeling at home in the world after crossing to the continent of Africa without leaving Europe. I went down to the old gate through which the guests would go as they descended to the beach that is no more. I sat close to the swimming pool. A high port tower in front of the hotel no longer seemed intrusive to my eyes that had begun to let the surroundings be. I loitered harmoniously, as the sun slowly sank behind the trees, and the garden was shaded, and it was evening. I saw no Yeatsian heron, but there was a myriad of small birds vividly inhabiting their garden world. I marked, against the background of the constant industrial monotone, the subtle nuance of their song.

Coming up to dusk, many big sea-birds, that I assumed were gulls, were chaotically filling the air above the trees, squawking. I wondered were they the birds that Yeats saw, and subsequently distilled to become figments of his imagination. I thought of him: that sometimes smiling public man, a publicly successful life behind him, and thoughts born at Algeciras of the death that awaited him. I lingered outside in the warm night, marvelling the phenomenon of the place. I was walking back in through the terrace when my phone rang with an unknown number. At first the person did not seem to get through. It rang again. When I answered it, it was a voice from home, telling me of the tragic death of a young woman, a beautiful soul, found drowned off Coney Island in Sligo Bay.

Before going inside, I fixed my attention briefly on the one star that was visible to me. I thought: one couldn't say the universe is without meaning as a microcosm of it, the human being, is so powerfully deeply drawn to seek it. Later, in bed the warmth of the night had me waking in the midst of dreams triggered by the out of the blue phone call, with a jumble of anxious images born of the disturbances of my past quotidian; anxiety too about my health, and fear that I might even give up the ghost on this my last night in Algeciras. I was awake for a long while, wondering would I be able to get back to sleep at all; and of course I thought of Yeats's Great Questioner: what, if I were asked, would I have to say?

It was still dark when I left the bed and opened the window of my room to hear the dawn chorus of the birds prevail for a while over the noise of human machines. The first glimmer was coming into the sky above the strait, and dawn was breaking upon those mingled seas.

———

The day after returning home, I attended the young woman's funeral in Sligo Cathedral. It was full to overflowing. Scattered amidst the young, there was the re-appearance of old familiar faces. Among them was the bishop emeritus who, although suffering from a serious illness, had come out of retirement for the occasion. In the midst of the Mass, the young woman's sister played on a tin whistle a traditional tune, for which many different words have been given over the ages, but there were no words on that day for the pure poignance of her playing. The bishop in his homily embodied more than expressed what was inspiring about his faith. He lauded the size of the congregation, compar-ing it with gatherings of the earliest Christians and, as he finished, he struck his hand on the lectern to emphasise his plea to God, to bring solace to the family in their grief.

Having followed in Yeats's footsteps to Algeciras, I followed in them to Rosses Point. I parked below the statue of a woman with arms outstretched that is a memorial to those lost at sea. The sun was sinking by the time I was walking the second beach. A dog came running down past me and into the sea.

It was a black and white collie, identical to my memory of the dog who used to be my companion on that shore, decades ago. He ran out into the water, splashing for the sake of it, and it was as if he was an emissary, appearing briefly and quietly, reminding me of a younger world. I loitered in the rocks at the end of the beach, remembering again the years of my youth, mulling memories.

Rosses' level shore: how could one speak of it after so long? I was drawn to it partly because it was beyond speech. The sea was quiet. The sky was reddening behind it. Long dark lines of water were surging, breaking into white in places that lengthened until they joined as they approached the shore. I conjured up Yeats's "Algeciras" on my phone, and thought, whether or not one has faith in the Great Questioner, in the end of the day, if one listens, one is faced with a question that has become one's own. What do you have to say?

I walked back beside the small waves softly landing. I remembered a line in a letter that Yeats wrote to Elizabeth Pelham, a few weeks before he died: "Man can embody truth but he cannot know it." I thought: you do not have to believe in God, or gods, to be able to imagine appearing before an ultimate tribunal, and the account you might give in the hope that your life might be redeemed.

Back at the beginning of the beach, I was sitting on the wall when a woman with young children came along. An older child, a dark-skinned girl, came up to her from the beach, saying, "Look. Look", holding out her hand on which were arrayed bright shells from Rosses' level shore.

I climbed up from the beach, and back the way I had come, looking across to Oyster Island and Coney, and the Metal Man beacon in the channel in front of them. A guide for mariners, the Metal Man had been set there in 1821, and was already old in the time of W.B. Yeats; his brother Jack figured it in several of his works; it is at the centre of an early painting that he called Memory Harbour.

The Metal Man: the man who never looks back towards Coney. His hand is always out, always in the one direction, slightly downward, pointing towards the channel. His face, a face from a child's comic book, simple, but as opaque as the Mona Lisa, set always in the one pronounced expression, from which one couldn't tell whether he was showing the way, or pointing towards hazards hidden beneath the surface of the water. Once again I tried to find a word for it. The only word that came to me was *baffled*. Why should he not be — frozen in his antique clothes, in the middle of the channel between an island and the fast-flowing human world? I waited until his light began to go on and off in bursts of three. On either side, Blackrock lighthouse and Oyster

Island lighthouse were flashing softly. An evening chill came on the air. I heard a boat leaving the harbour. I could barely see its helmsman in the twilight as he headed across towards Coney. I could hear the engine reversing as it came in to the harbour there. In the background was the rhythmic rush of the surf on the far side of the island. As I walked back the boat was returning. There were two figures now, their voices raised as they chatted above the engine. I saw them disembarking at the quay, but they had disappeared by the time I passed it on my way up to where I had parked my car. I drove home in the darkness.

A retired social worker, Gerard McCarthy was born in Dublin in 1949 and now lives in Sligo. He studied Philosophy at University College Dublin. His first published essays have all appeared in issues of Irish Pages. *He divides his time between his Sligo residence, an old schoolhouse on Collanmore Island in Clew Bay, and various travels to the Mediterranean and other peripheries of Europe.* Old Istanbul & Other Essays, *his first book, is published by The Irish Pages Press in early 2021.*

NEW FROM
THE IRISH PAGES PRESS

—

Old Istanbul & Other Essays
By Gerard McCarthy

This is the first book of essays by a major new Irish non-fiction writer from the West of Ireland, comparable to the celebrated Kilkenny essayist Hubert Butler first published by The Lilliput Press and subsequently widely acclaimed. McCarthy's writing is no less distinguished than Butler's.

He writes of the extraordinarily subtle mix of his essays:

> *"Perhaps the Philosophers who had the most enduring influence on me were the contrary figures of Nietzsche and Marcus Aurelius. The reading of each was an antidote to the other, but I was drawn to both by an instinctive affinity. They were augmented subsequently by the gargantuan figure of Michel de Montaigne. My interest has continued to be in the region where Philosophy merges into Literature, with a preference for a language of metaphor rather than of abstract reasoning. These eight essays were written over the course of more than a decade. The fact that they have all been published in the one place, by the good offices of Irish Pages, has allowed me see the continuity between them, and to hope that they might be seen by the reader to form a unity."*

NEW FROM
THE IRISH PAGES PRESS

—

Trump Rant

By Chris Agee

Caustically humorous and polemically compulsive, *Trump Rant* is a work of meticulous political portraiture: a deep-delving and epoch-spanning investigation into the nature of power in American life, made luminous by Agee's nuanced, exploratory understanding of authoritarian drift and thwarted democratic aspiration in a number of world-historical contexts, from Belfast to the Balkans to the formerly Confederate South. Free-roaming in its breadth of reference and tonal range, the *Rant* is at once viscerally personal and unsettlingly resonant, infused throughout with an almost hypnotic sense of scale, largesse, and historical moment.

"What a profusion of insults and vituperation, what a cornucopia of abuse, reproach, contempt, disgust and political and psychological analysis. What an abundance of inventiveness and unfailing imagination and versatility. I am reminded of the copious, imaginative and colourful execration one finds in Shakespeare. Agee's rant could only have been done by a poet with authentic delight in language and a proper poet's audacity. It has a poet's command of cultural allusions too. I admire all these qualities a lot, and enjoyed it immensely. Altogether this little book of outrage is splendid."

Chris Preddle, *poet*

NEW FROM
THE IRISH PAGES PRESS

—

Ben Dorain:
a conversation with a mountain
By Garry MacKenzie

Ben Dorain: a conversation with a mountain draws on the work of an eighteenth-century Gaelic poem by Duncan Bàn MacIntyre, rendering it into English. Where it does so, this is not to present MacIntyre's poetry per se to an English-language reader, as is customary with a translation or version. Instead, the sections of *Ben Dorain* which draw upon MacIntyre's poem incorporate that earlier work into a whole which is completely new.

"*Garry MacKenzie is acutely aware of the implications of Duncan àn MacIntrye's poem for our times. He is also aware of the impossibility of a writer today not working intertextually. MacKenzie is analytical and furthers his knowledge of the natural history of deer through study. If Donnchadh Bàn's stance is subsumed in the words, structure and music of the poem, MacKenzie's meaning literally appears intertextually, between his translation of Donnchadh Bàn and his own and others' writing. He has conversed with many aspects of the poem and has created another poem, I feel, of equal mystery and potency. Donnchadh's grounds have become MacKenzie's variations.*"

Meg Bateman, *poet and scholar*

NEW FROM
THE IRISH PAGES PRESS

—

Kilclief & Other Essays
By Patricia Craig

This long-awaited selection of essays and reviews from one of Ireland's leading critics brings together a wealth of reflection, observation and astute literary comment. It ranges in time from William Carleton to Edna O'Brien, and in subject matter from recent Irish poetry to ghosts, children's books and MI5. Patricia Craig has some important points to make, and makes them with cogency and wit. Always readable and entertaining (and sometimes controversial), she is possibly the only female non-academic Northern Irish critic who has consistently, and over a long period, contributed to every leading UK and Irish publication (and a couple in the US).

"Patricia Craig is not only Ireland's greatest reader, she is also ... line by line, page by page, one of its finest, wittiest writers."

Glenn Patterson, *novelist*